M. NIGHT SHYAMALAN FILM
THE LAST AIRBENDER
PREQUEL
ZUKO'S STORY

Story by Dave Roman & Alison Wilgus

Art by Nina Matsumoto

Based on the series *Avatar: The Last Airbender*
created by Michael Dante DiMartino and
Bryan Konietzko. Based on the screenplay
written by M. Night Shyamalan.

Ballantine B

A Del Rey Manga Trade Paperback Original

Published in the United States by Del Rey, an imprint of The Random House Publishing Group, a division of Random House, Inc., New York.

DEL REY is a registered trademark and the Del Rey colophon is a trademark of Random House, Inc.

ISBN 978-0-345-51854-5

Printed in the United States of America

www.delreymanga.com

9 8 7 6 5 4 3 2 1

CONTENTS

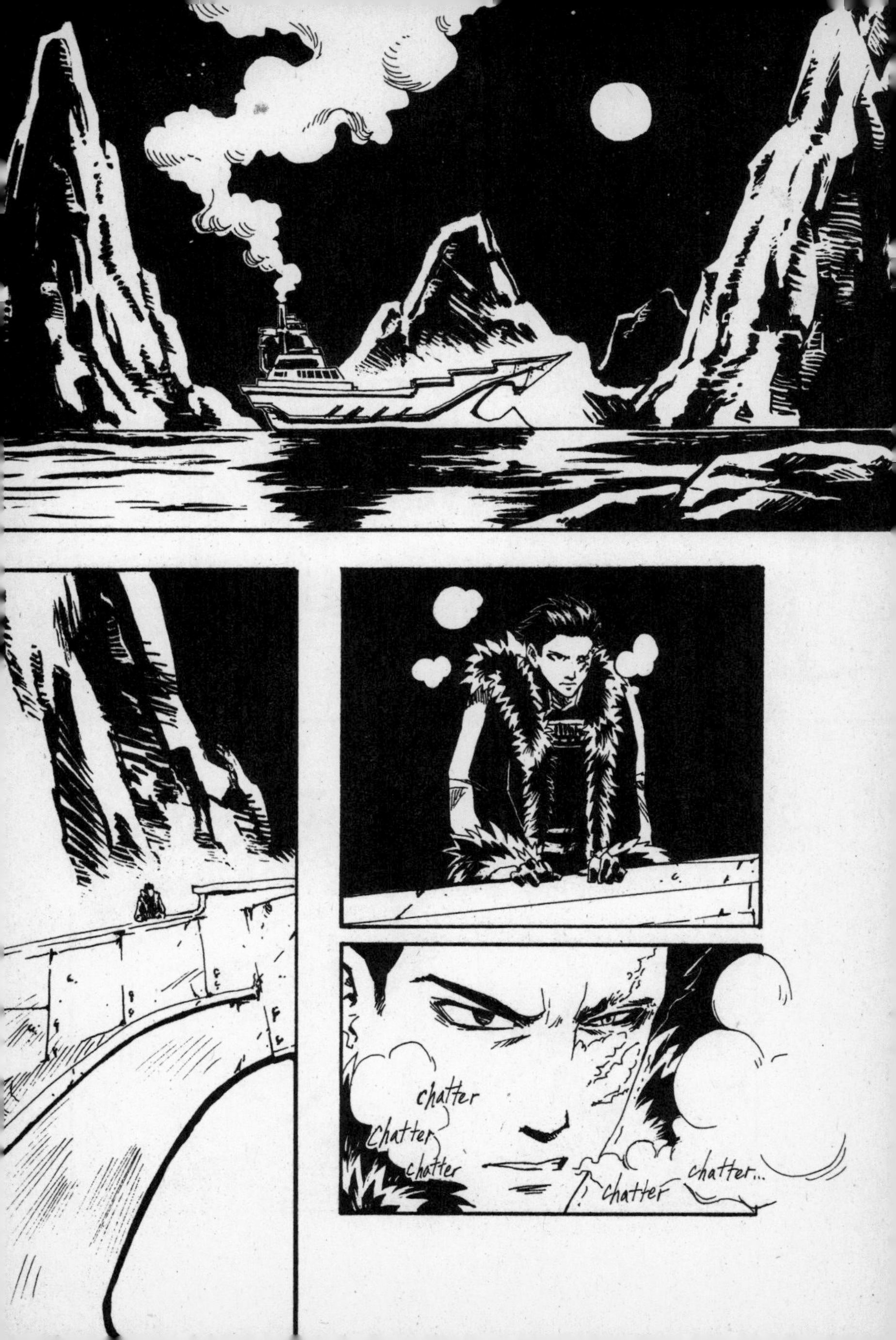
chatter
chatter
chatter
chatter
chatter...

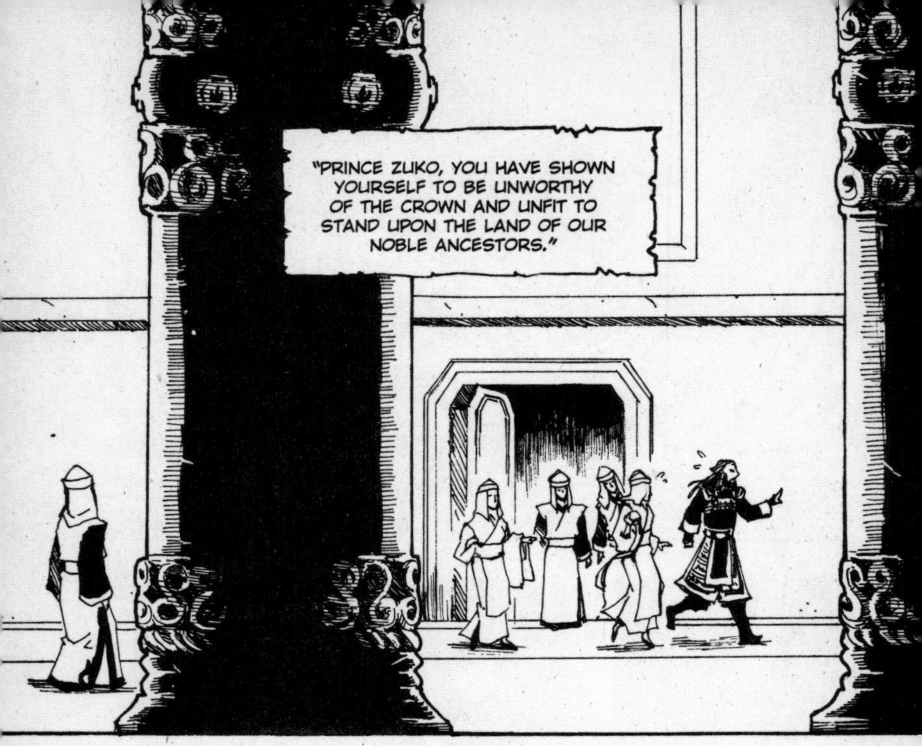
"PRINCE ZUKO, YOU HAVE SHOWN YOURSELF TO BE UNWORTHY OF THE CROWN AND UNFIT TO STAND UPON THE LAND OF OUR NOBLE ANCESTORS."

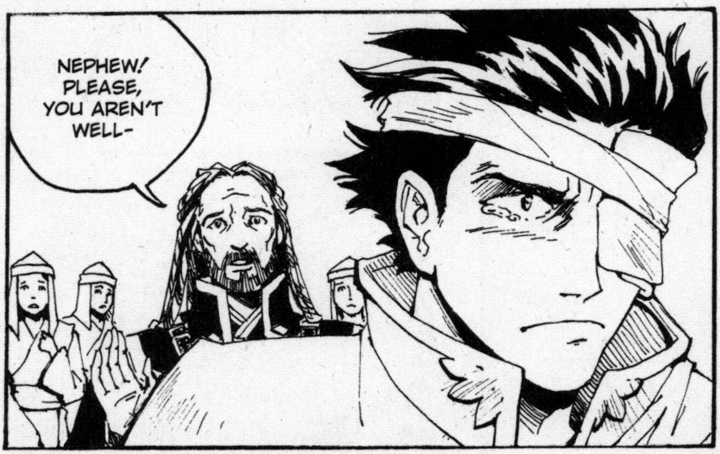
NEPHEW! PLEASE, YOU AREN'T WELL-

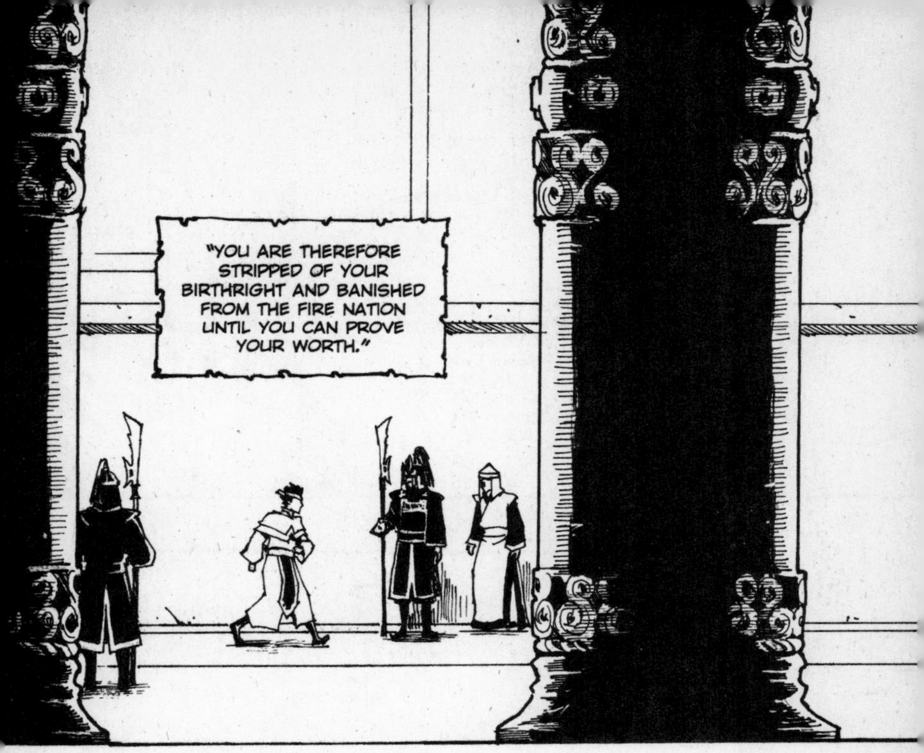
"YOU ARE THEREFORE STRIPPED OF YOUR BIRTHRIGHT AND BANISHED FROM THE FIRE NATION UNTIL YOU CAN PROVE YOUR WORTH."

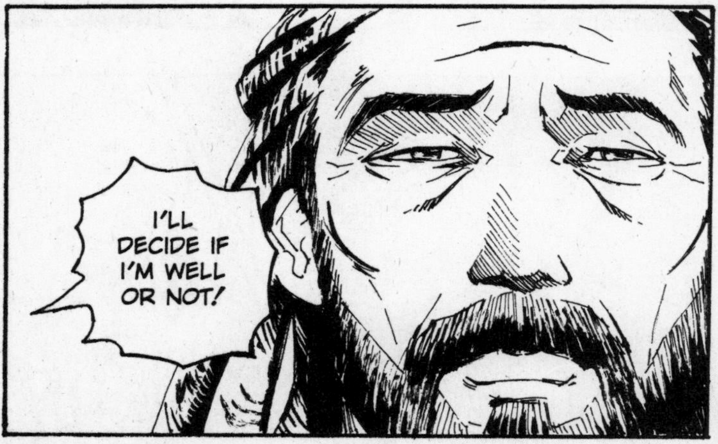
I'LL DECIDE IF I'M WELL OR NOT!

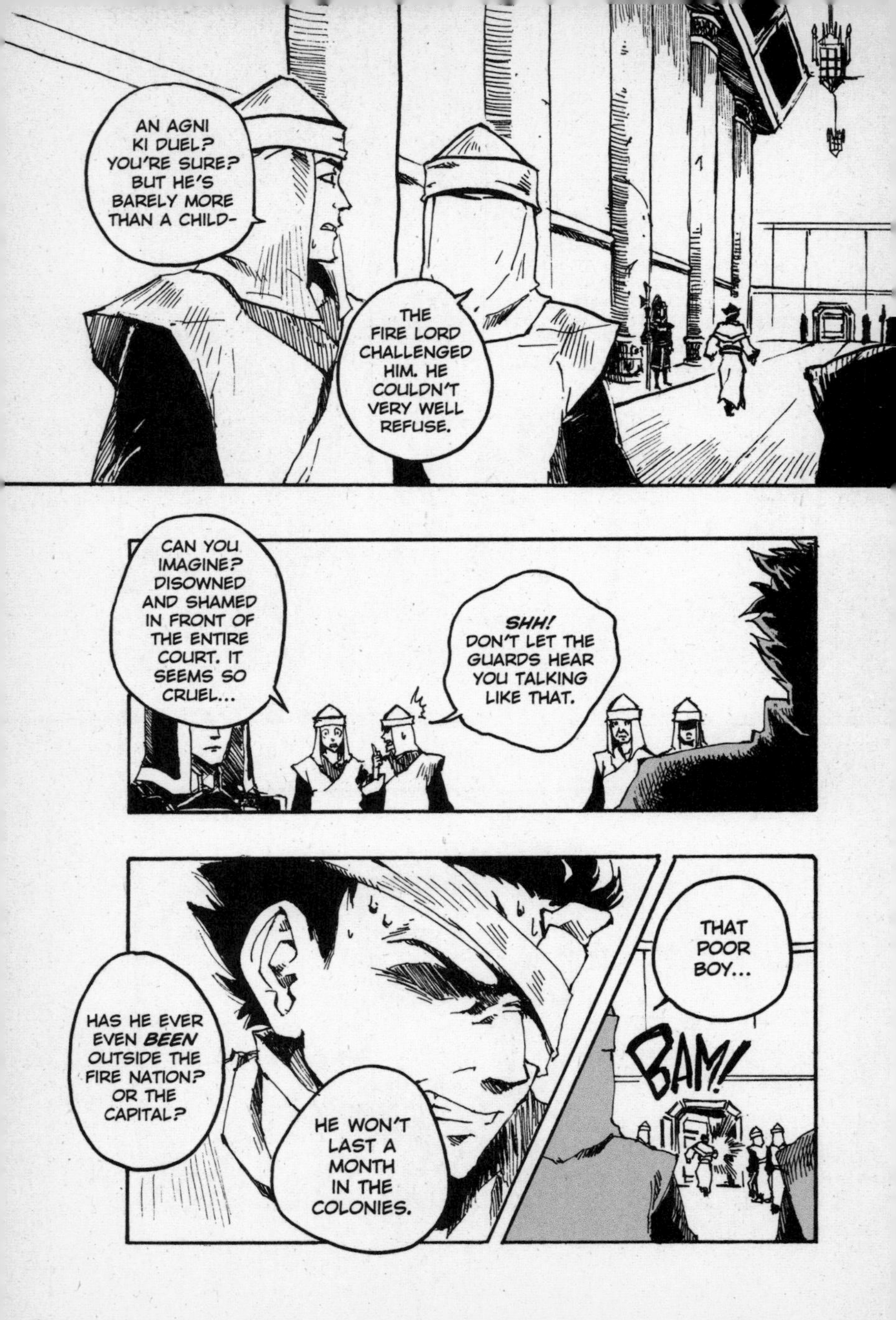
AN AGNI KI DUEL? YOU'RE SURE? BUT HE'S BARELY MORE THAN A CHILD-
THE FIRE LORD CHALLENGED HIM. HE COULDN'T VERY WELL REFUSE.
CAN YOU IMAGINE? DISOWNED AND SHAMED IN FRONT OF THE ENTIRE COURT. IT SEEMS SO CRUEL...
SHH! DON'T LET THE GUARDS HEAR YOU TALKING LIKE THAT.
HAS HE EVER EVEN BEEN OUTSIDE THE FIRE NATION? OR THE CAPITAL?
HE WON'T LAST A MONTH IN THE COLONIES.
THAT POOR BOY...
BAM!

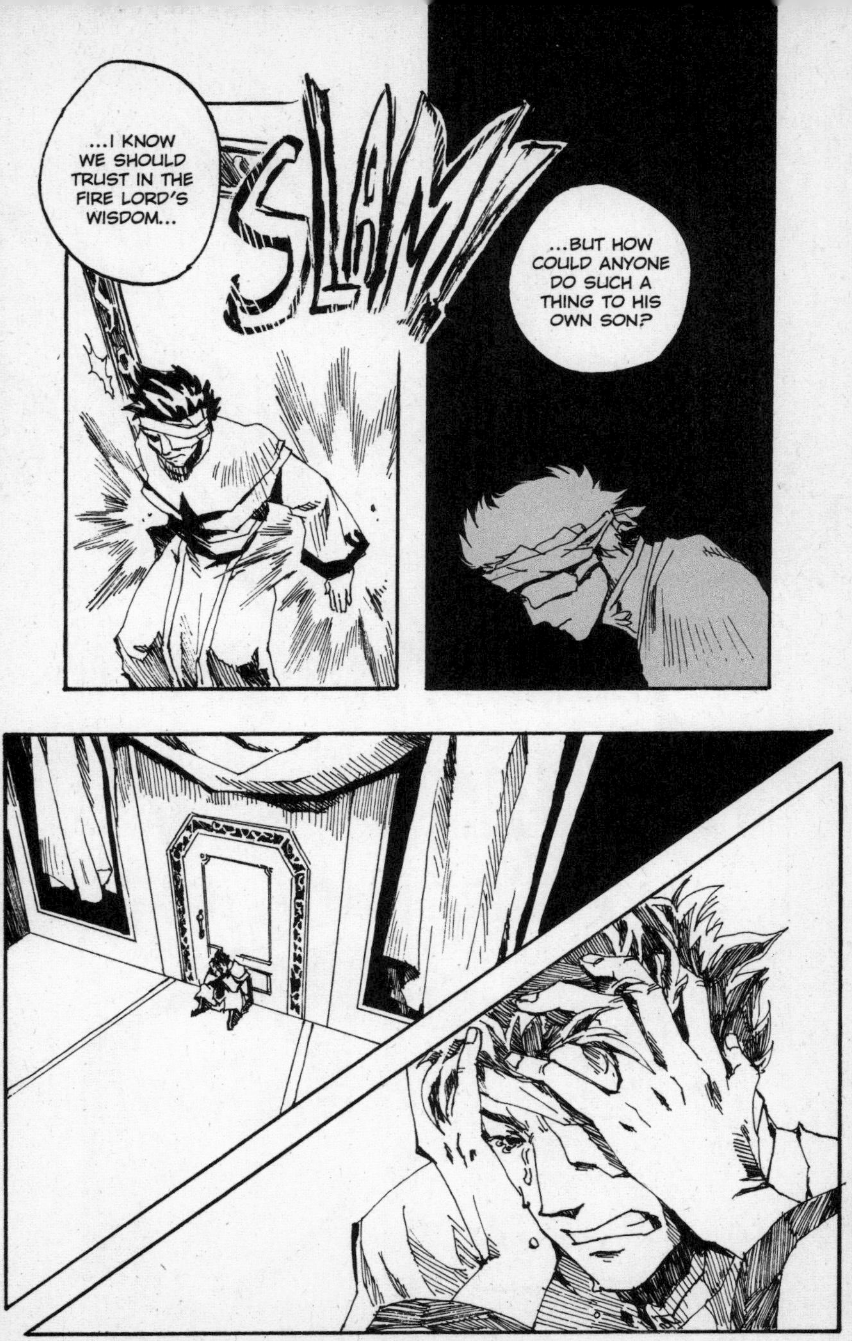
...I KNOW WE SHOULD TRUST IN THE FIRE LORD'S WISDOM...
SLAM
...BUT HOW COULD ANYONE DO SUCH A THING TO HIS OWN SON?

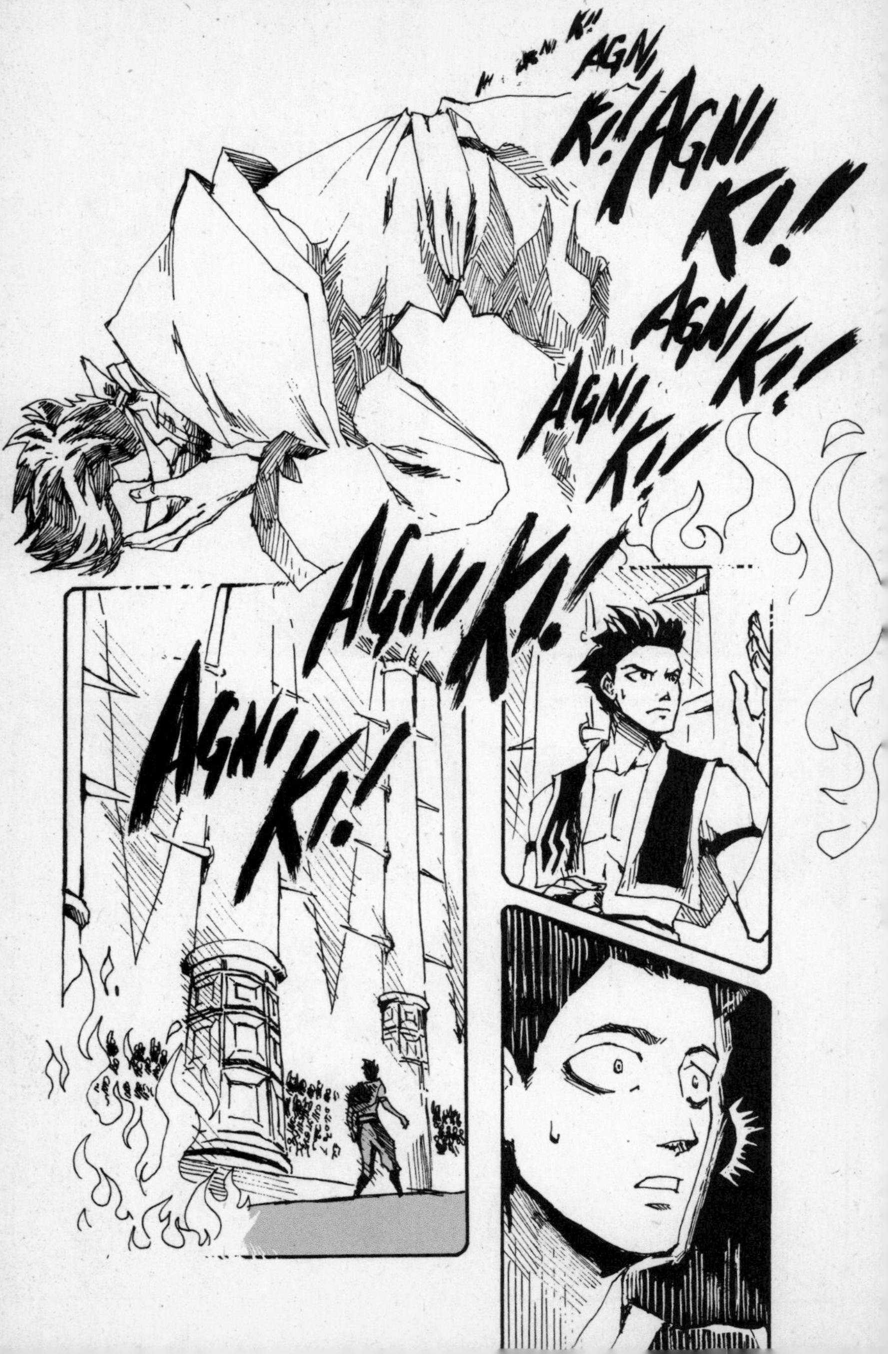
AGNI KI!! AGNI KI!! AGNI KI!! AGNI KI!! AGNI KI!! AGNI KI!! AGNI KI!!

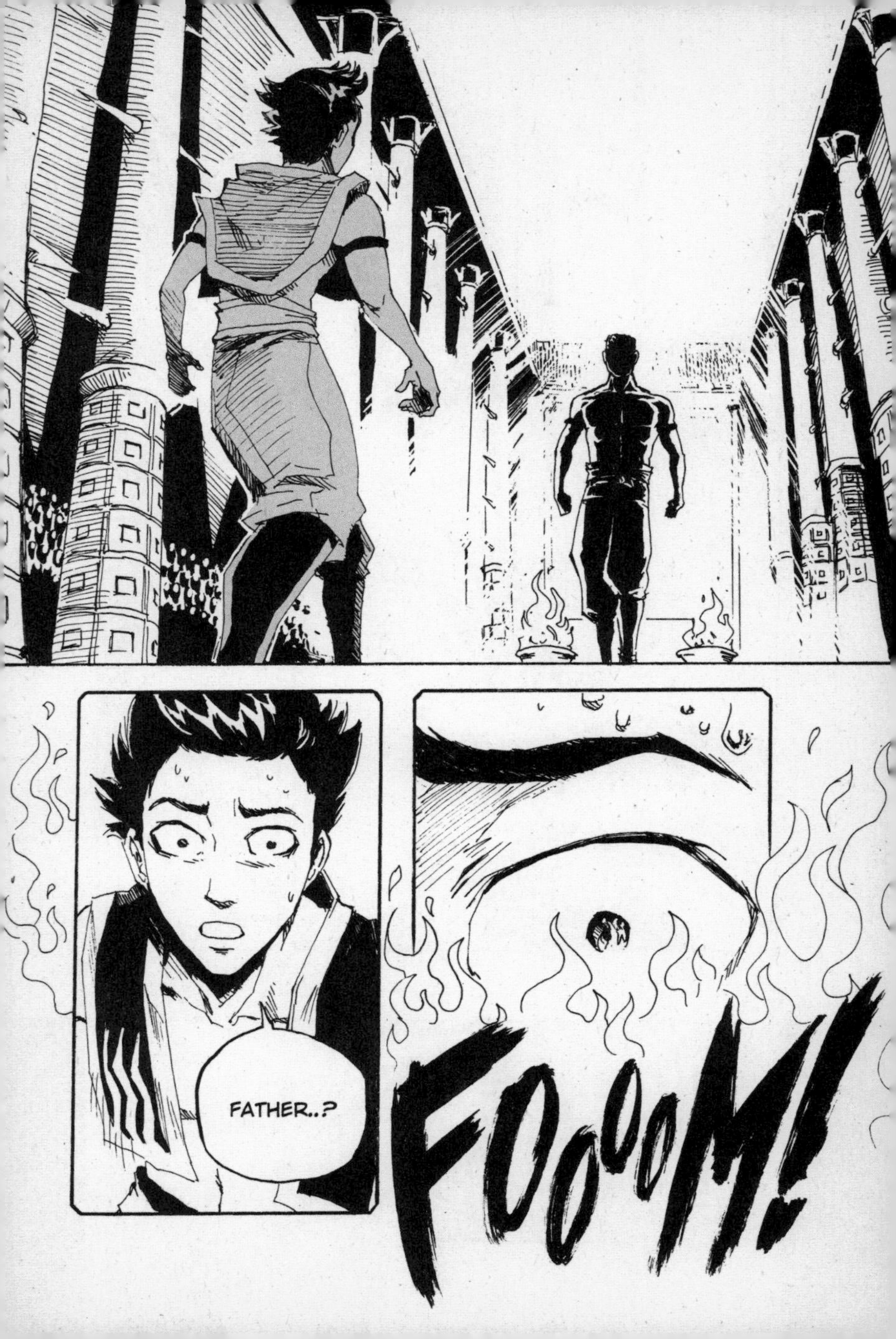
FATHER..?
FOOOOM!!

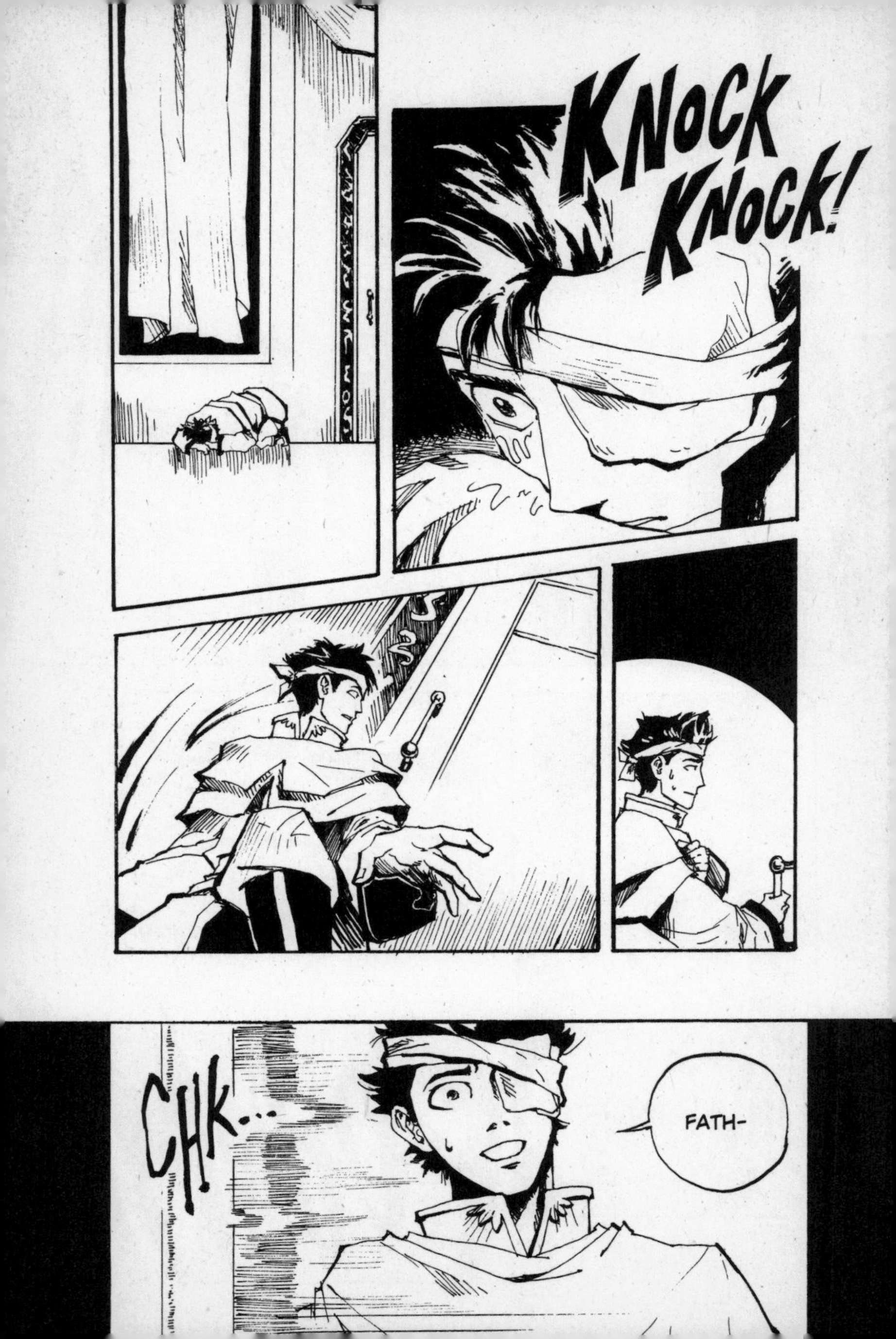
KNOCK KNOCK!
CHK...
FATH-

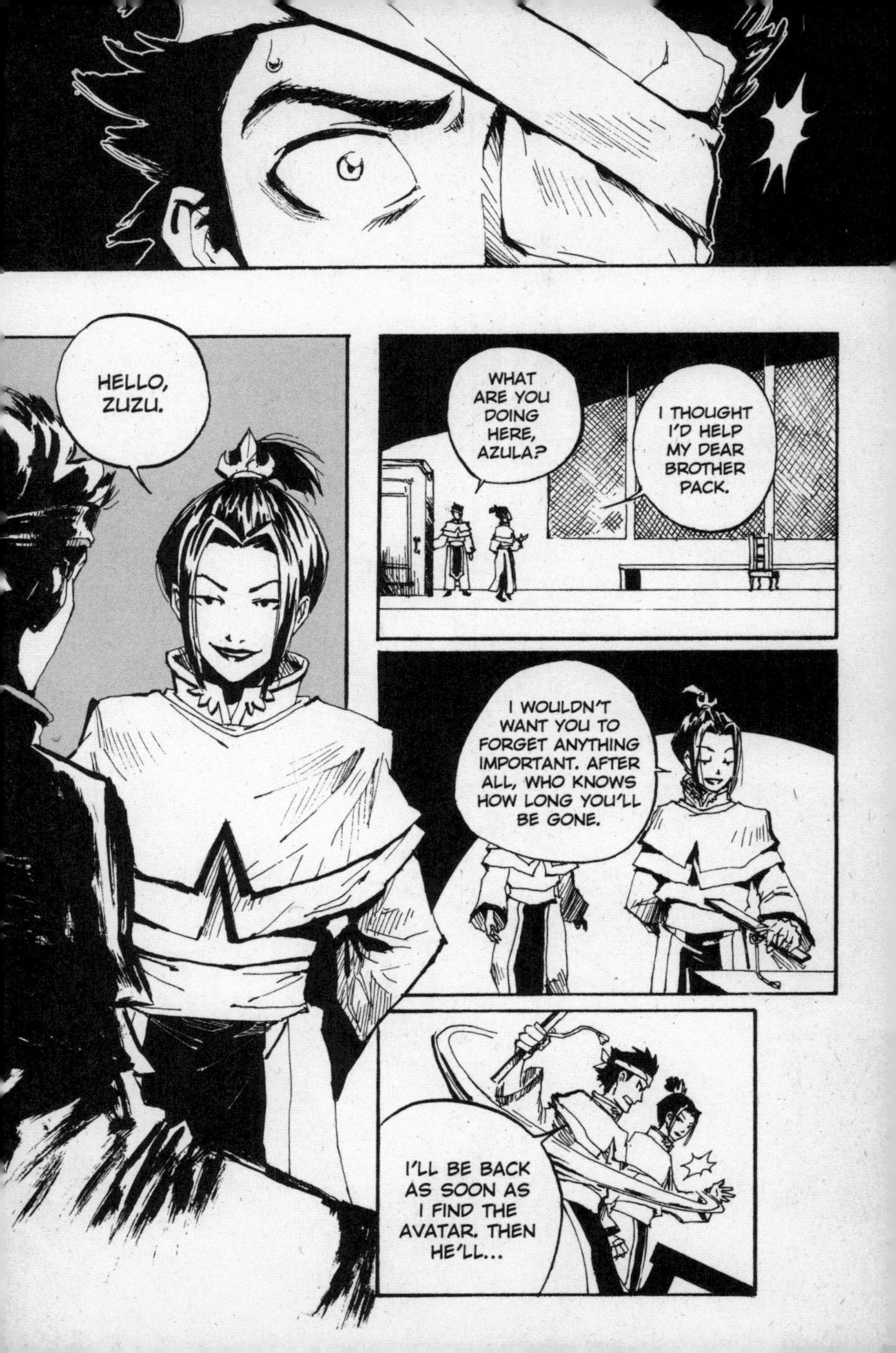
HELLO, ZUZU.
WHAT ARE YOU DOING HERE, AZULA?
I THOUGHT I'D HELP MY DEAR BROTHER PACK.
I WOULDN'T WANT YOU TO FORGET ANYTHING IMPORTANT. AFTER ALL, WHO KNOWS HOW LONG YOU'LL BE GONE.
I'LL BE BACK AS SOON AS I FIND THE AVATAR. THEN HE'LL...

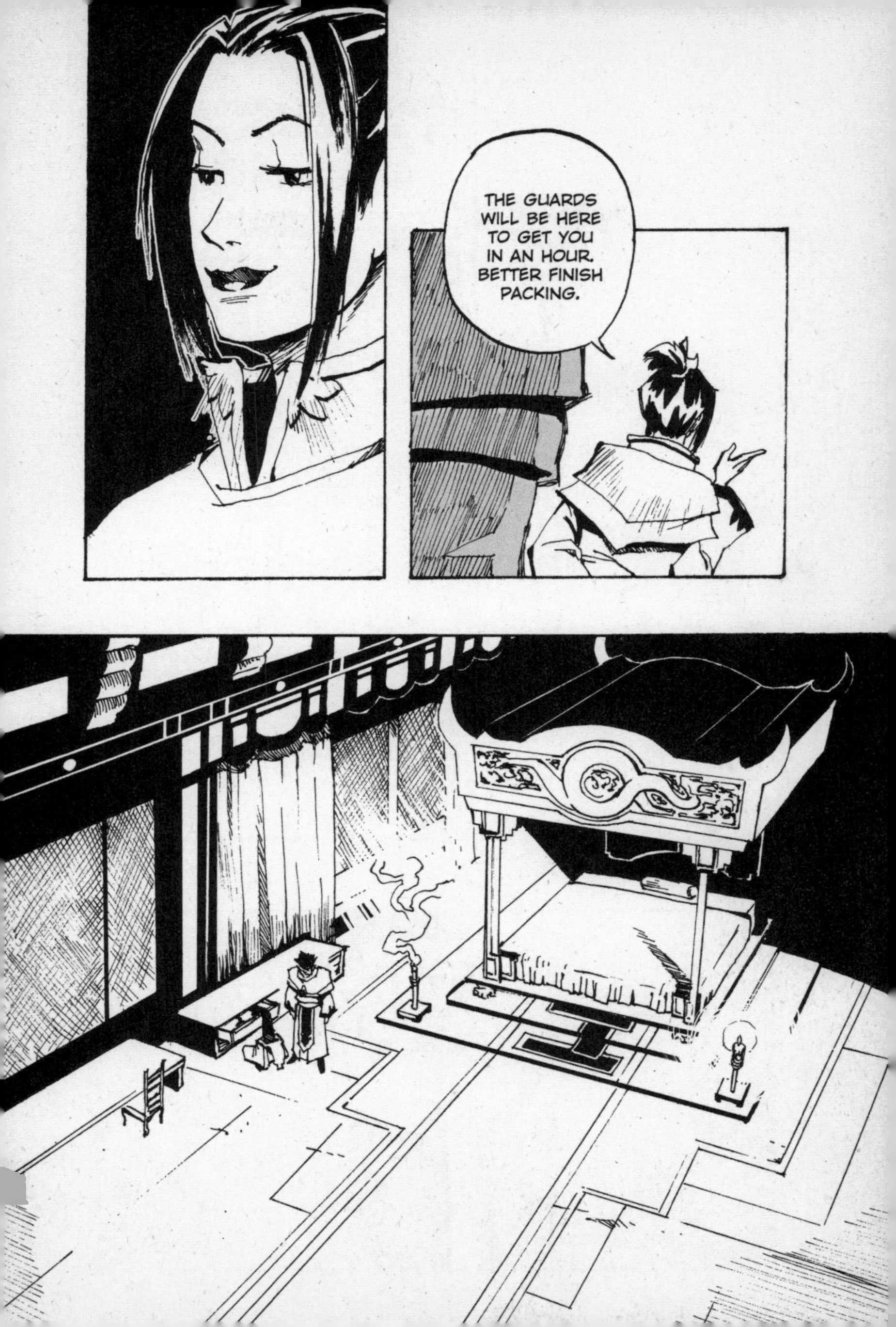
THE GUARDS WILL BE HERE TO GET YOU IN AN HOUR. BETTER FINISH PACKING.

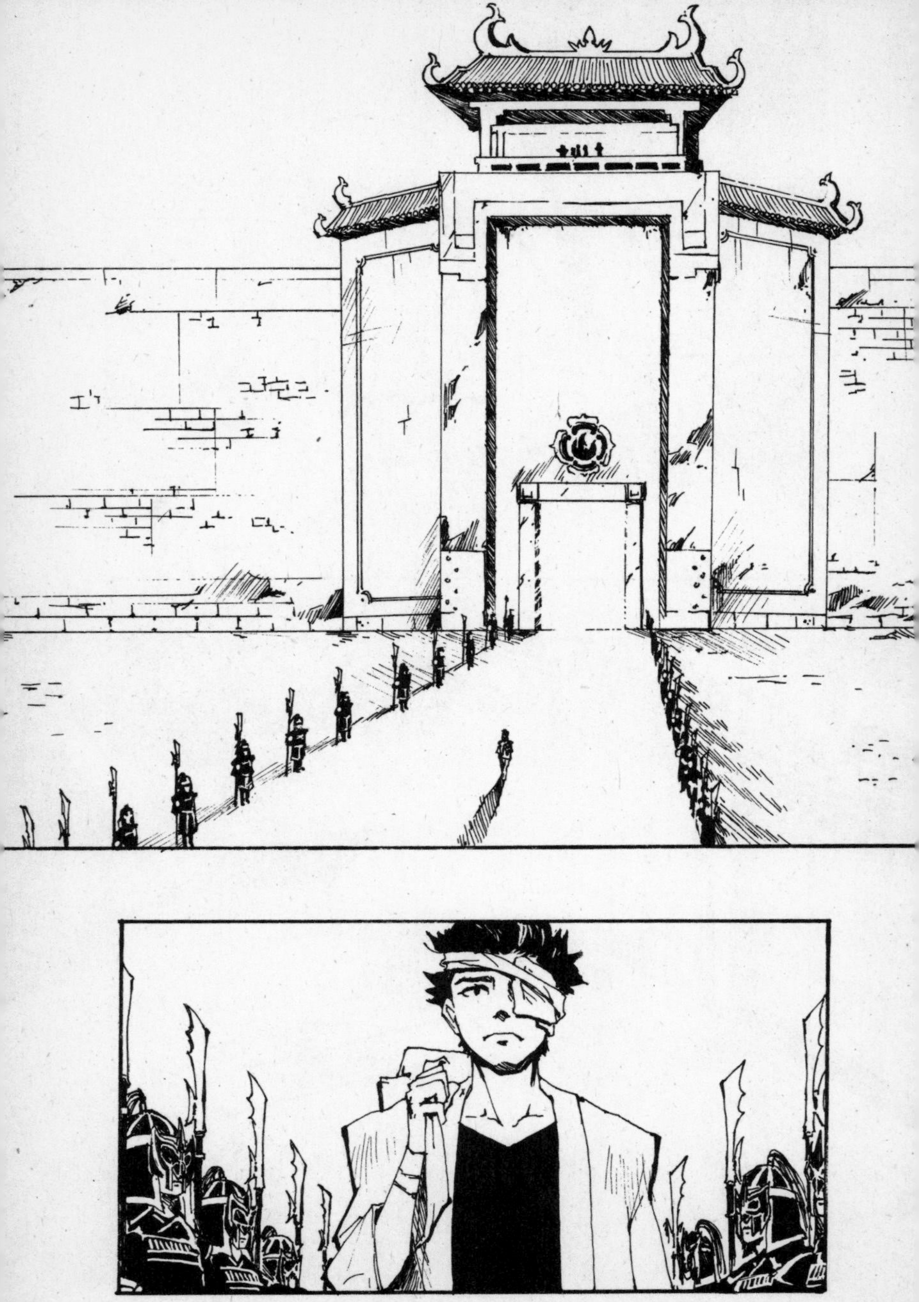

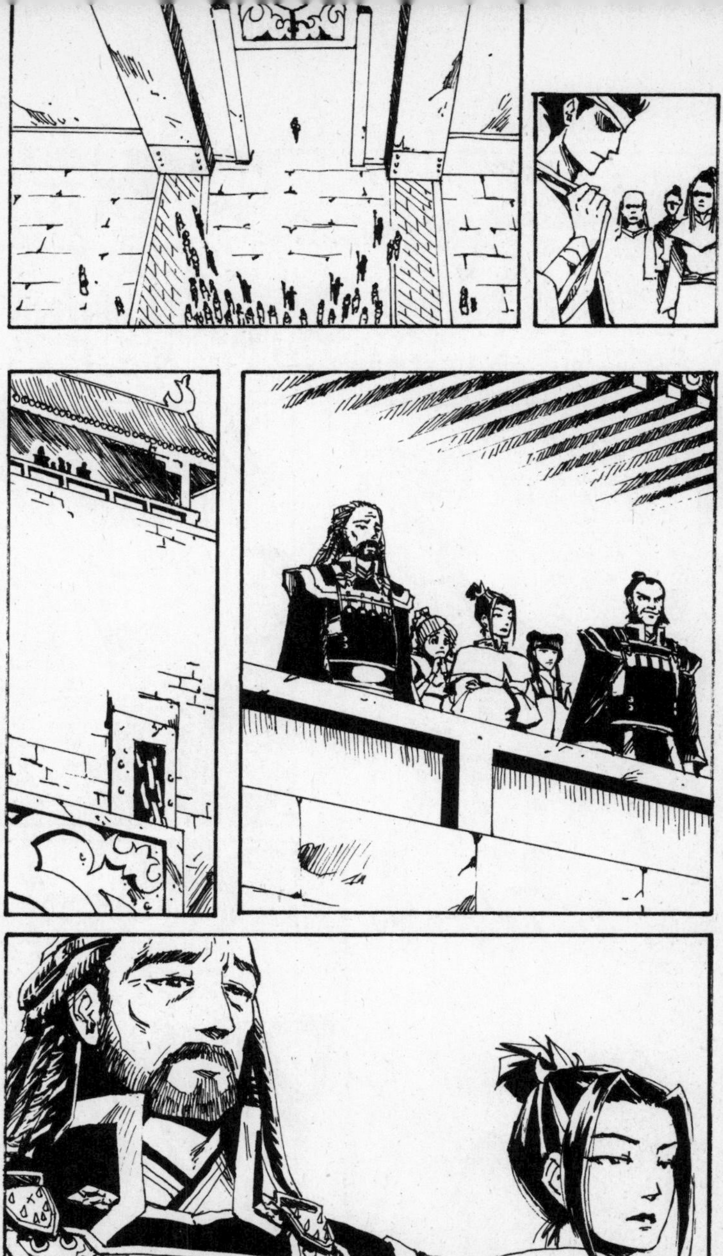

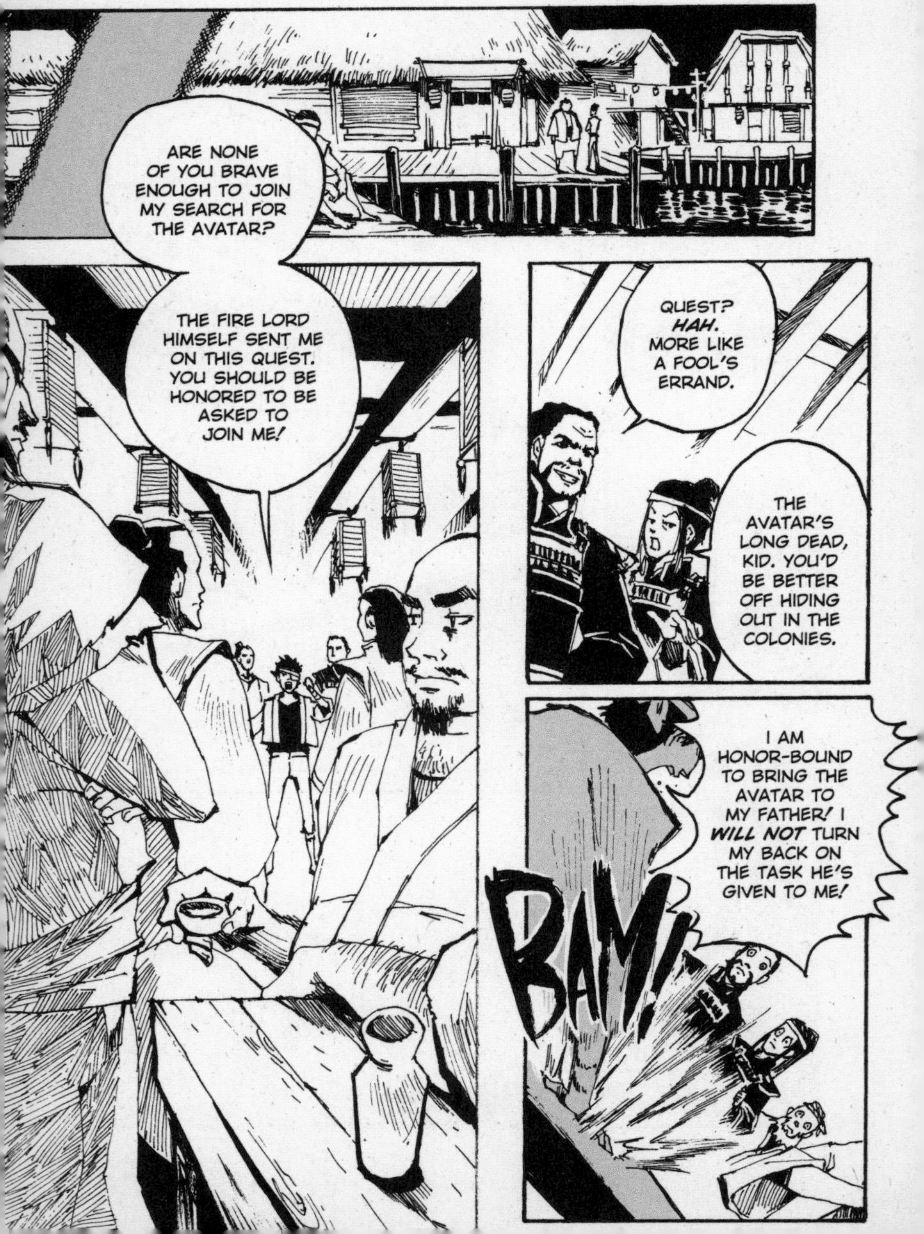
ARE NONE OF YOU BRAVE ENOUGH TO JOIN MY SEARCH FOR THE AVATAR?
THE FIRE LORD HIMSELF SENT ME ON THIS QUEST. YOU SHOULD BE HONORED TO BE ASKED TO JOIN ME!
QUEST? *HAH*. MORE LIKE A FOOL'S ERRAND.
THE AVATAR'S LONG DEAD, KID. YOU'D BE BETTER OFF HIDING OUT IN THE COLONIES.
I AM HONOR-BOUND TO BRING THE AVATAR TO MY FATHER! I *WILL NOT* TURN MY BACK ON THE TASK HE'S GIVEN TO ME!
BAM!

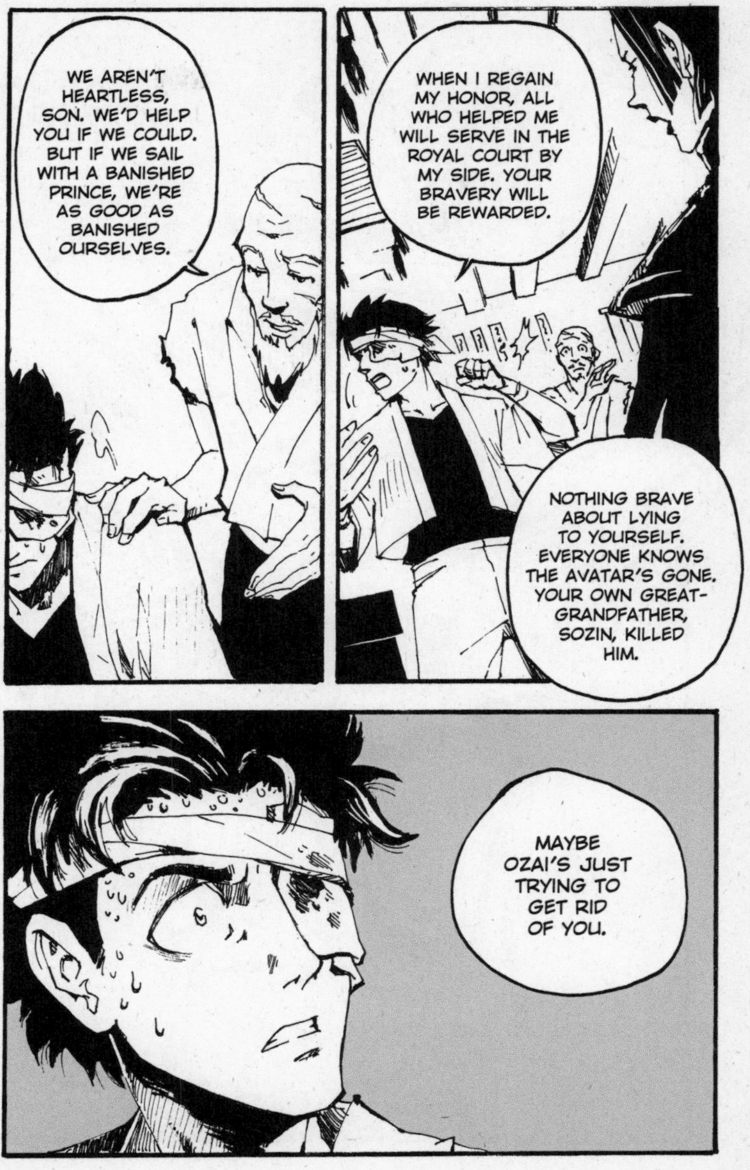
WE AREN'T HEARTLESS, SON. WE'D HELP YOU IF WE COULD. BUT IF WE SAIL WITH A BANISHED PRINCE, WE'RE AS GOOD AS BANISHED OURSELVES.
WHEN I REGAIN MY HONOR, ALL WHO HELPED ME WILL SERVE IN THE ROYAL COURT BY MY SIDE. YOUR BRAVERY WILL BE REWARDED.
NOTHING BRAVE ABOUT LYING TO YOURSELF. EVERYONE KNOWS THE AVATAR'S GONE. YOUR OWN GREAT-GRANDFATHER, SOZIN, KILLED HIM.
MAYBE OZAI'S JUST TRYING TO GET RID OF YOU.

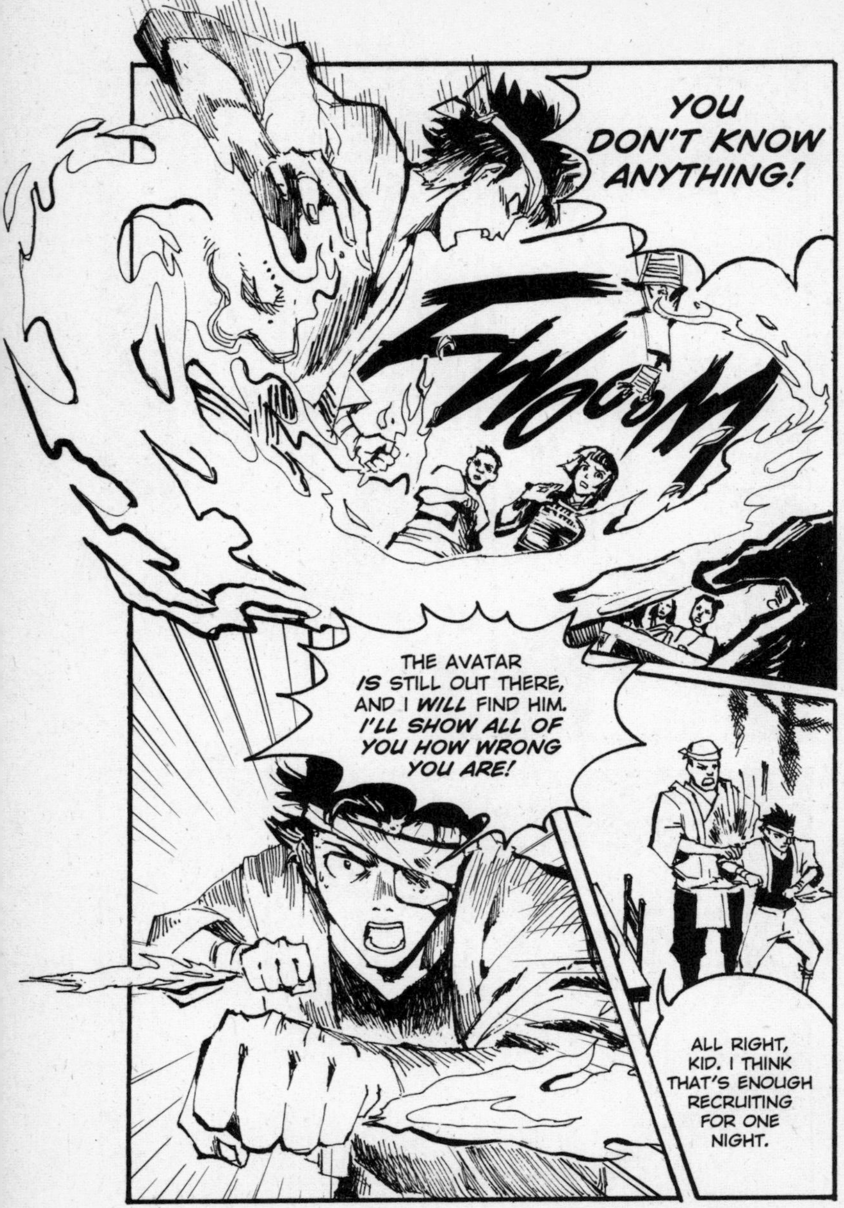
YOU DON'T KNOW ANYTHING!
FWOOOM
THE AVATAR *IS* STILL OUT THERE, AND I *WILL* FIND HIM. ***I'LL SHOW ALL OF YOU HOW WRONG YOU ARE!***
ALL RIGHT, KID. I THINK THAT'S ENOUGH RECRUITING FOR ONE NIGHT.

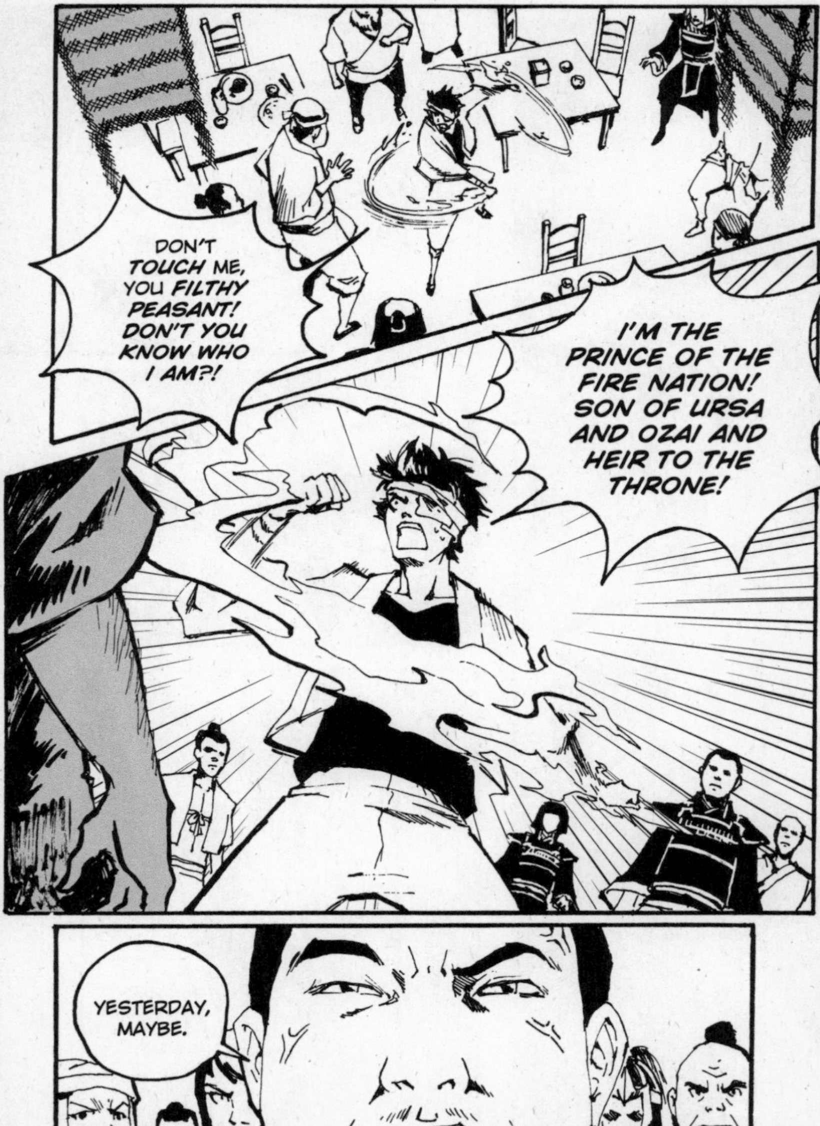
DON'T *TOUCH* ME, YOU *FILTHY PEASANT! DON'T YOU KNOW WHO I AM?!*
I'M THE PRINCE OF THE FIRE NATION! SON OF URSA AND OZAI AND HEIR TO THE THRONE!
YESTERDAY, MAYBE.

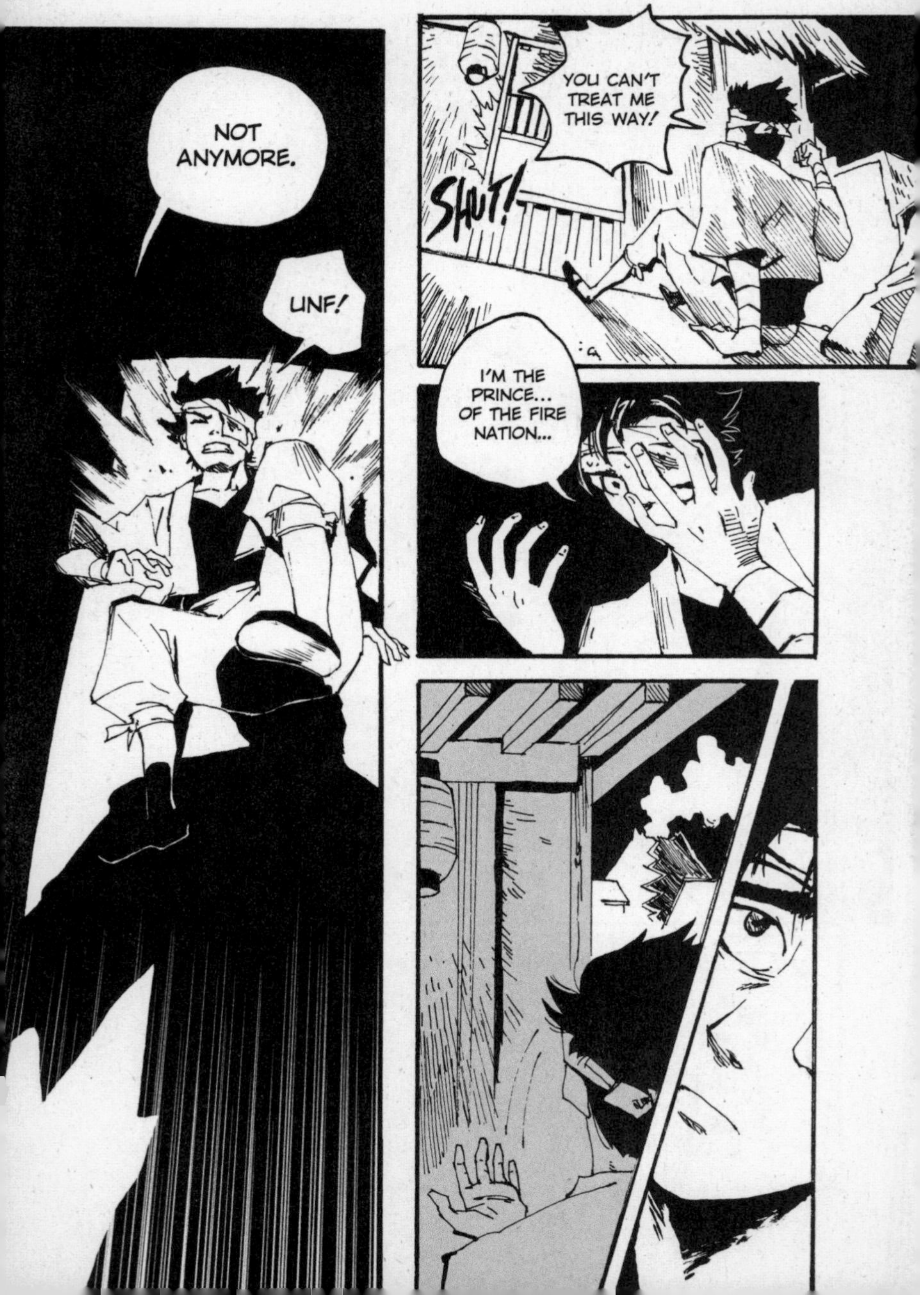
NOT ANYMORE.
UNF!
YOU CAN'T TREAT ME THIS WAY!
SHUT!
I'M THE PRINCE... OF THE FIRE NATION...

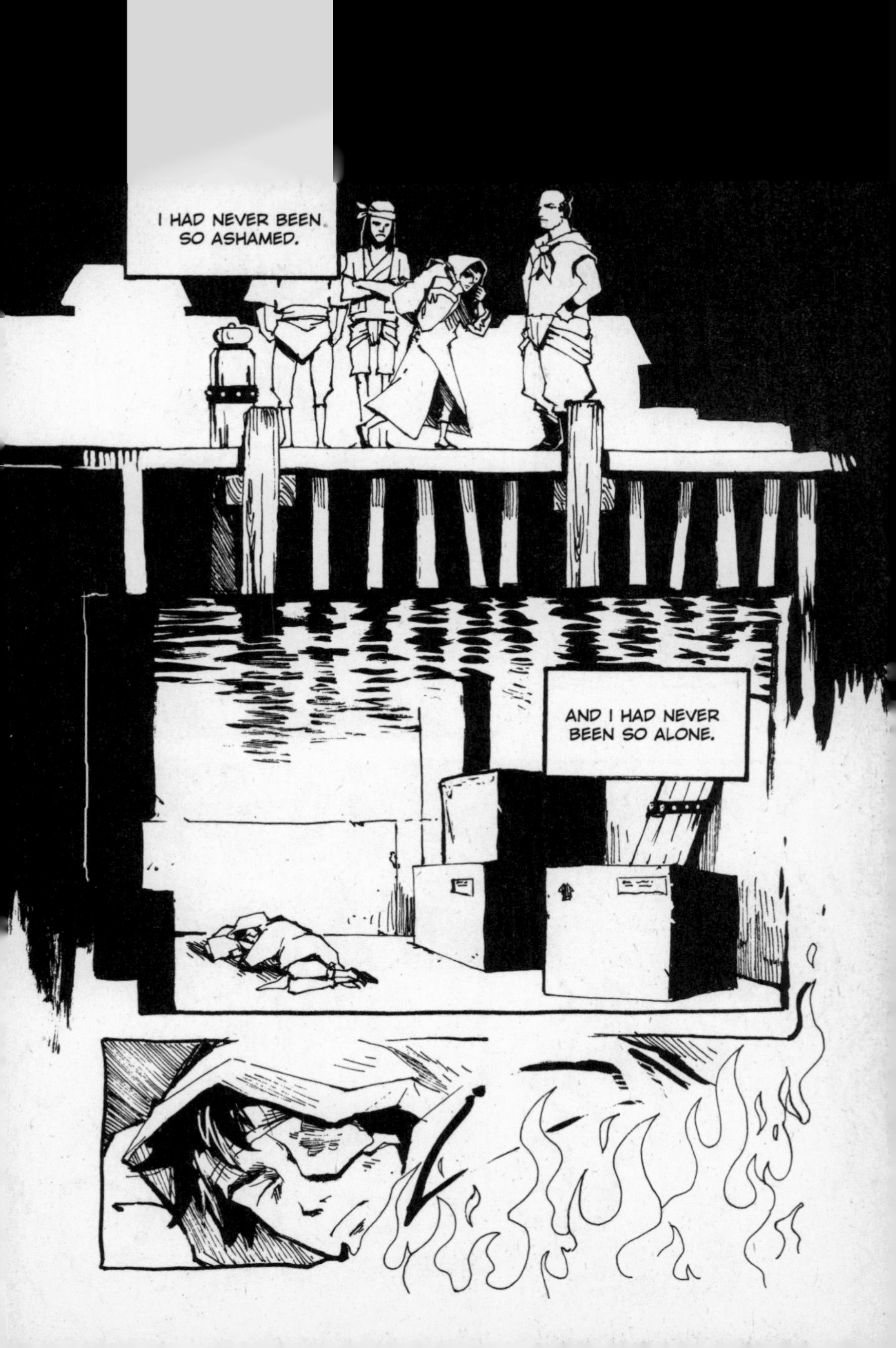
I HAD NEVER BEEN SO ASHAMED.
AND I HAD NEVER BEEN SO ALONE.

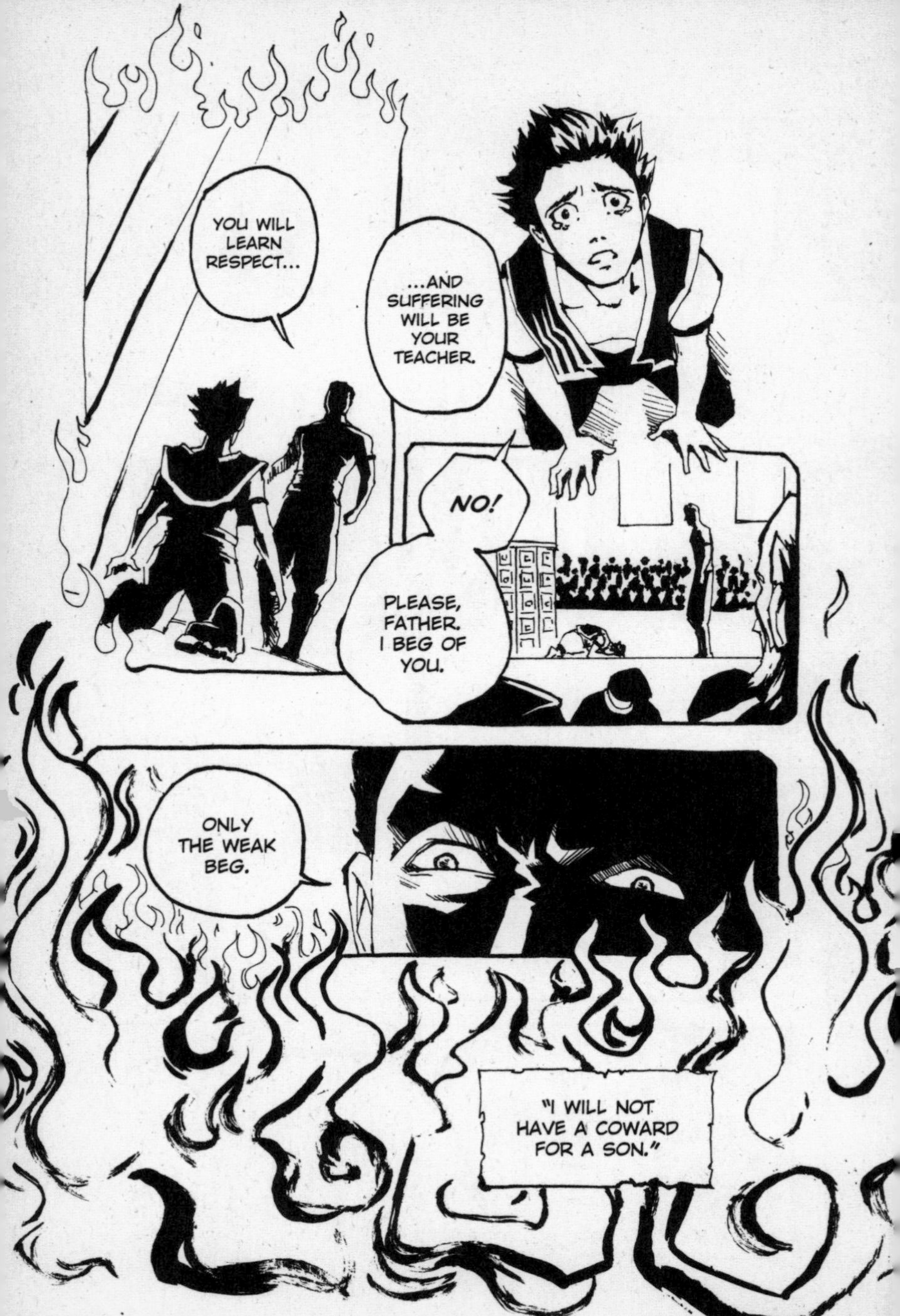
YOU WILL LEARN RESPECT...
...AND SUFFERING WILL BE YOUR TEACHER.
NO!
PLEASE, FATHER. I BEG OF YOU.
ONLY THE WEAK BEG.
"I WILL NOT HAVE A COWARD FOR A SON."

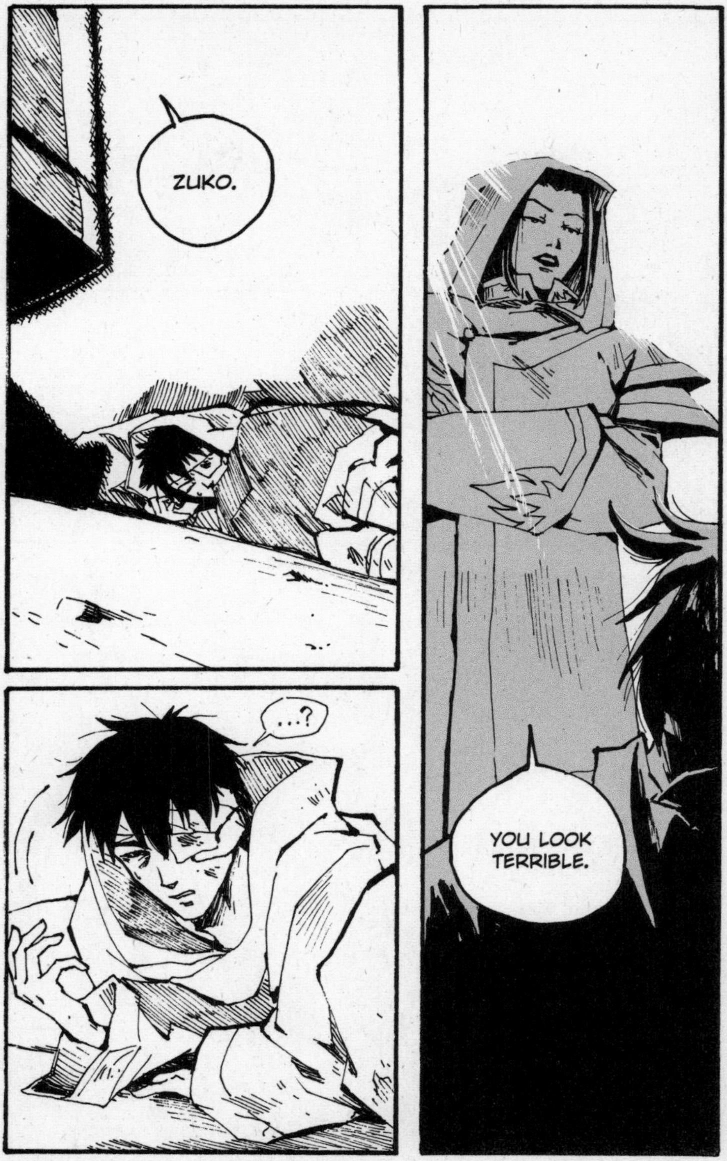
ZUKO.
...?
YOU LOOK TERRIBLE.

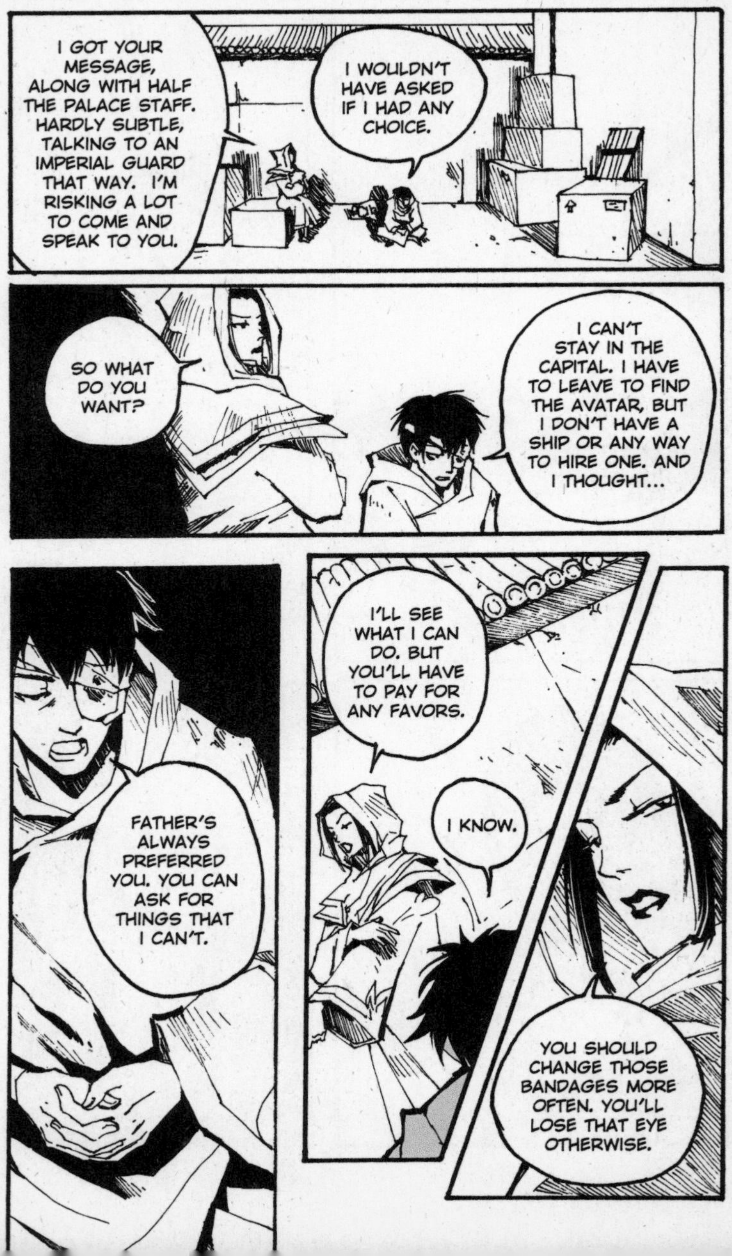
I GOT YOUR MESSAGE, ALONG WITH HALF THE PALACE STAFF. HARDLY SUBTLE, TALKING TO AN IMPERIAL GUARD THAT WAY. I'M RISKING A LOT TO COME AND SPEAK TO YOU.
I WOULDN'T HAVE ASKED IF I HAD ANY CHOICE.
SO WHAT DO YOU WANT?
I CAN'T STAY IN THE CAPITAL. I HAVE TO LEAVE TO FIND THE AVATAR, BUT I DON'T HAVE A SHIP OR ANY WAY TO HIRE ONE. AND I THOUGHT...
FATHER'S ALWAYS PREFERRED YOU. YOU CAN ASK FOR THINGS THAT I CAN'T.
I'LL SEE WHAT I CAN DO. BUT YOU'LL HAVE TO PAY FOR ANY FAVORS.
I KNOW.
YOU SHOULD CHANGE THOSE BANDAGES MORE OFTEN. YOU'LL LOSE THAT EYE OTHERWISE.

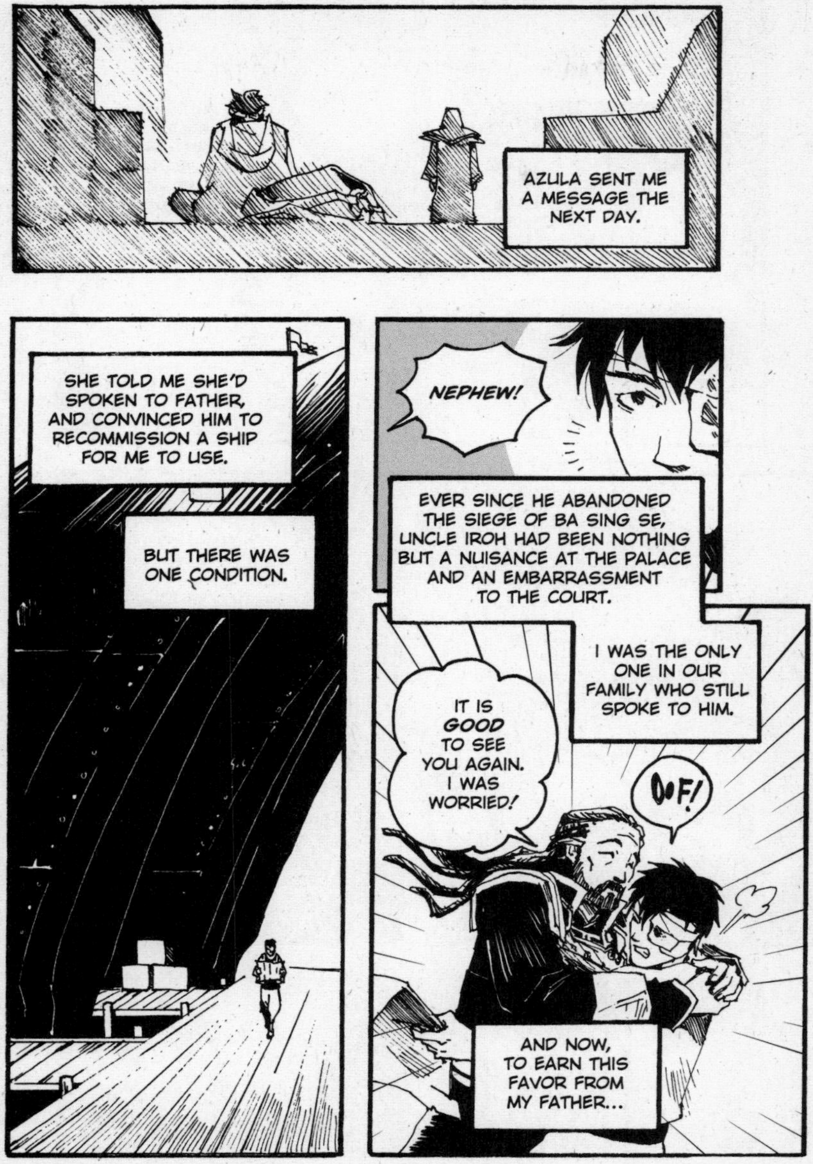
AZULA SENT ME A MESSAGE THE NEXT DAY.
SHE TOLD ME SHE'D SPOKEN TO FATHER, AND CONVINCED HIM TO RECOMMISSION A SHIP FOR ME TO USE.
BUT THERE WAS ONE CONDITION.
NEPHEW!
EVER SINCE HE ABANDONED THE SIEGE OF BA SING SE, UNCLE IROH HAD BEEN NOTHING BUT A NUISANCE AT THE PALACE AND AN EMBARRASSMENT TO THE COURT.
I WAS THE ONLY ONE IN OUR FAMILY WHO STILL SPOKE TO HIM.
IT IS *GOOD* TO SEE YOU AGAIN. I WAS WORRIED!
OOF!
AND NOW, TO EARN THIS FAVOR FROM MY FATHER...

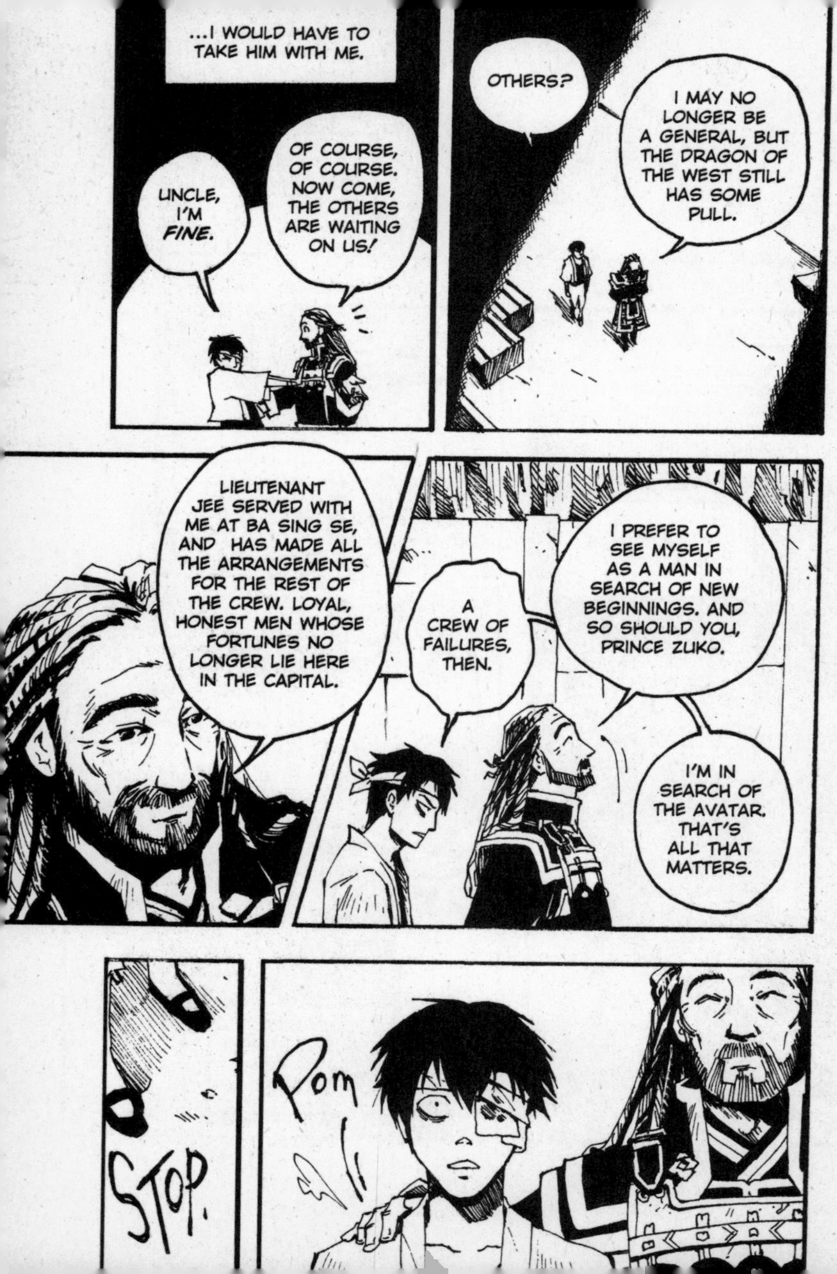
...I WOULD HAVE TO TAKE HIM WITH ME.
UNCLE, I'M *FINE*.
OF COURSE, OF COURSE. NOW COME, THE OTHERS ARE WAITING ON US!
OTHERS?
I MAY NO LONGER BE A GENERAL, BUT THE DRAGON OF THE WEST STILL HAS SOME PULL.
LIEUTENANT JEE SERVED WITH ME AT BA SING SE, AND HAS MADE ALL THE ARRANGEMENTS FOR THE REST OF THE CREW. LOYAL, HONEST MEN WHOSE FORTUNES NO LONGER LIE HERE IN THE CAPITAL.
A CREW OF FAILURES, THEN.
I PREFER TO SEE MYSELF AS A MAN IN SEARCH OF NEW BEGINNINGS. AND SO SHOULD YOU, PRINCE ZUKO.
I'M IN SEARCH OF THE AVATAR. THAT'S ALL THAT MATTERS.
STOP.
Pom

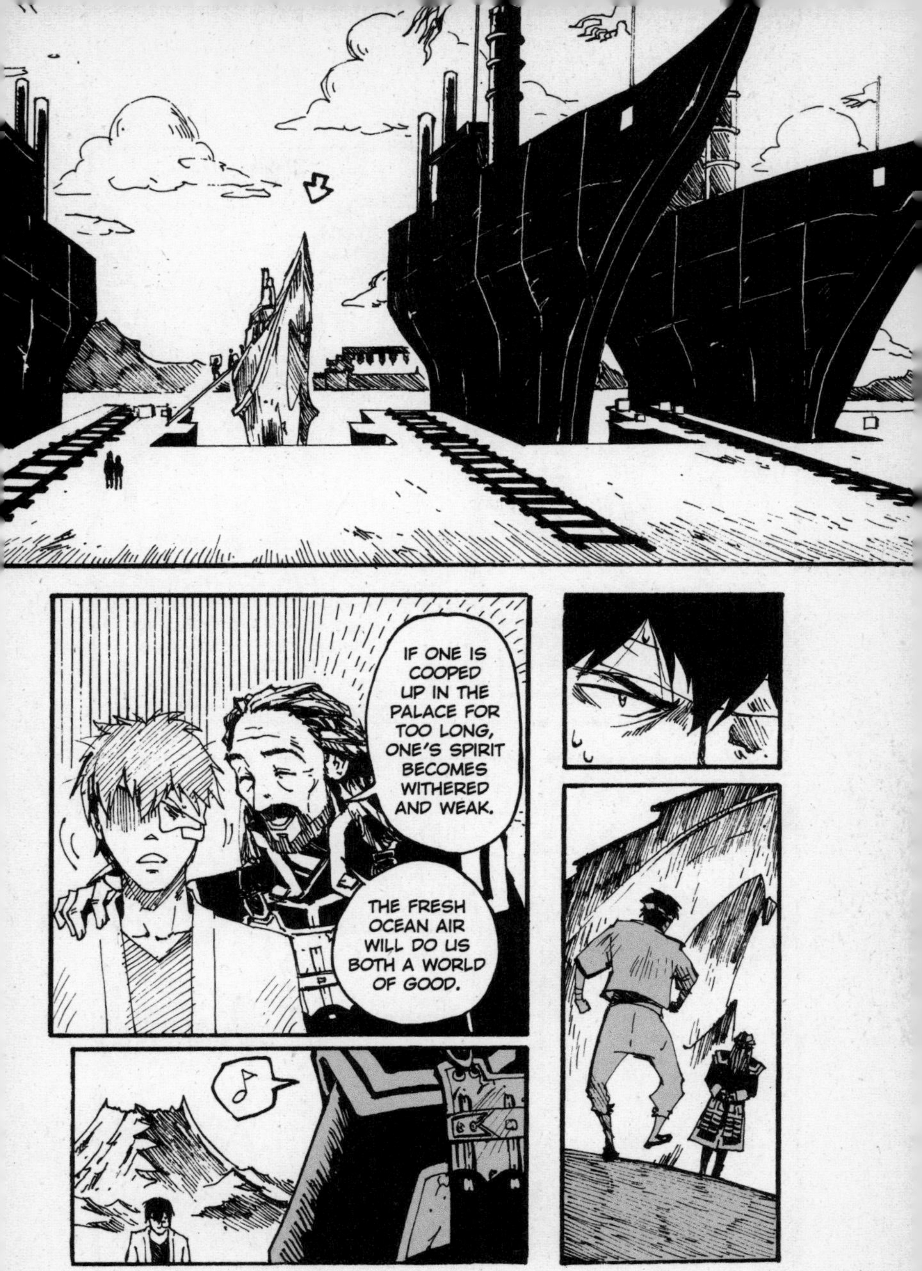
IF ONE IS COOPED UP IN THE PALACE FOR TOO LONG, ONE'S SPIRIT BECOMES WITHERED AND WEAK.
THE FRESH OCEAN AIR WILL DO US BOTH A WORLD OF GOOD.
♪

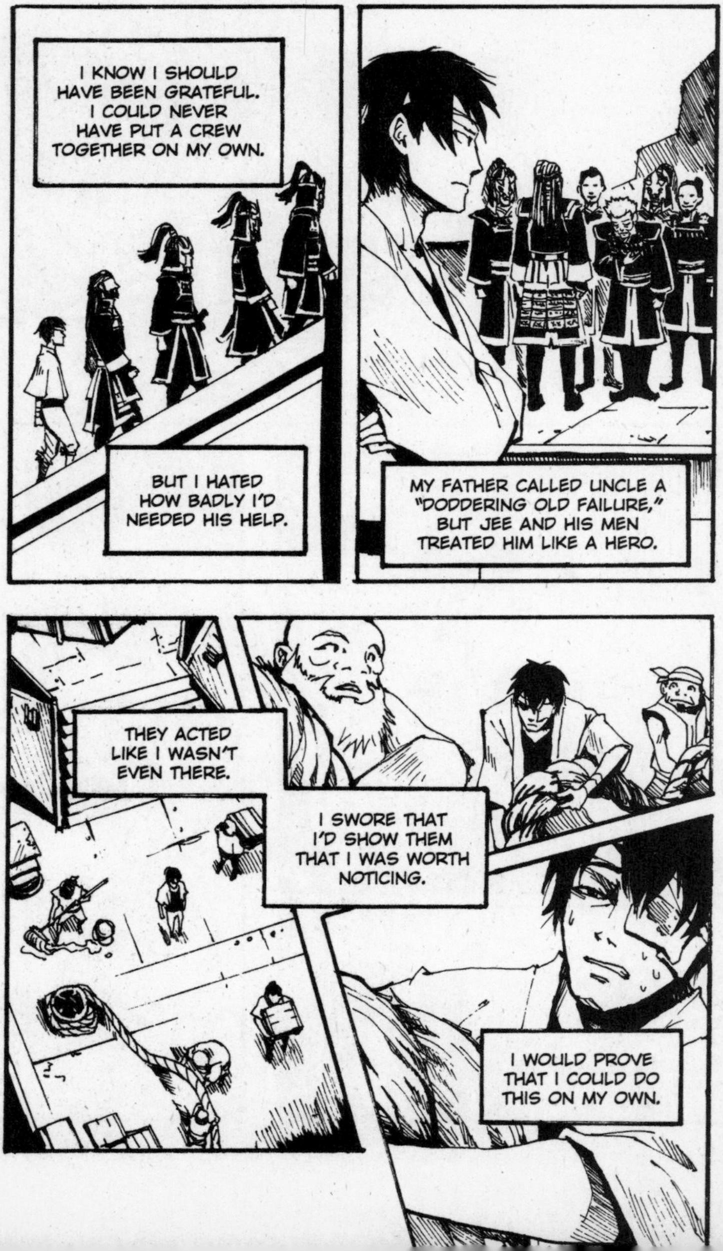
I KNOW I SHOULD HAVE BEEN GRATEFUL. I COULD NEVER HAVE PUT A CREW TOGETHER ON MY OWN.
BUT I HATED HOW BADLY I'D NEEDED HIS HELP.
MY FATHER CALLED UNCLE A "DODDERING OLD FAILURE," BUT JEE AND HIS MEN TREATED HIM LIKE A HERO.
THEY ACTED LIKE I WASN'T EVEN THERE.
I SWORE THAT I'D SHOW THEM THAT I WAS WORTH NOTICING.
I WOULD PROVE THAT I COULD DO THIS ON MY OWN.

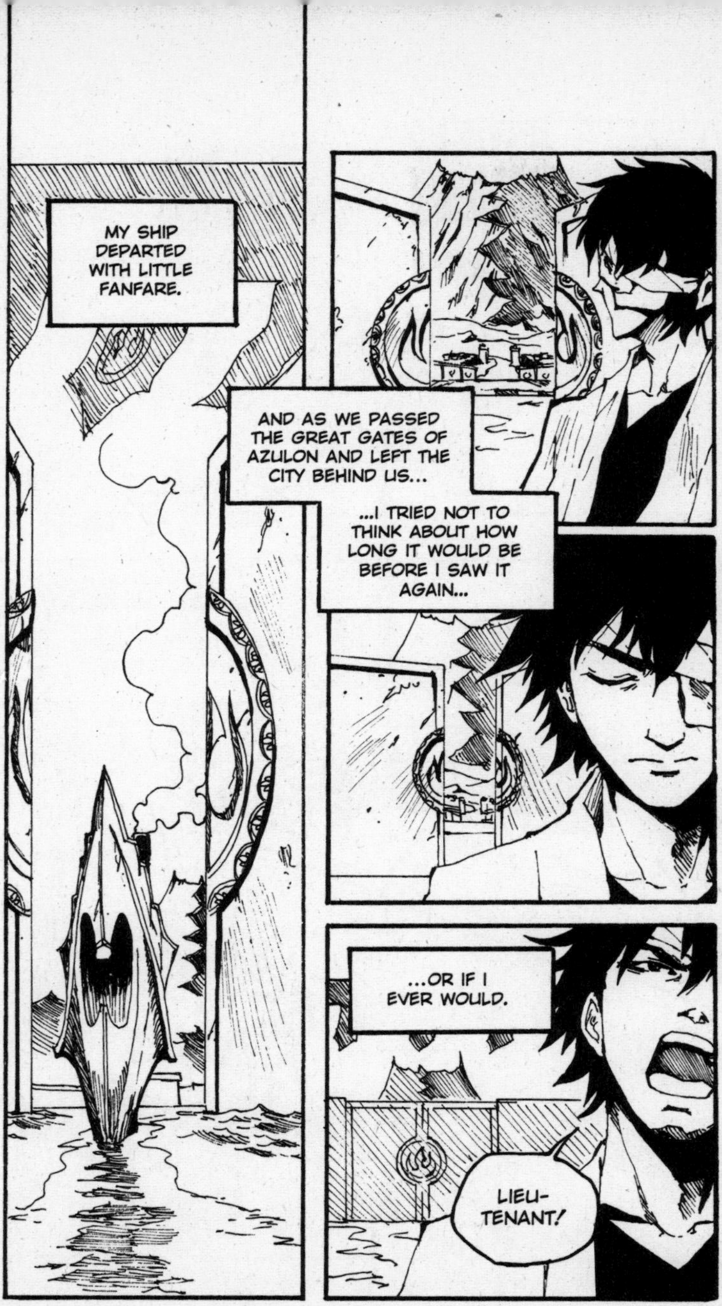
MY SHIP DEPARTED WITH LITTLE FANFARE.
AND AS WE PASSED THE GREAT GATES OF AZULON AND LEFT THE CITY BEHIND US...
...I TRIED NOT TO THINK ABOUT HOW LONG IT WOULD BE BEFORE I SAW IT AGAIN...
...OR IF I EVER WOULD.
LIEU-TENANT!

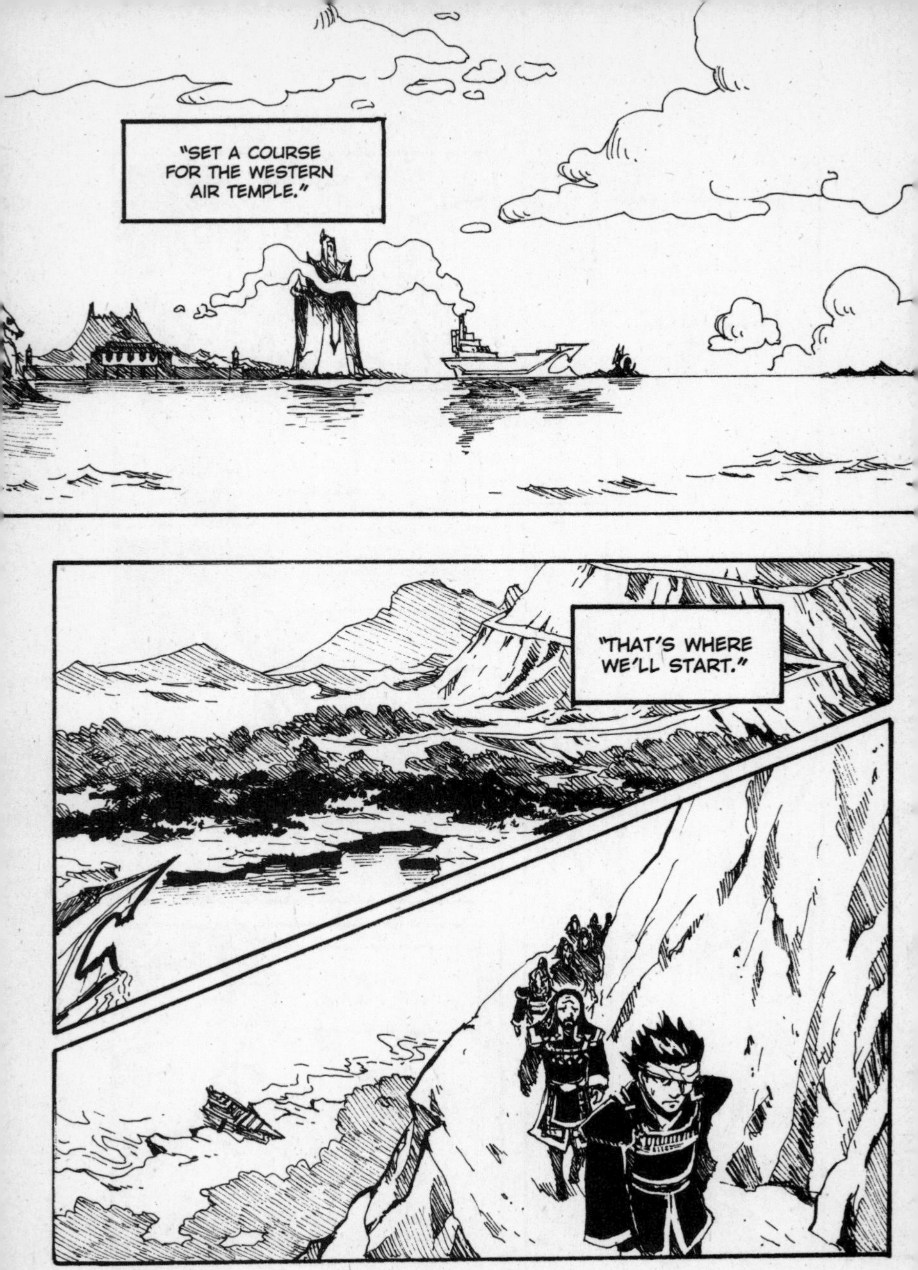
"SET A COURSE FOR THE WESTERN AIR TEMPLE."
"THAT'S WHERE WE'LL START."

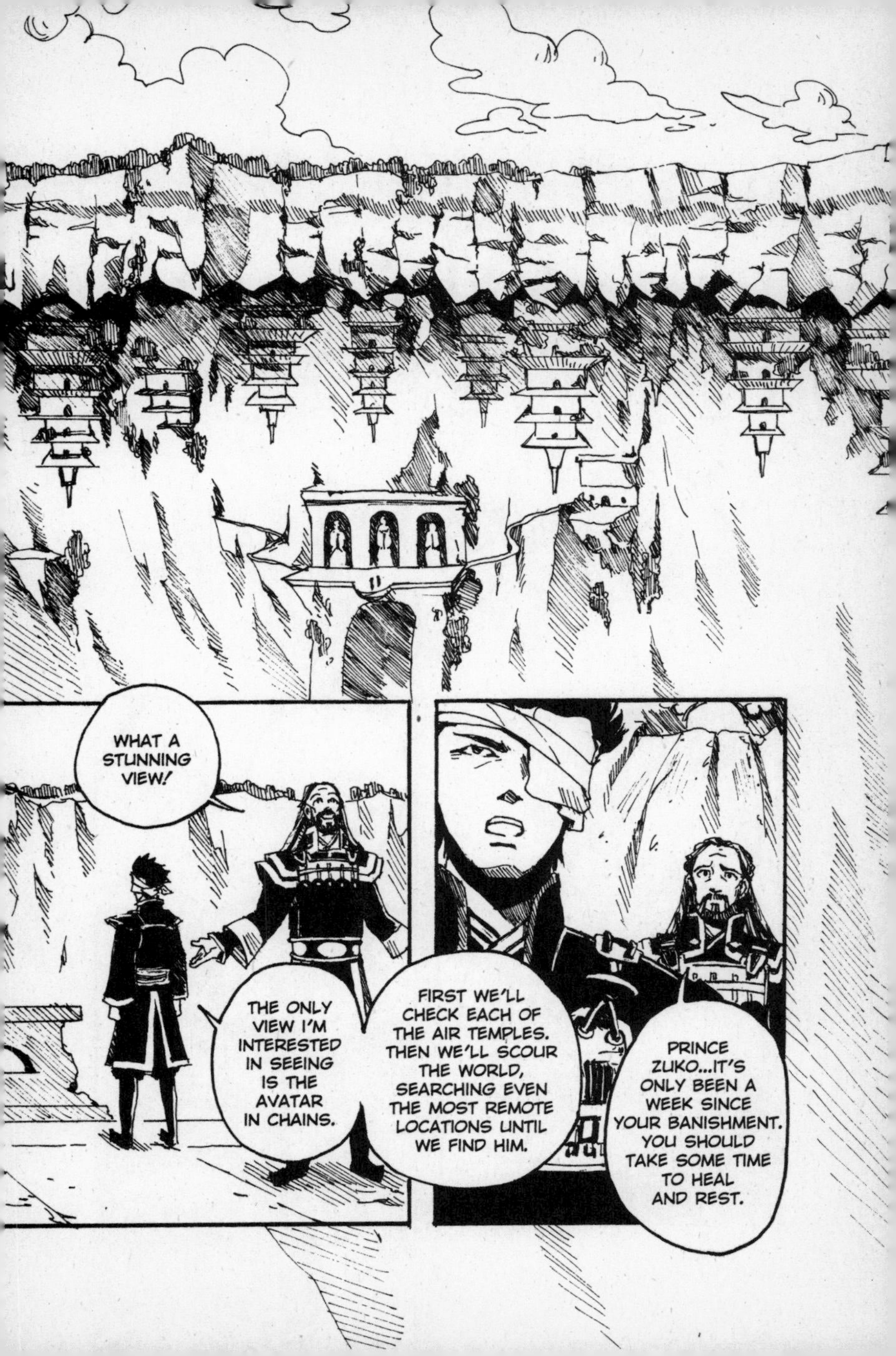
WHAT A STUNNING VIEW!
THE ONLY VIEW I'M INTERESTED IN SEEING IS THE AVATAR IN CHAINS.
FIRST WE'LL CHECK EACH OF THE AIR TEMPLES. THEN WE'LL SCOUR THE WORLD, SEARCHING EVEN THE MOST REMOTE LOCATIONS UNTIL WE FIND HIM.
PRINCE ZUKO...IT'S ONLY BEEN A WEEK SINCE YOUR BANISHMENT. YOU SHOULD TAKE SOME TIME TO HEAL AND REST.

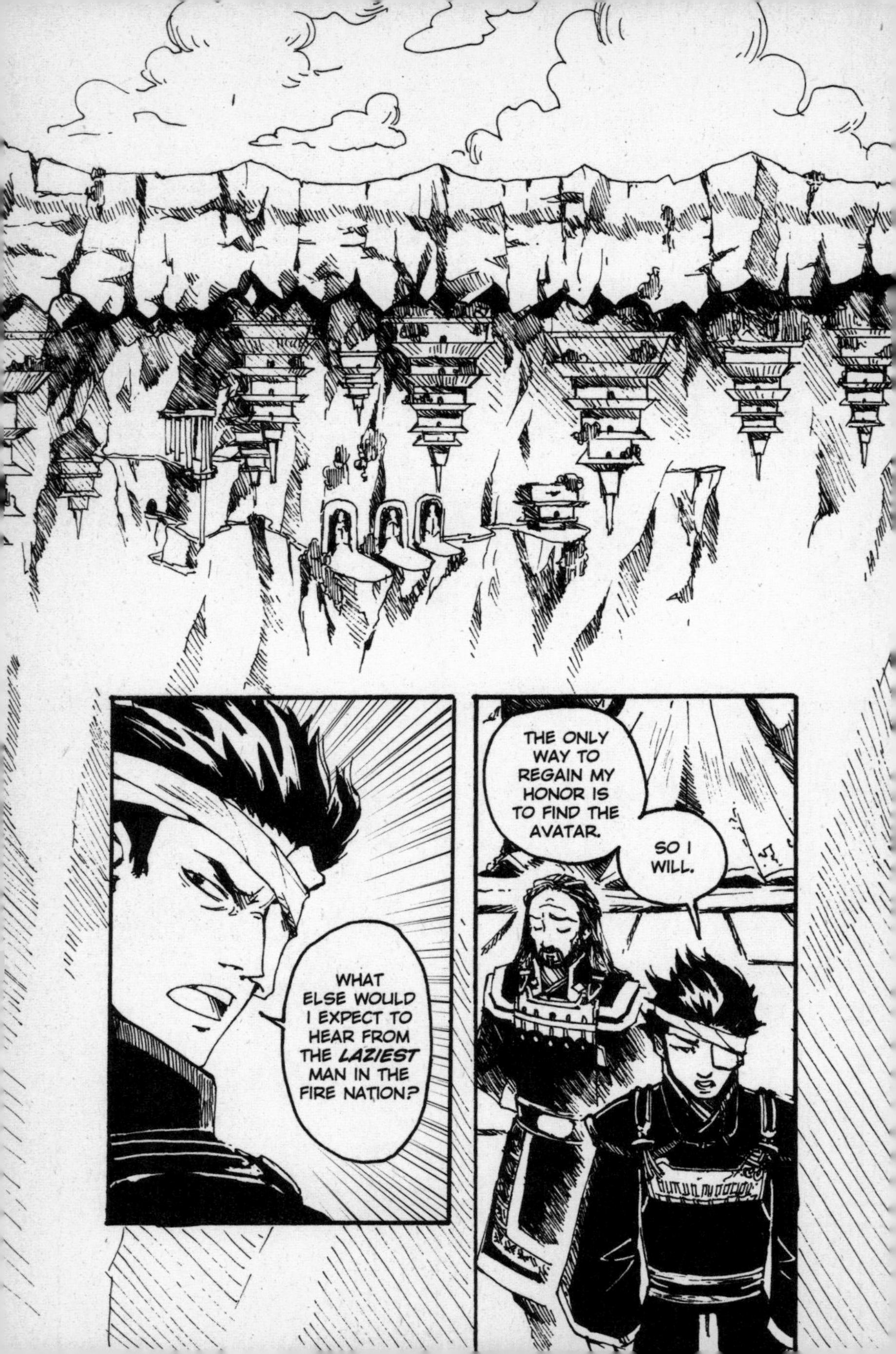
WHAT ELSE WOULD I EXPECT TO HEAR FROM THE *LAZIEST* MAN IN THE FIRE NATION?
THE ONLY WAY TO REGAIN MY HONOR IS TO FIND THE AVATAR.
SO I WILL.

I WOULD NOT PRESUME TO TELL YOU HOW TO CONDUCT YOUR SEARCH, NEPHEW. BUT YOU WERE TOLD VERY LITTLE ABOUT THE AVATAR WHEN YOU WERE A BOY.

PERHAPS IF YOU KNEW MORE ABOUT THE LIVES HE HAS ALREADY LED, YOU WOULD HAVE A CLEARER PICTURE OF WHAT YOU ARE SEARCHING *FOR.*

HOW MANY HUNDRED-YEAR-OLD AIRBENDERS DO YOU THINK THERE ARE? I KNOW ENOUGH.

THE PREVIOUS AVATAR, ROKU, LIVED AT THE FIRE TEMPLE ON CRESCENT ISLAND FOR SEVERAL YEARS. THE SAGES THERE KNOW MORE ABOUT HIM THAN ANYONE ELSE IN THE WORLD.

THAT ISLAND IS *WEEKS* OFF-COURSE!

BUT GOING MAY SAVE YOU *YEARS* OF FRUITLESS EFFORT. IT CANNOT HURT TO ASK.

FINE. IF IT'LL KEEP YOU FROM NAGGING ME.

I ONLY NAG BECAUSE I CARE, NEPHEW.

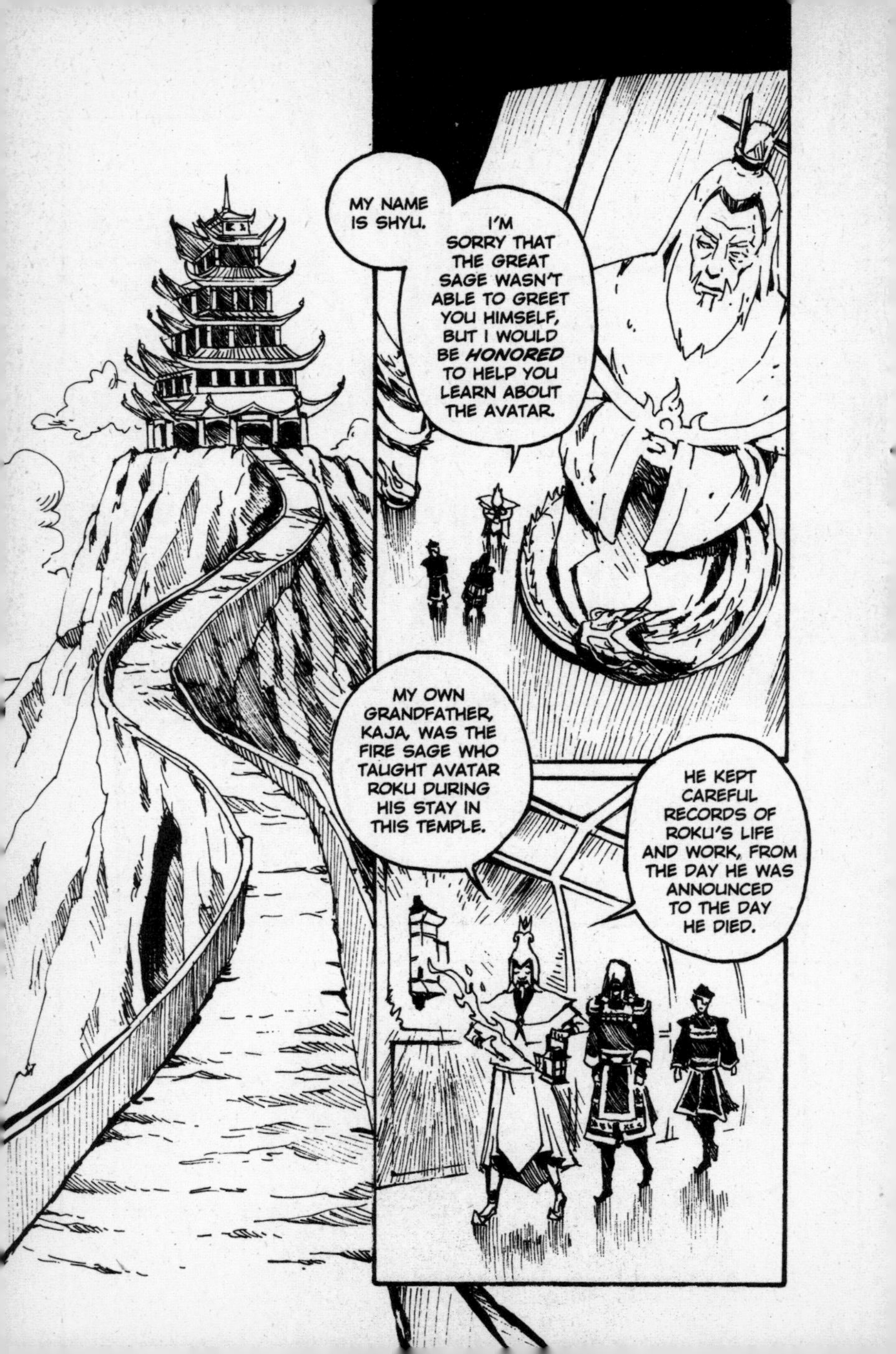
MY NAME IS SHYU.
I'M SORRY THAT THE GREAT SAGE WASN'T ABLE TO GREET YOU HIMSELF, BUT I WOULD BE *HONORED* TO HELP YOU LEARN ABOUT THE AVATAR.
MY OWN GRANDFATHER, KAJA, WAS THE FIRE SAGE WHO TAUGHT AVATAR ROKU DURING HIS STAY IN THIS TEMPLE.
HE KEPT CAREFUL RECORDS OF ROKU'S LIFE AND WORK, FROM THE DAY HE WAS ANNOUNCED TO THE DAY HE DIED.

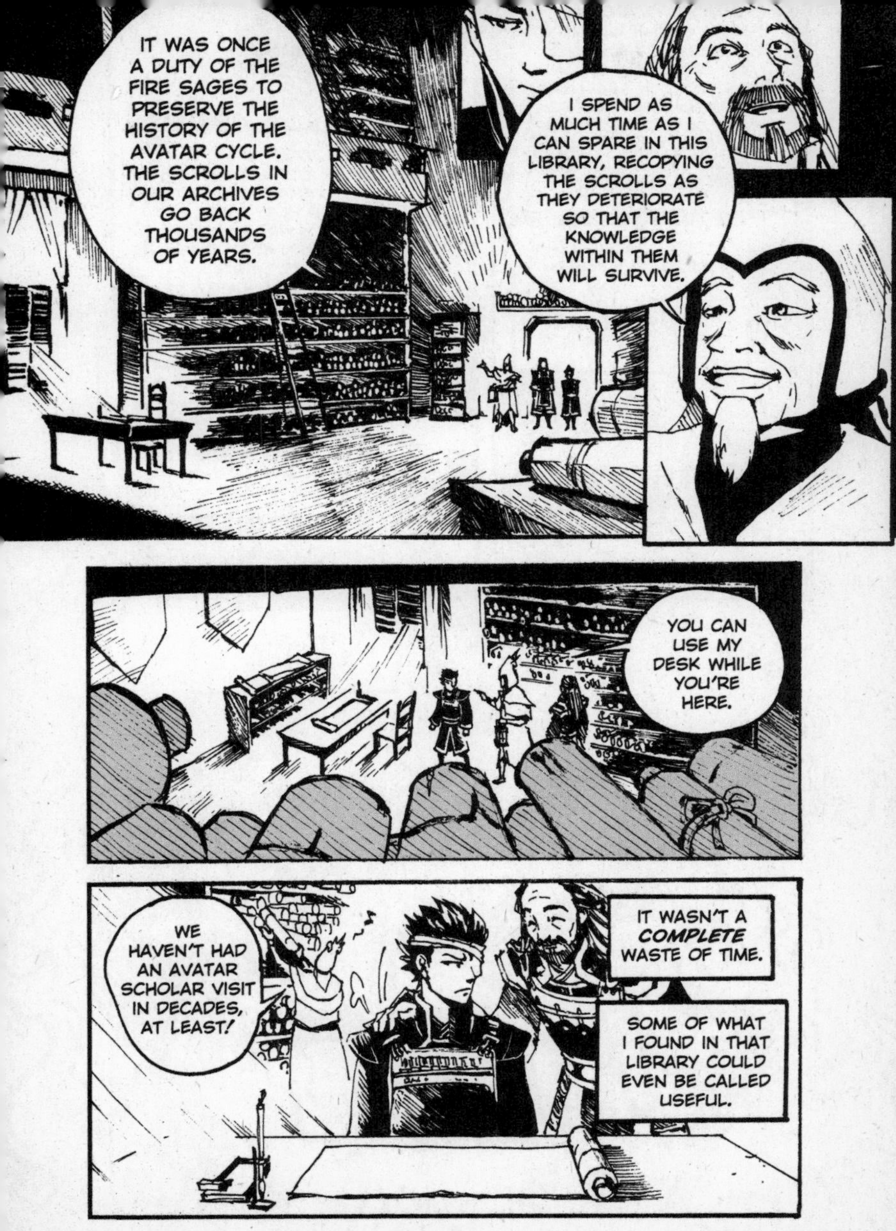
IT WAS ONCE A DUTY OF THE FIRE SAGES TO PRESERVE THE HISTORY OF THE AVATAR CYCLE. THE SCROLLS IN OUR ARCHIVES GO BACK THOUSANDS OF YEARS.
I SPEND AS MUCH TIME AS I CAN SPARE IN THIS LIBRARY, RECOPYING THE SCROLLS AS THEY DETERIORATE SO THAT THE KNOWLEDGE WITHIN THEM WILL SURVIVE.
YOU CAN USE MY DESK WHILE YOU'RE HERE.
WE HAVEN'T HAD AN AVATAR SCHOLAR VISIT IN DECADES, AT LEAST!
IT WASN'T A *COMPLETE* WASTE OF TIME.
SOME OF WHAT I FOUND IN THAT LIBRARY COULD EVEN BE CALLED USEFUL.

AVATAR YANGCHEN BUILT A HERMITAGE NEAR THE EASTERN AIR TEMPLE, AND SPENT HER LATER YEARS THERE IN SECLUSION. AVATAR KYOSHI LIVED FOR TWO-HUNDRED AND THIRTY YEARS — MUCH OLDER THAN THE CURRENT AVATAR WOULD BE.

MOST VALUABLE OF ALL WERE THE TESTS — WAYS YOU COULD TELL FOR SURE IF SOMEONE WAS THE AVATAR OR NOT.

BUT THE MAJORITY OF IT WAS DRY, DUSTY KNOW-LEDGE ABOUT PEOPOLE WHO HAD DIED HUNDREDS OF YEARS AGO; WARS AND TREATIES BETWEEN KINGDOMS THAT NO LONGER EXISTED; ENDLESS LISTS OF BIRTHS AND DEATHS AND MARRIAGES.

THE REST WAS OUTDATED PHILOSOPHY, ABOUT KEEPING THE NATIONS IN BALANCE AND MAINTAINING A CONNECTION WITH THE SPIRIT WORLD — DULL AT BEST AND OUTRIGHT TRAITOROUS AT WORST.

MY MIND WANDERED.

Fssh...

CRACKLE

Fssh...

CRACKLE

FOOOOM

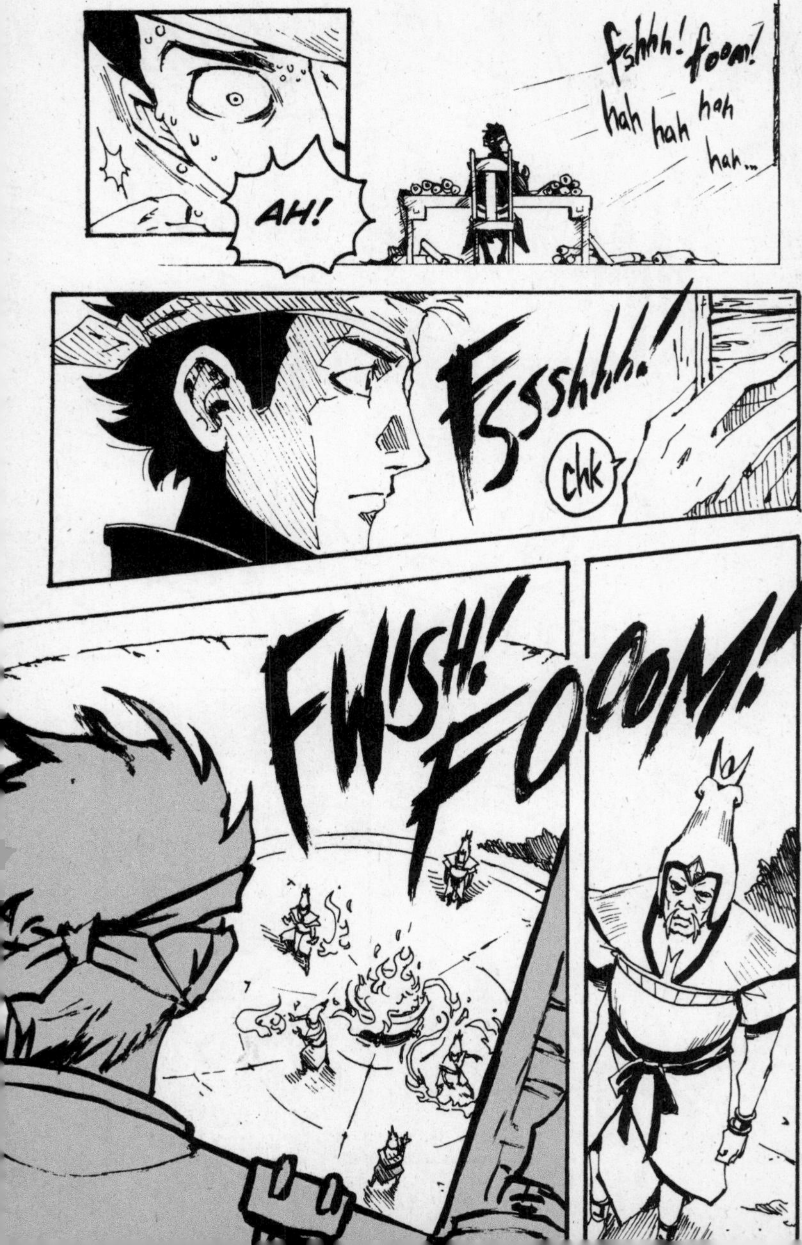
AH!
fshhh! foom!
hah hah hah hah...
Fssshhh!
chk
FWISH! FOOOOM!

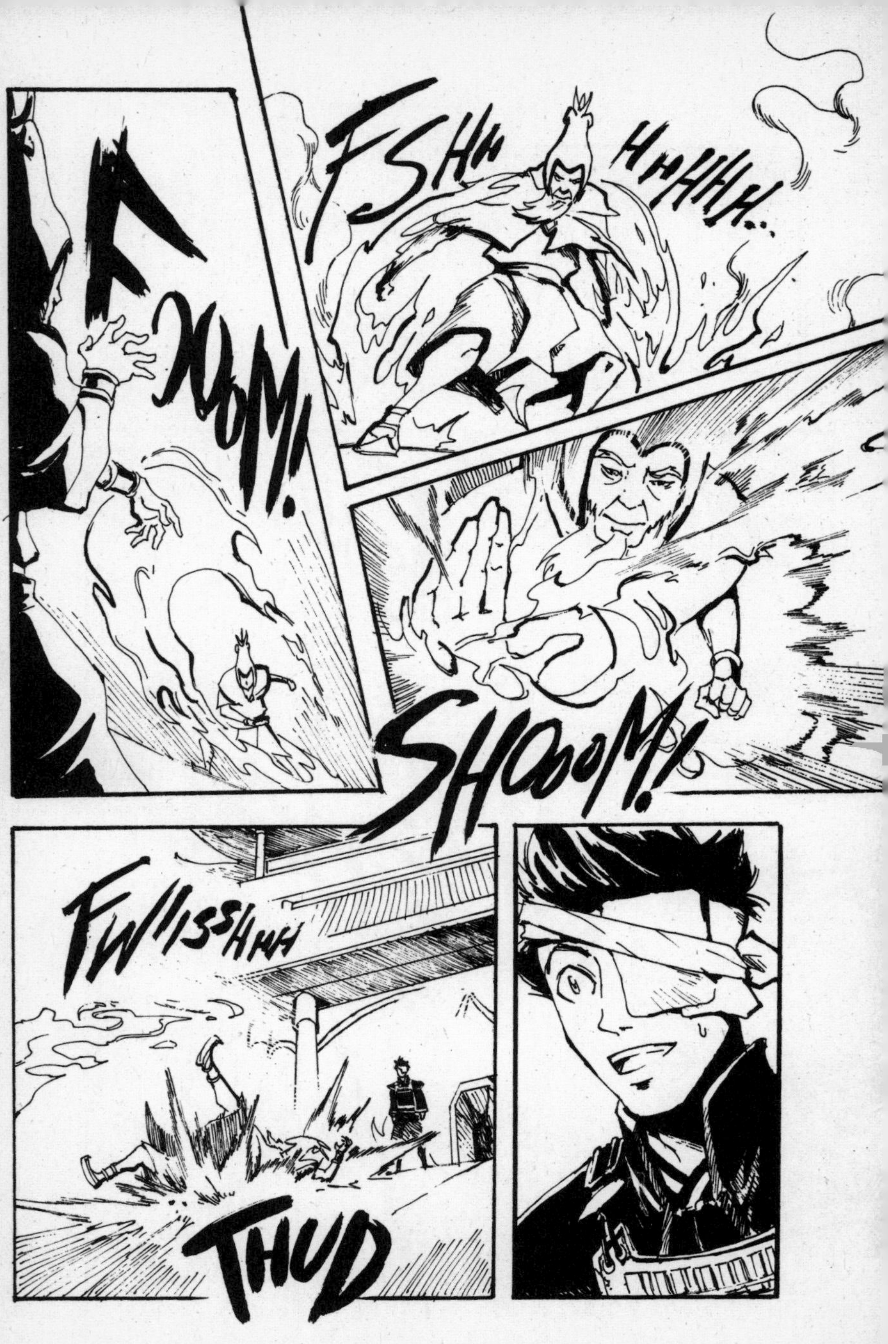

FWOOM!
FSHHHHHHH...
SHOOOM!
FWISSHHH
THUD

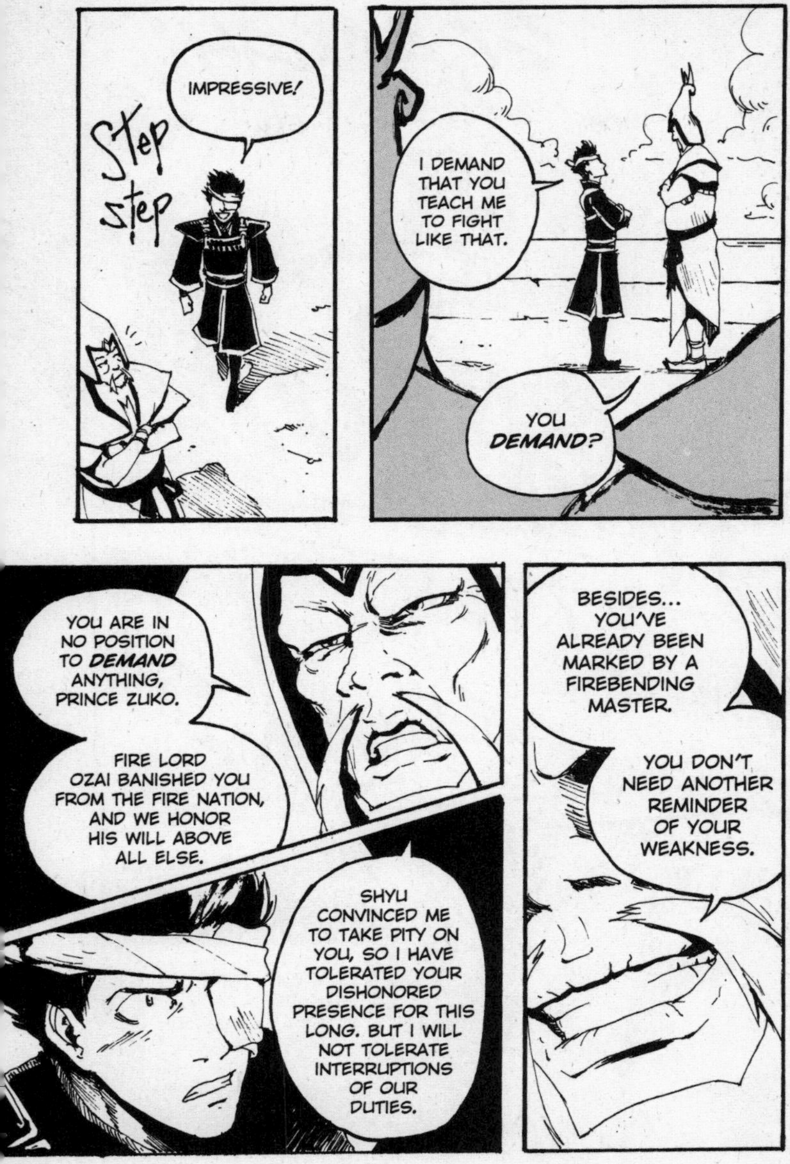
STEP STEP
IMPRESSIVE!
I DEMAND THAT YOU TEACH ME TO FIGHT LIKE THAT.
YOU DEMAND?
YOU ARE IN NO POSITION TO DEMAND ANYTHING, PRINCE ZUKO.
FIRE LORD OZAI BANISHED YOU FROM THE FIRE NATION, AND WE HONOR HIS WILL ABOVE ALL ELSE.
SHYU CONVINCED ME TO TAKE PITY ON YOU, SO I HAVE TOLERATED YOUR DISHONORED PRESENCE FOR THIS LONG. BUT I WILL NOT TOLERATE INTERRUPTIONS OF OUR DUTIES.
BESIDES... YOU'VE ALREADY BEEN MARKED BY A FIREBENDING MASTER.
YOU DON'T NEED ANOTHER REMINDER OF YOUR WEAKNESS.

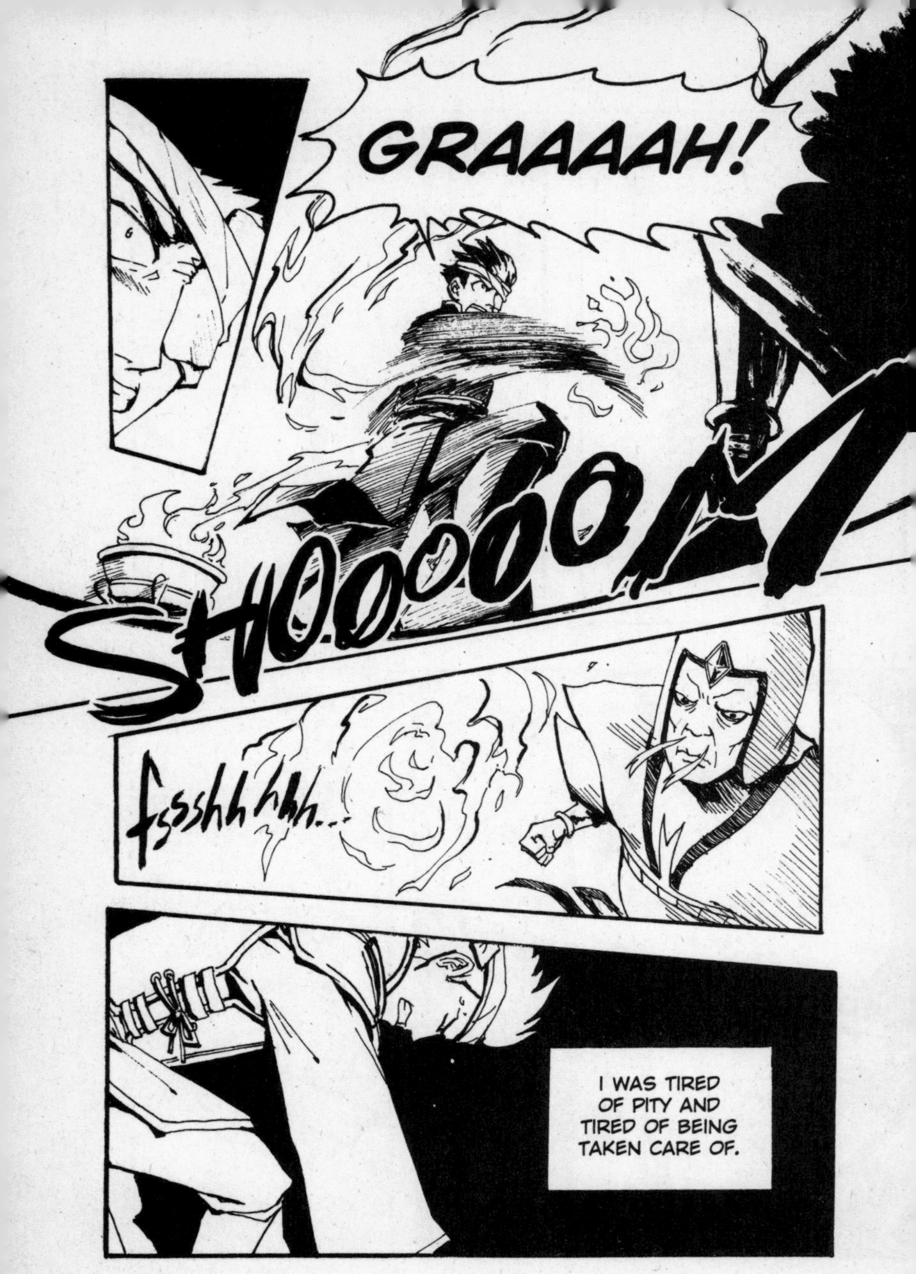
GRAAAAH!
SHOOOOOOM
fssshhhhh...
I WAS TIRED OF PITY AND TIRED OF BEING TAKEN CARE OF.

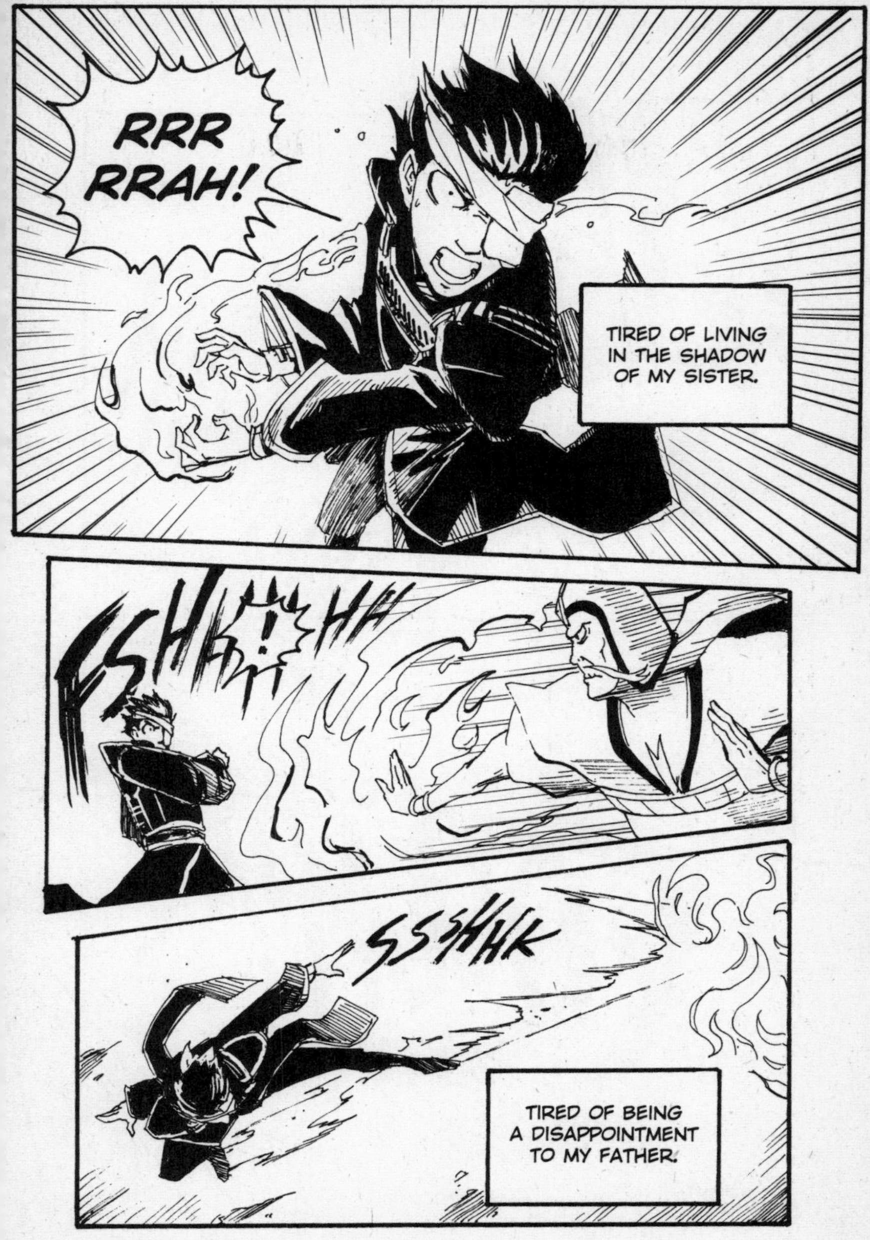
RRR RRAH!
TIRED OF LIVING IN THE SHADOW OF MY SISTER.
FSHHHHHA
SSSHHK
TIRED OF BEING A DISAPPOINTMENT TO MY FATHER.

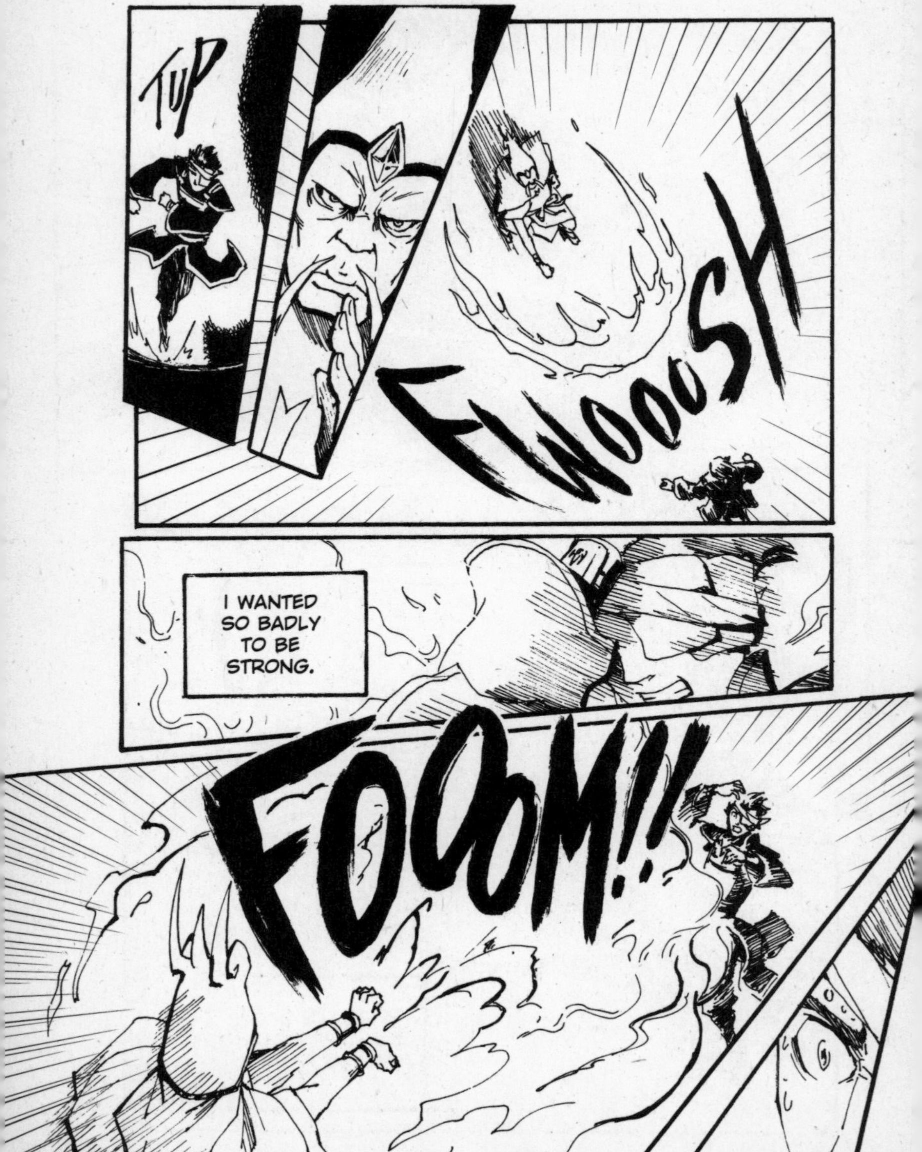
TUP
FWOOOSH
I WANTED SO BADLY TO BE STRONG.
FOOOM!!

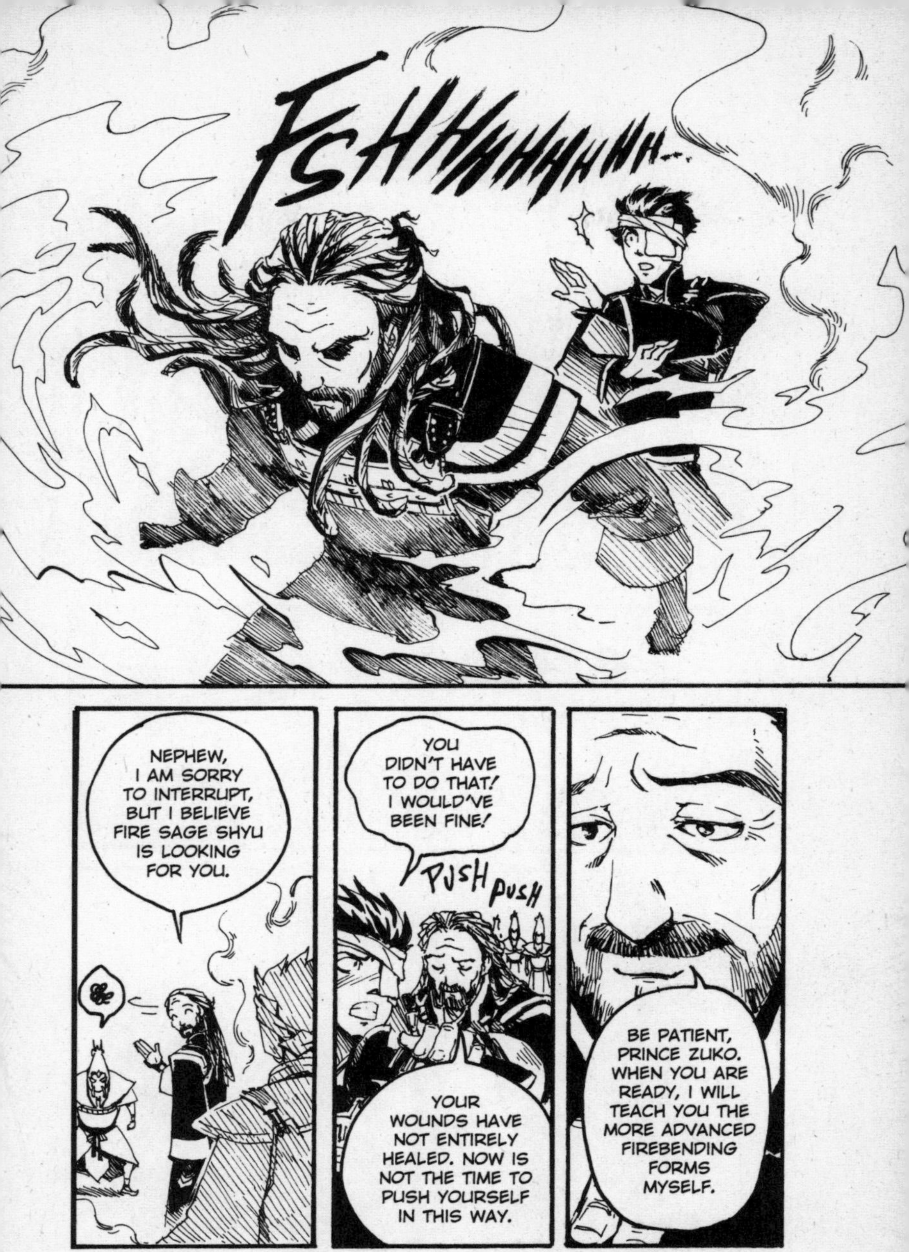
FSHHHHHHHHHH...
NEPHEW, I AM SORRY TO INTERRUPT, BUT I BELIEVE FIRE SAGE SHYU IS LOOKING FOR YOU.
YOU DIDN'T HAVE TO DO THAT! I WOULD'VE BEEN FINE!
PUSH PUSH
YOUR WOUNDS HAVE NOT ENTIRELY HEALED. NOW IS NOT THE TIME TO PUSH YOURSELF IN THIS WAY.
BE PATIENT, PRINCE ZUKO. WHEN YOU ARE READY, I WILL TEACH YOU THE MORE ADVANCED FIREBENDING FORMS MYSELF.

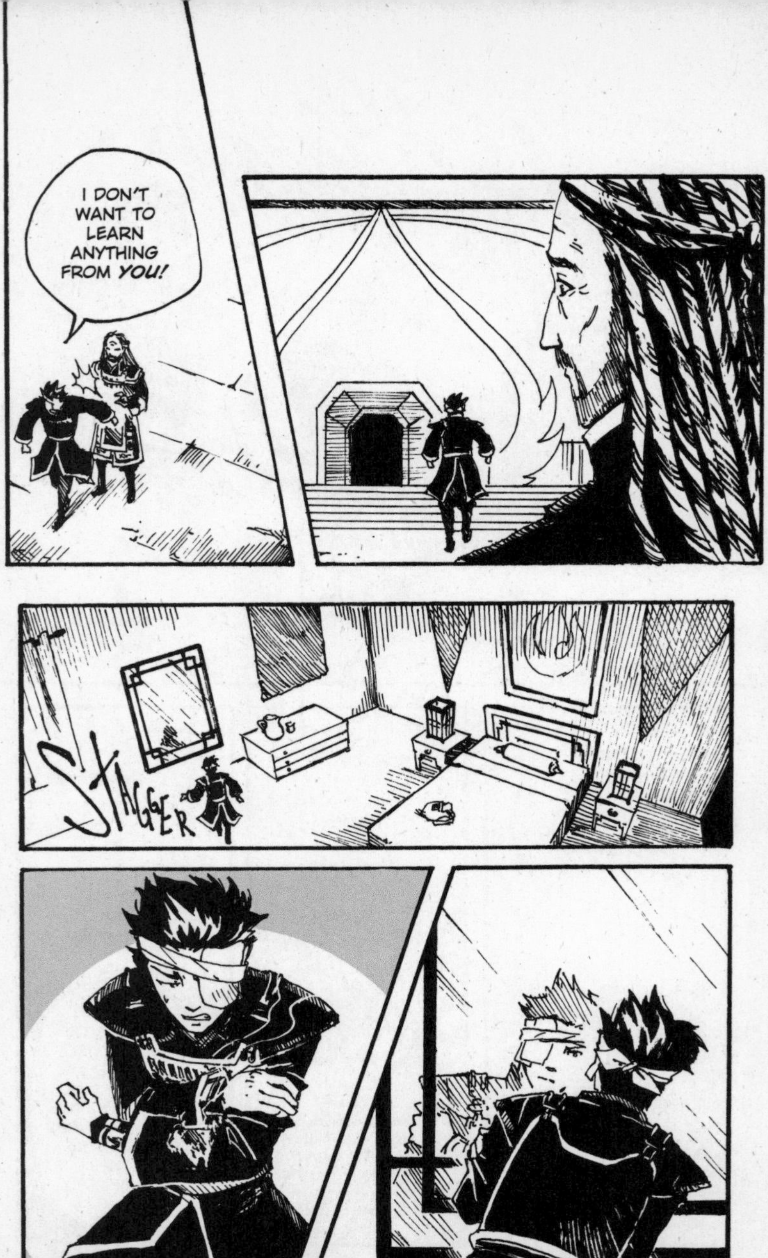
I DON'T WANT TO LEARN ANYTHING FROM *YOU!*
STAGGER

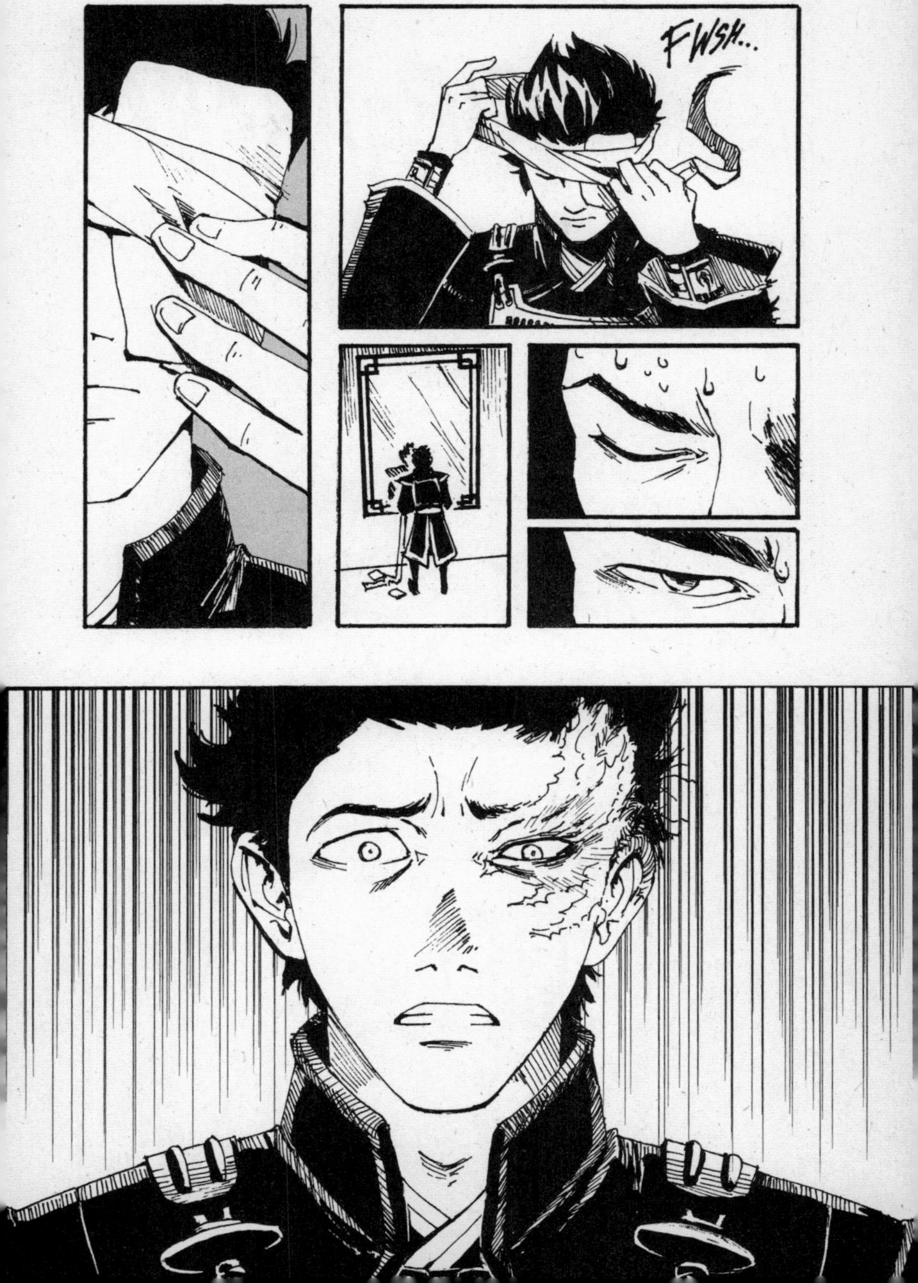
FWSH...

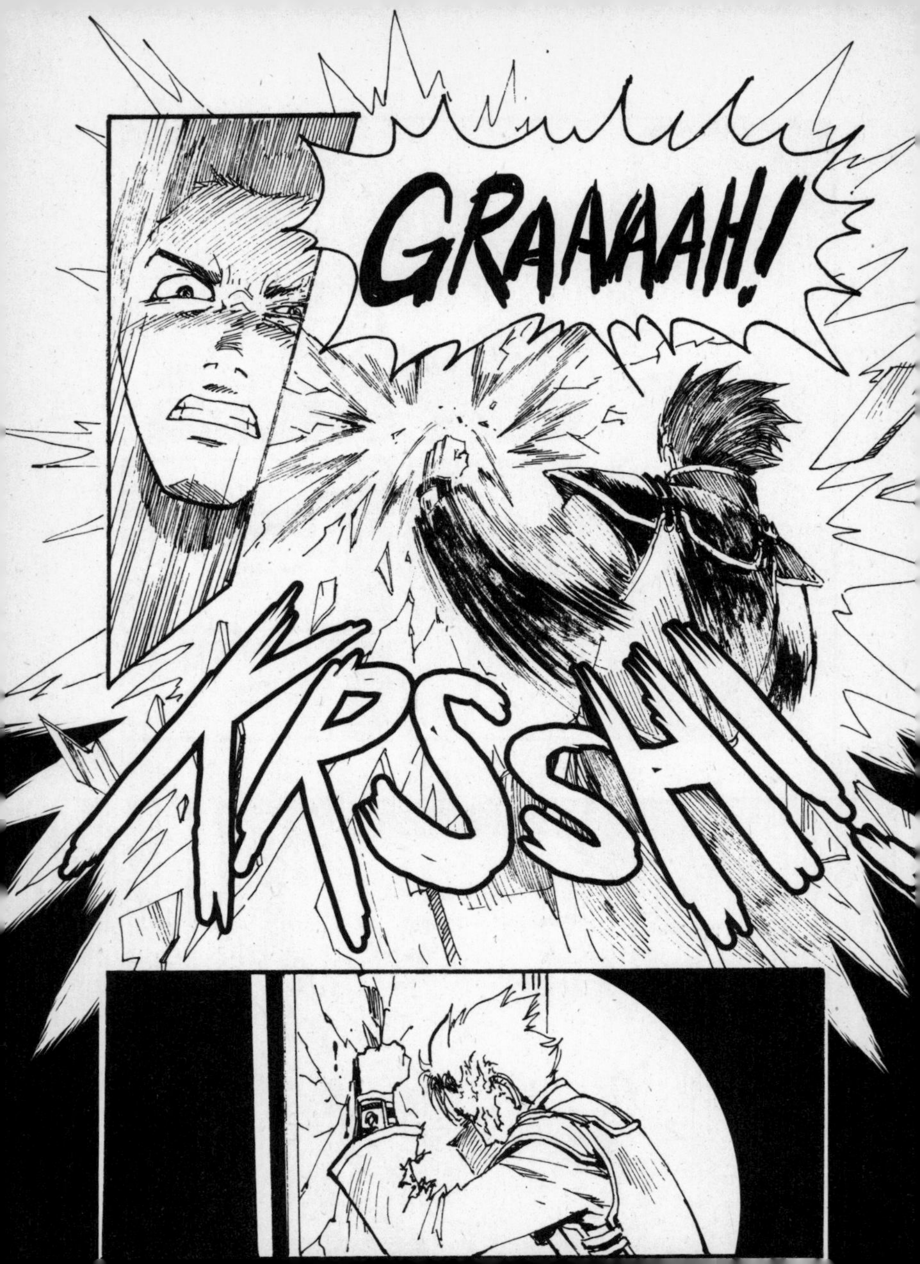
GRAAAAH!
KRSSH!

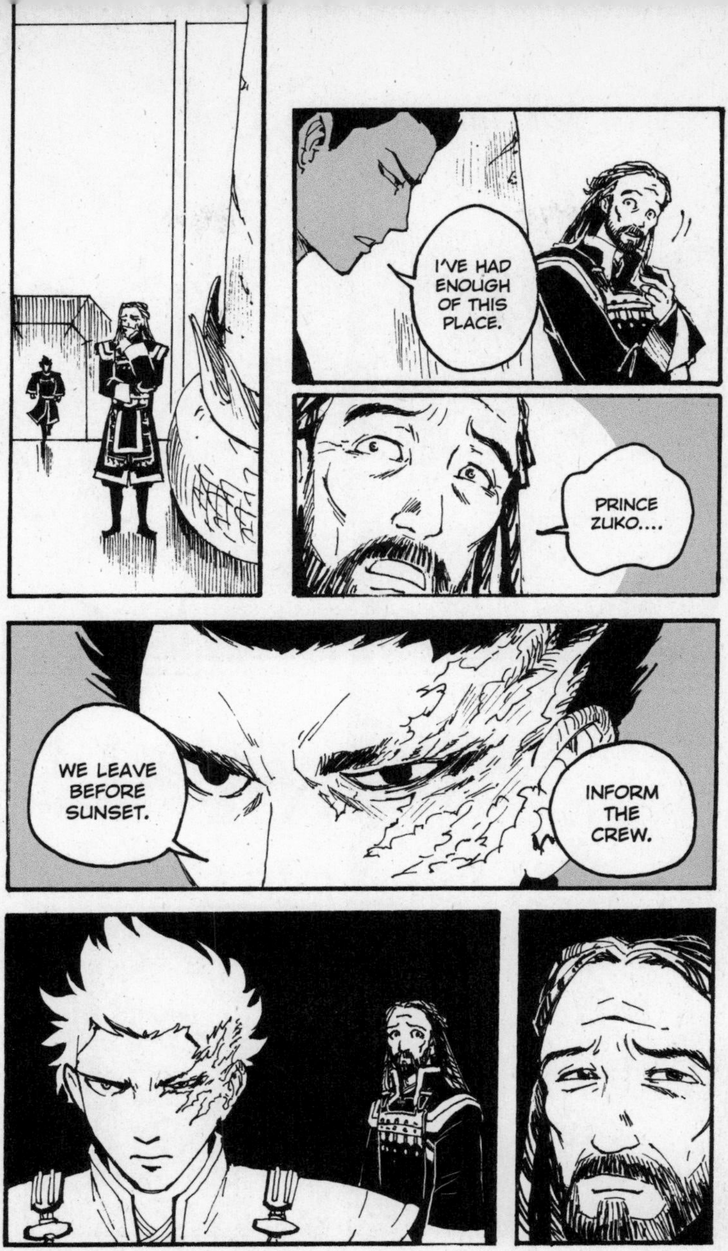
I'VE HAD ENOUGH OF THIS PLACE.
PRINCE ZUKO....
WE LEAVE BEFORE SUNSET.
INFORM THE CREW.

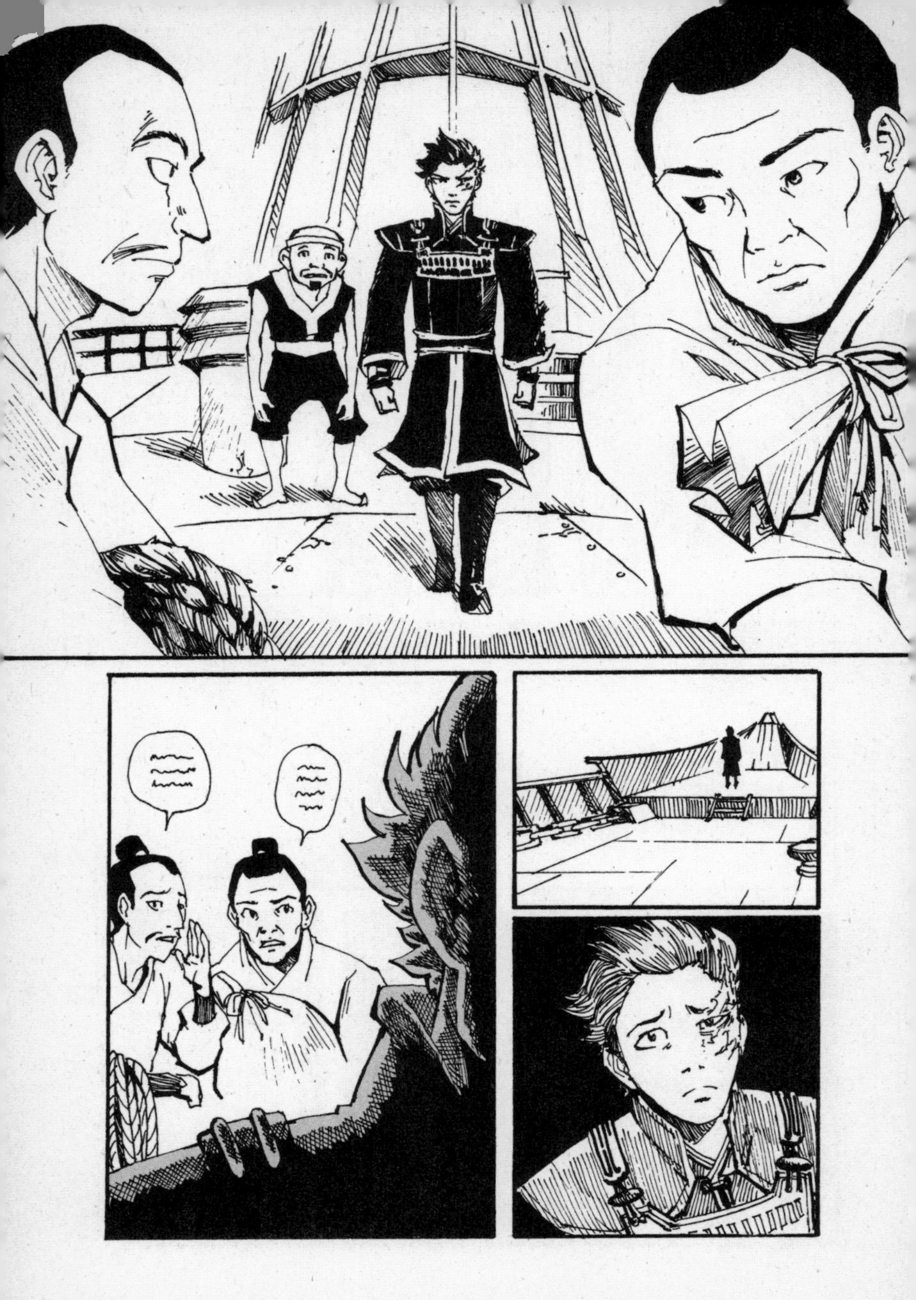

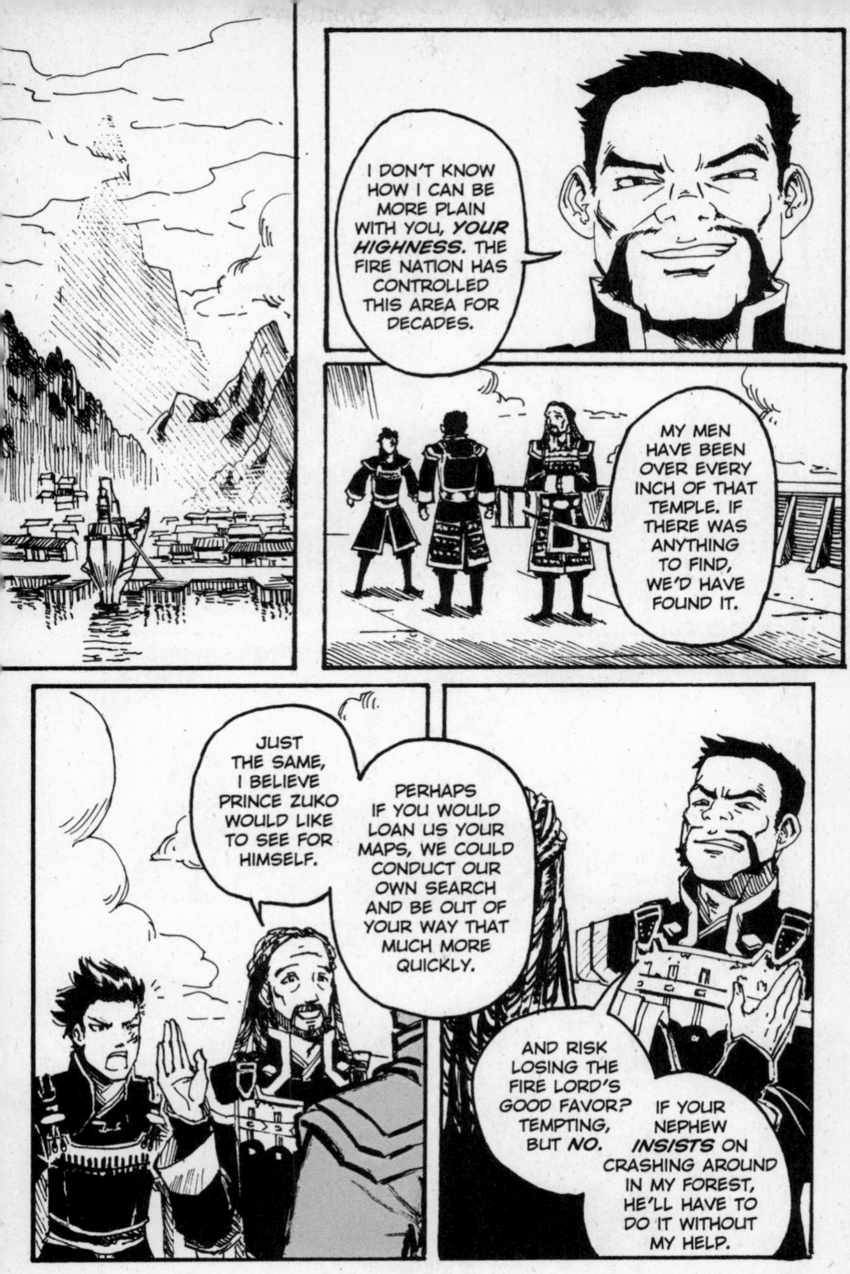
I DON'T KNOW HOW I CAN BE MORE PLAIN WITH YOU, *YOUR HIGHNESS.* THE FIRE NATION HAS CONTROLLED THIS AREA FOR DECADES.
MY MEN HAVE BEEN OVER EVERY INCH OF THAT TEMPLE. IF THERE WAS ANYTHING TO FIND, WE'D HAVE FOUND IT.
JUST THE SAME, I BELIEVE PRINCE ZUKO WOULD LIKE TO SEE FOR HIMSELF.
PERHAPS IF YOU WOULD LOAN US YOUR MAPS, WE COULD CONDUCT OUR OWN SEARCH AND BE OUT OF YOUR WAY THAT MUCH MORE QUICKLY.
AND RISK LOSING THE FIRE LORD'S GOOD FAVOR? TEMPTING, BUT *NO.*
IF YOUR NEPHEW *INSISTS* ON CRASHING AROUND IN MY FOREST, HE'LL HAVE TO DO IT WITHOUT MY HELP.

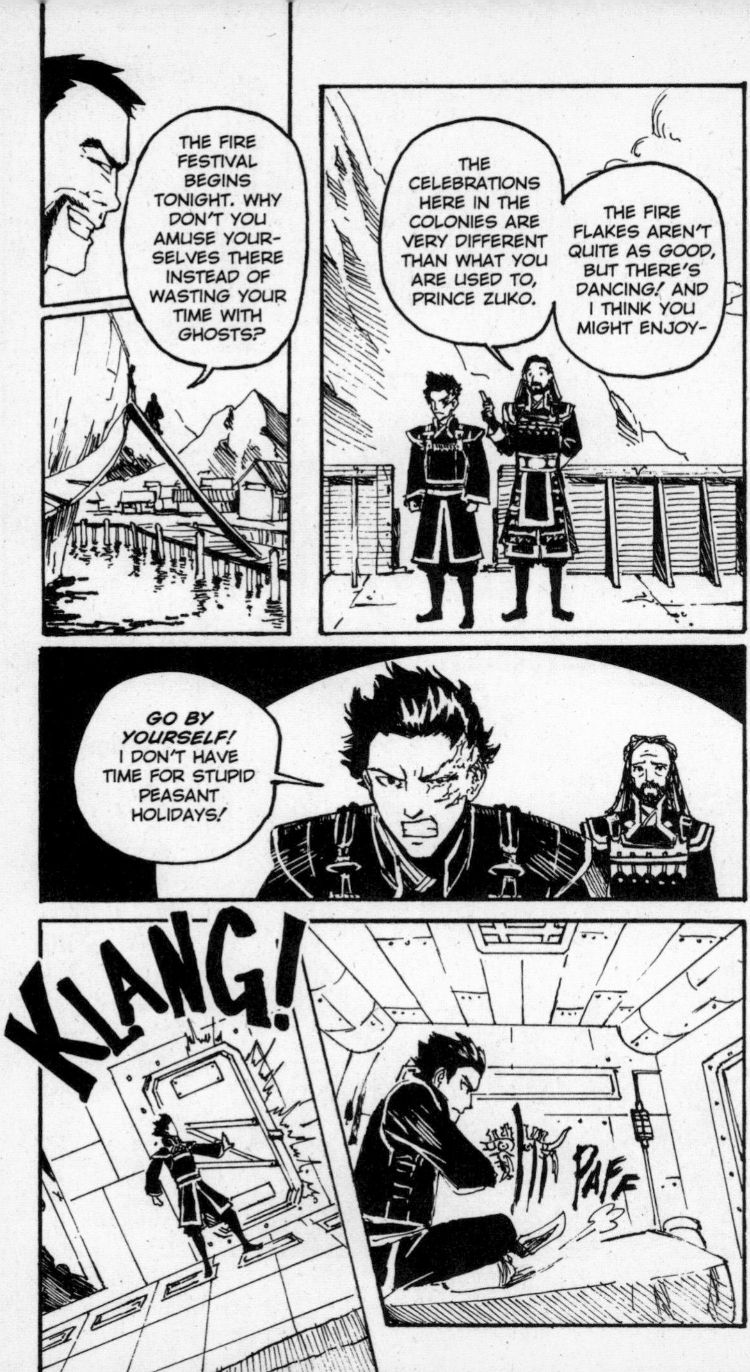
THE FIRE FESTIVAL BEGINS TONIGHT. WHY DON'T YOU AMUSE YOUR-SELVES THERE INSTEAD OF WASTING YOUR TIME WITH GHOSTS?
THE CELEBRATIONS HERE IN THE COLONIES ARE VERY DIFFERENT THAN WHAT YOU ARE USED TO, PRINCE ZUKO.
THE FIRE FLAKES AREN'T QUITE AS GOOD, BUT THERE'S DANCING! AND I THINK YOU MIGHT ENJOY-
GO BY YOURSELF! I DON'T HAVE TIME FOR STUPID PEASANT HOLIDAYS!
KLANG!
PAFF

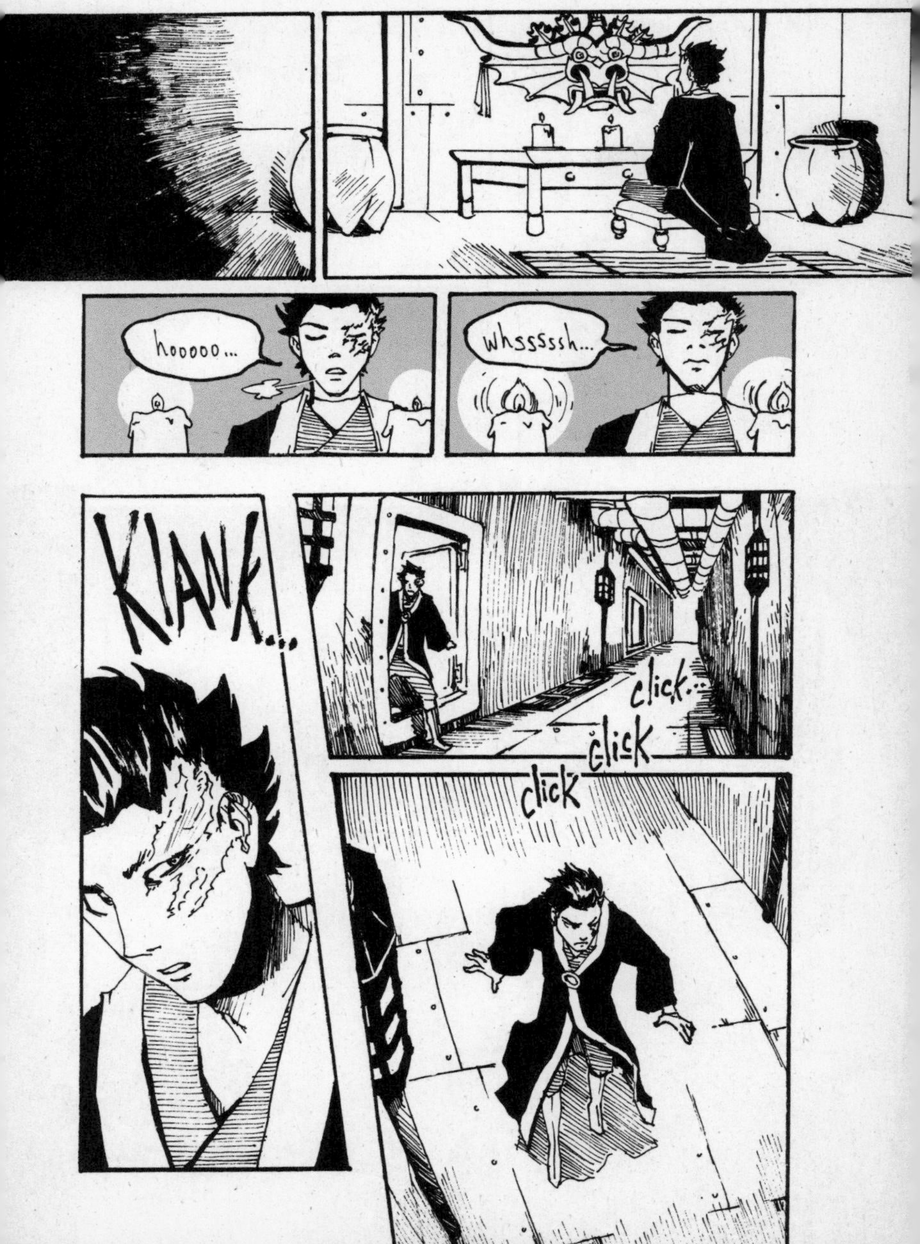
hooooo...
whssssssh...
KLANK...
click...
click
click

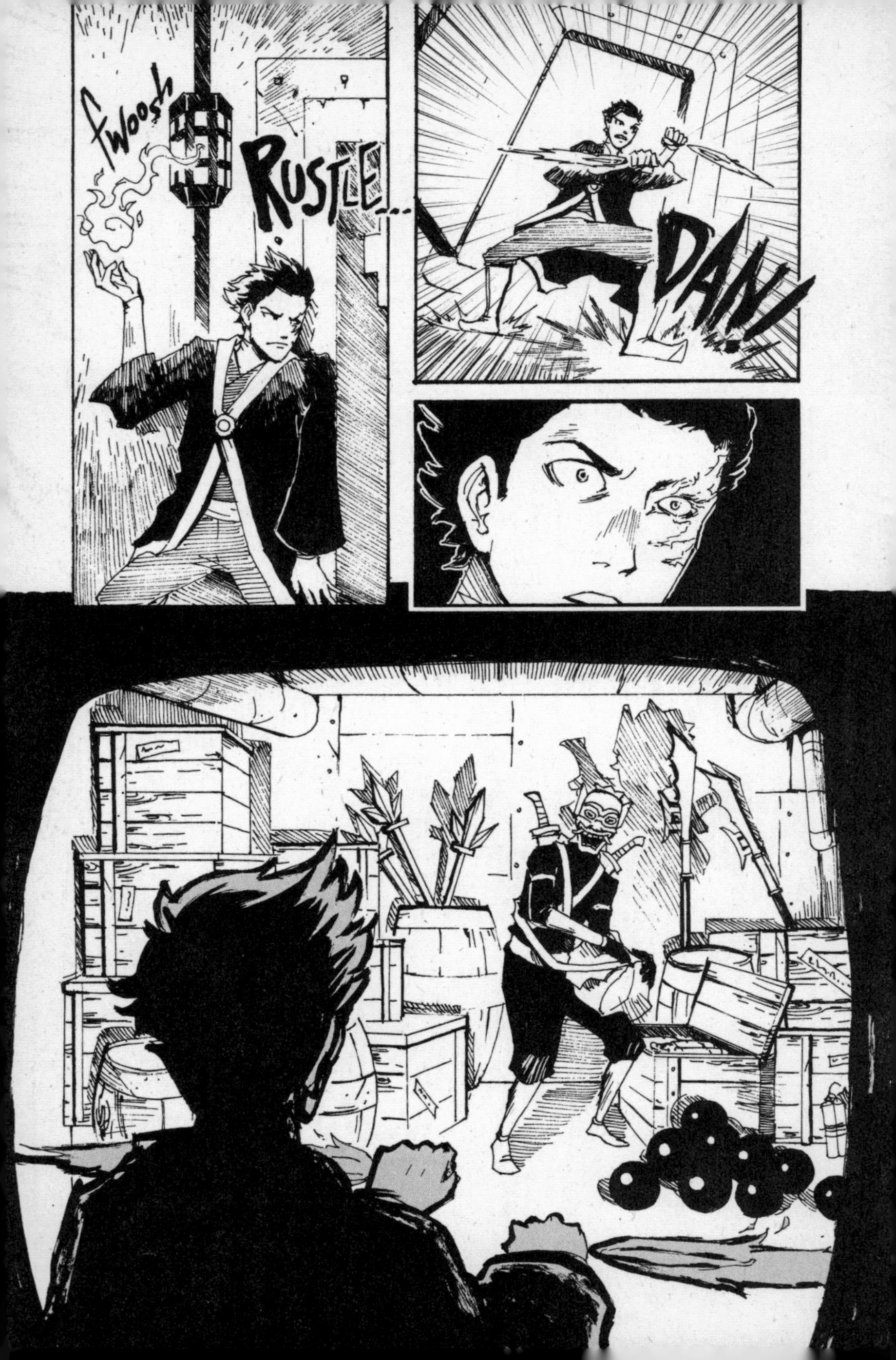
fwoosh
RUSTLE...
DAN!!

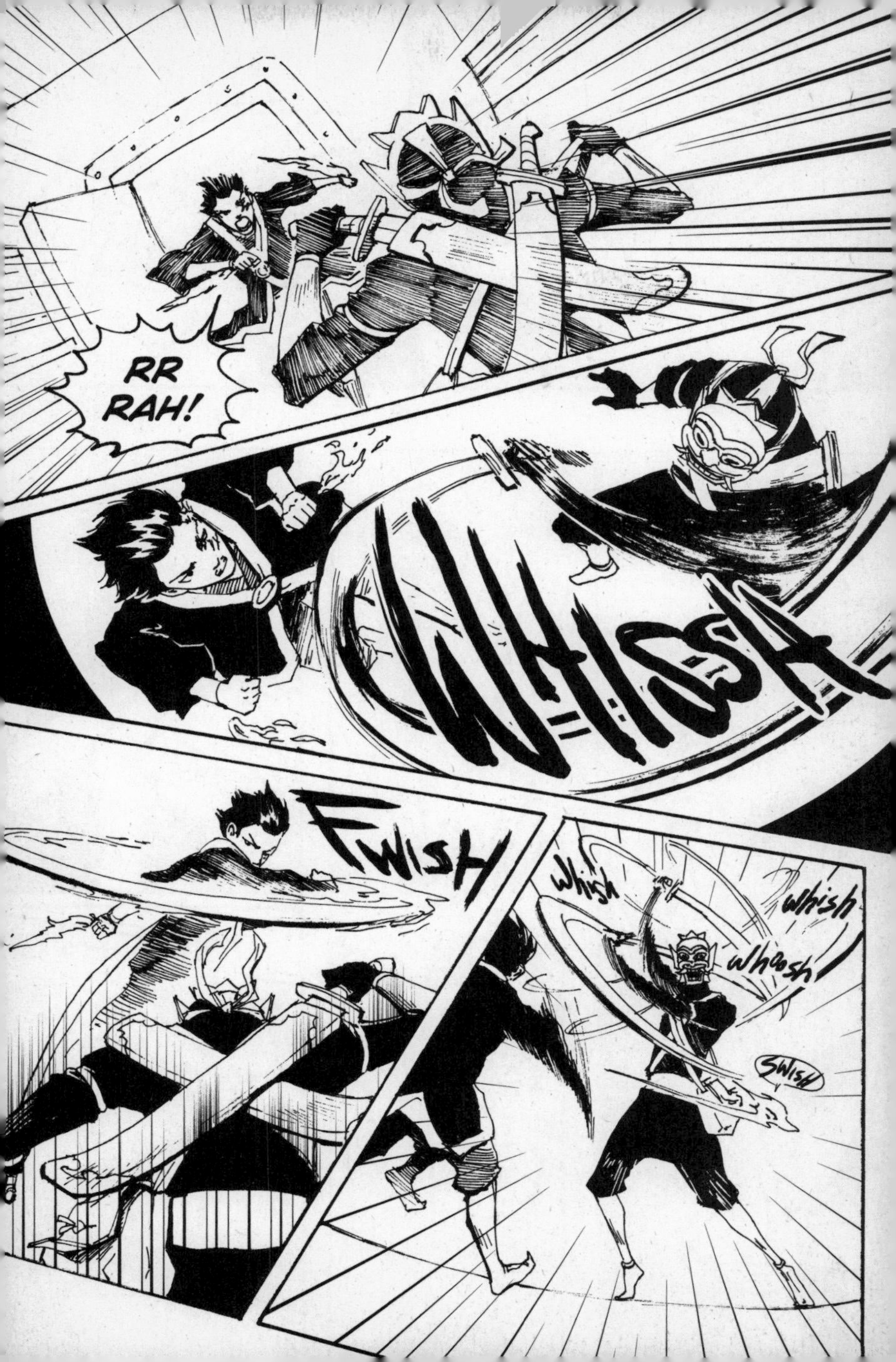
RR RAH!
WHISH
FWISH
whish
whish
whoosh
SWISH

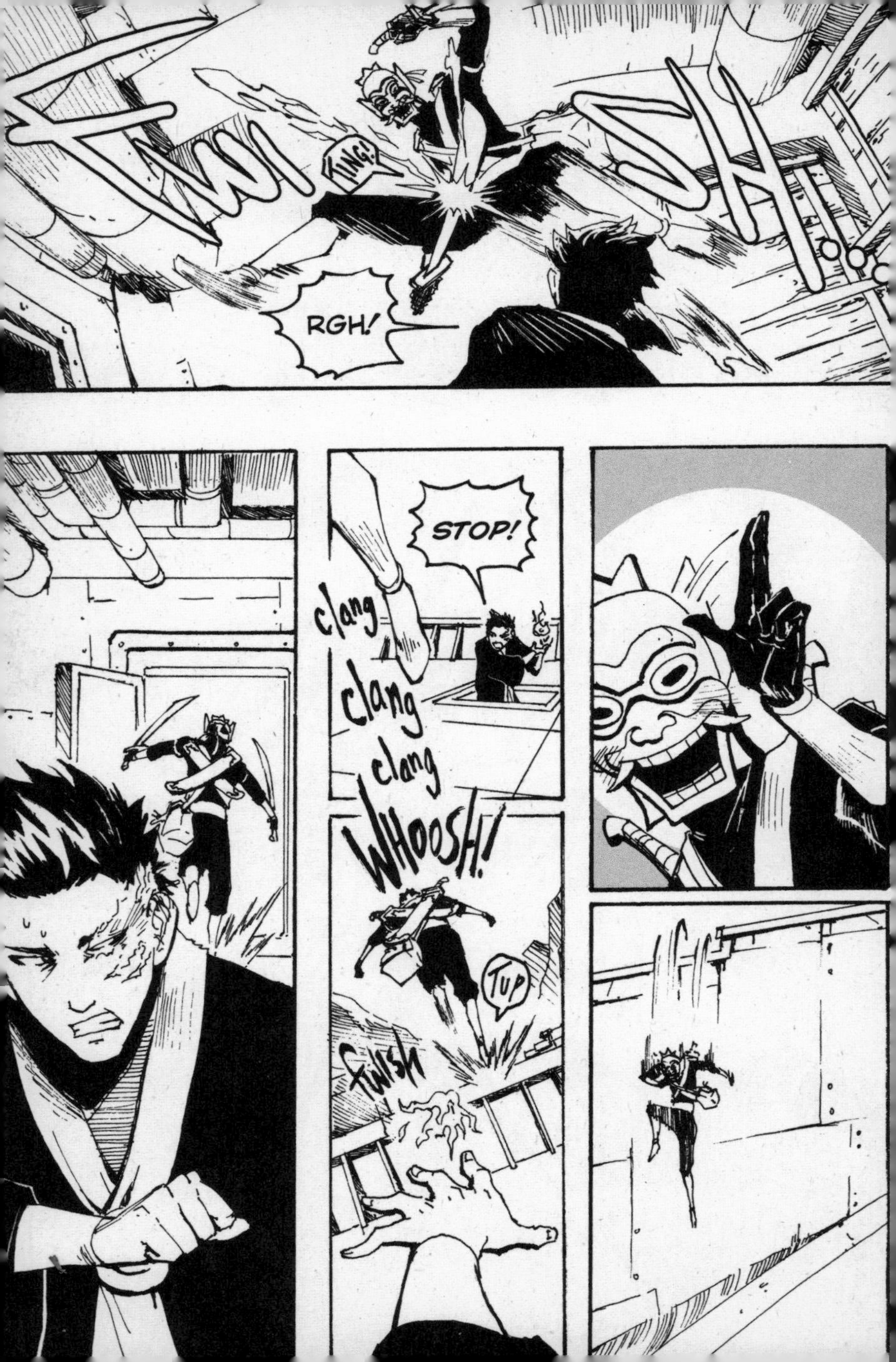
ING!
RGH!
STOP!
clang
clang
clang
WHOOSH!
TUP
fwish

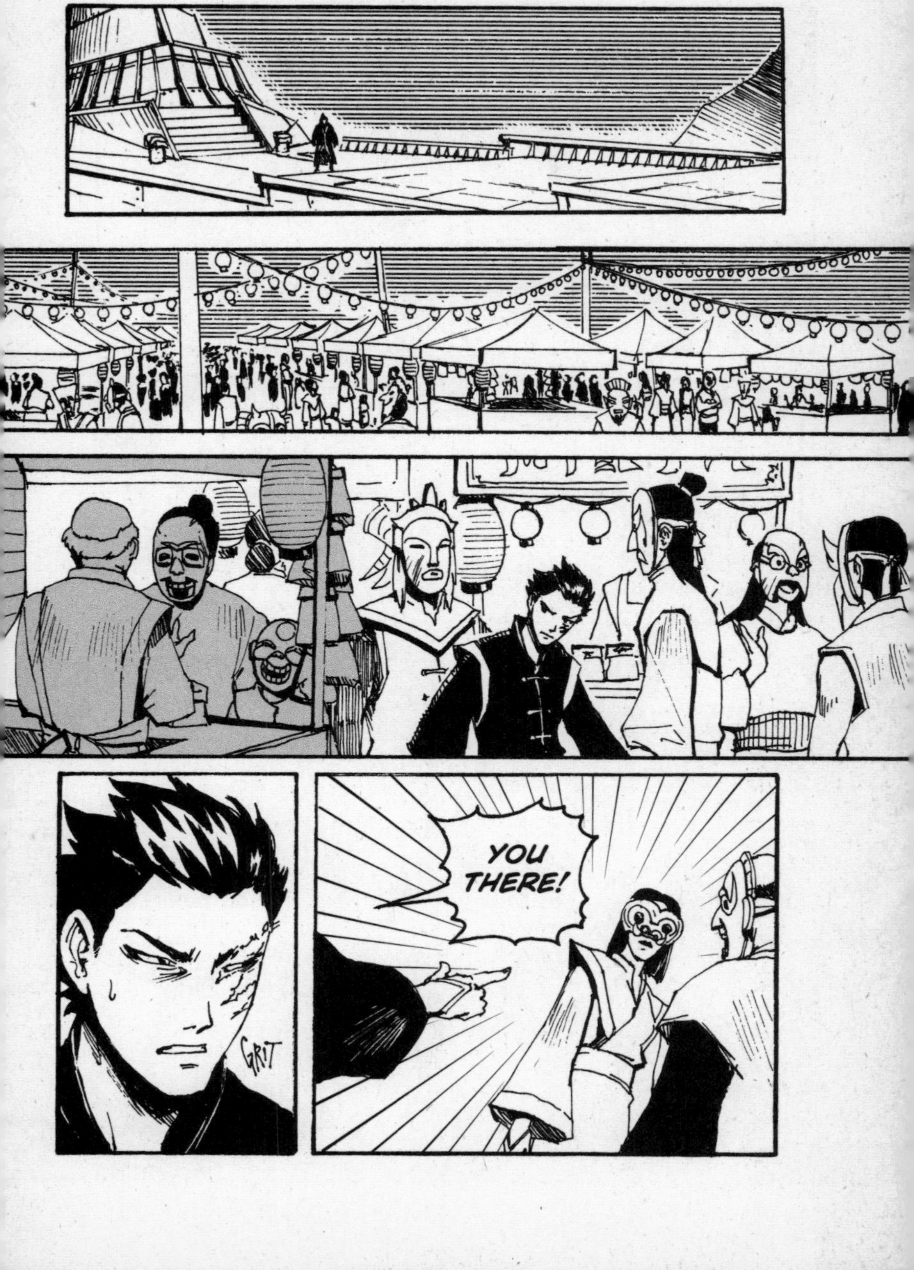
GRIT
YOU THERE!

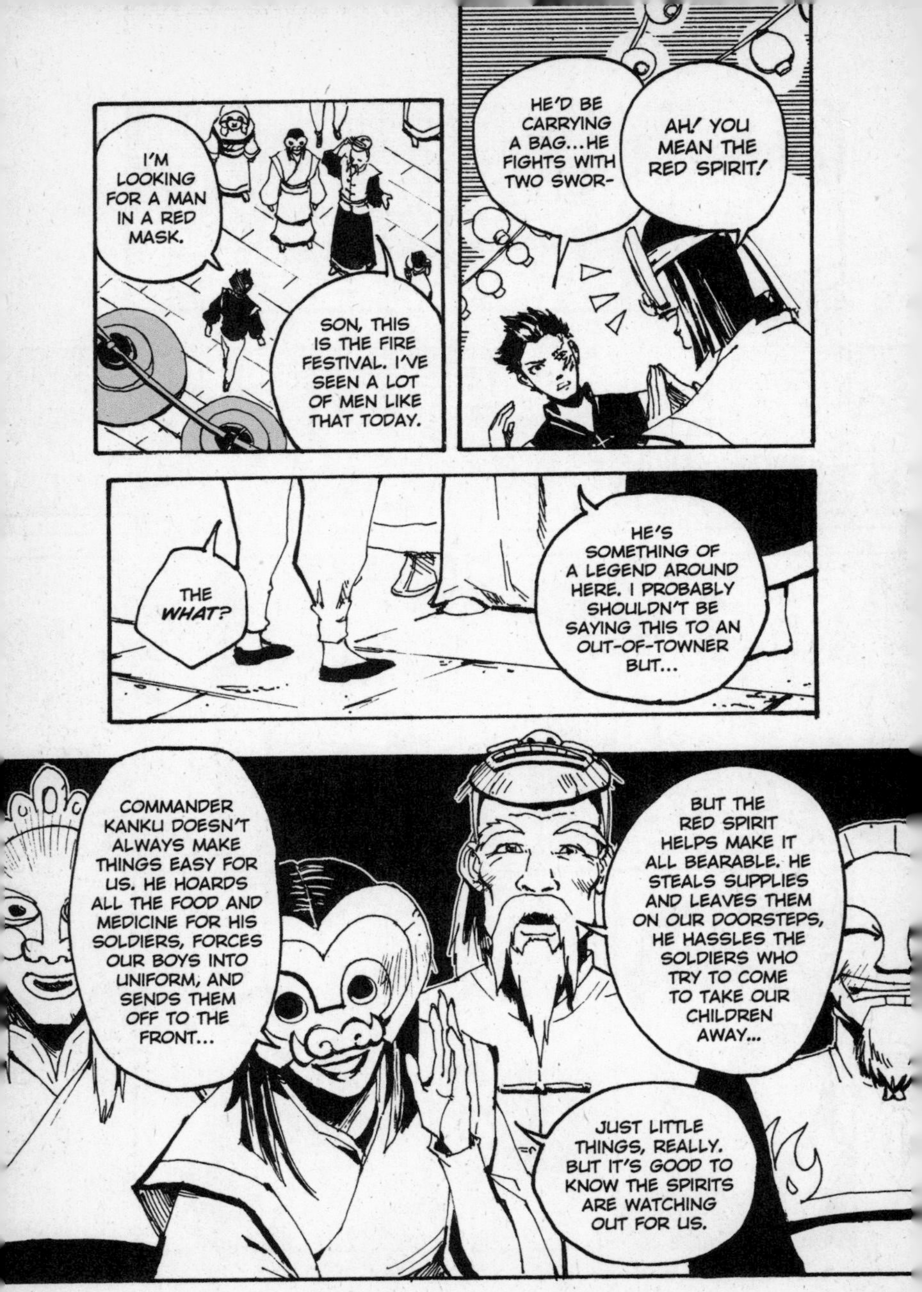
I'M LOOKING FOR A MAN IN A RED MASK.
SON, THIS IS THE FIRE FESTIVAL. I'VE SEEN A LOT OF MEN LIKE THAT TODAY.
HE'D BE CARRYING A BAG...HE FIGHTS WITH TWO SWOR-
AH! YOU MEAN THE RED SPIRIT!
THE *WHAT?*
HE'S SOMETHING OF A LEGEND AROUND HERE. I PROBABLY SHOULDN'T BE SAYING THIS TO AN OUT-OF-TOWNER BUT...
COMMANDER KANKU DOESN'T ALWAYS MAKE THINGS EASY FOR US. HE HOARDS ALL THE FOOD AND MEDICINE FOR HIS SOLDIERS, FORCES OUR BOYS INTO UNIFORM, AND SENDS THEM OFF TO THE FRONT...
BUT THE RED SPIRIT HELPS MAKE IT ALL BEARABLE. HE STEALS SUPPLIES AND LEAVES THEM ON OUR DOORSTEPS, HE HASSLES THE SOLDIERS WHO TRY TO COME TO TAKE OUR CHILDREN AWAY...
JUST LITTLE THINGS, REALLY. BUT IT'S GOOD TO KNOW THE SPIRITS ARE WATCHING OUT FOR US.

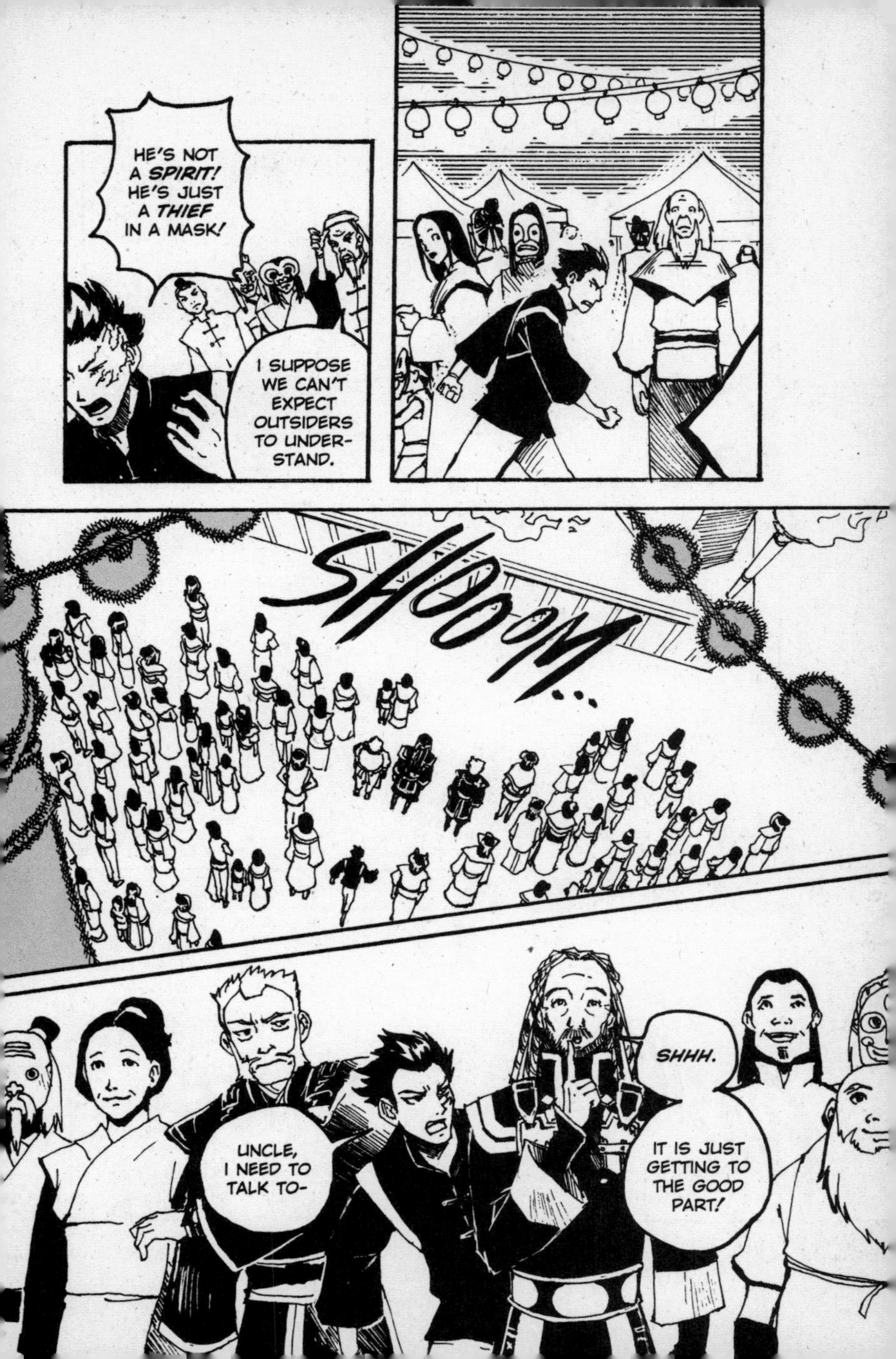
HE'S NOT A *SPIRIT!* HE'S JUST A *THIEF* IN A MASK!
I SUPPOSE WE CAN'T EXPECT OUTSIDERS TO UNDER-STAND.
SHOOOM...
UNCLE, I NEED TO TALK TO-
SHHH.
IT IS JUST GETTING TO THE GOOD PART!

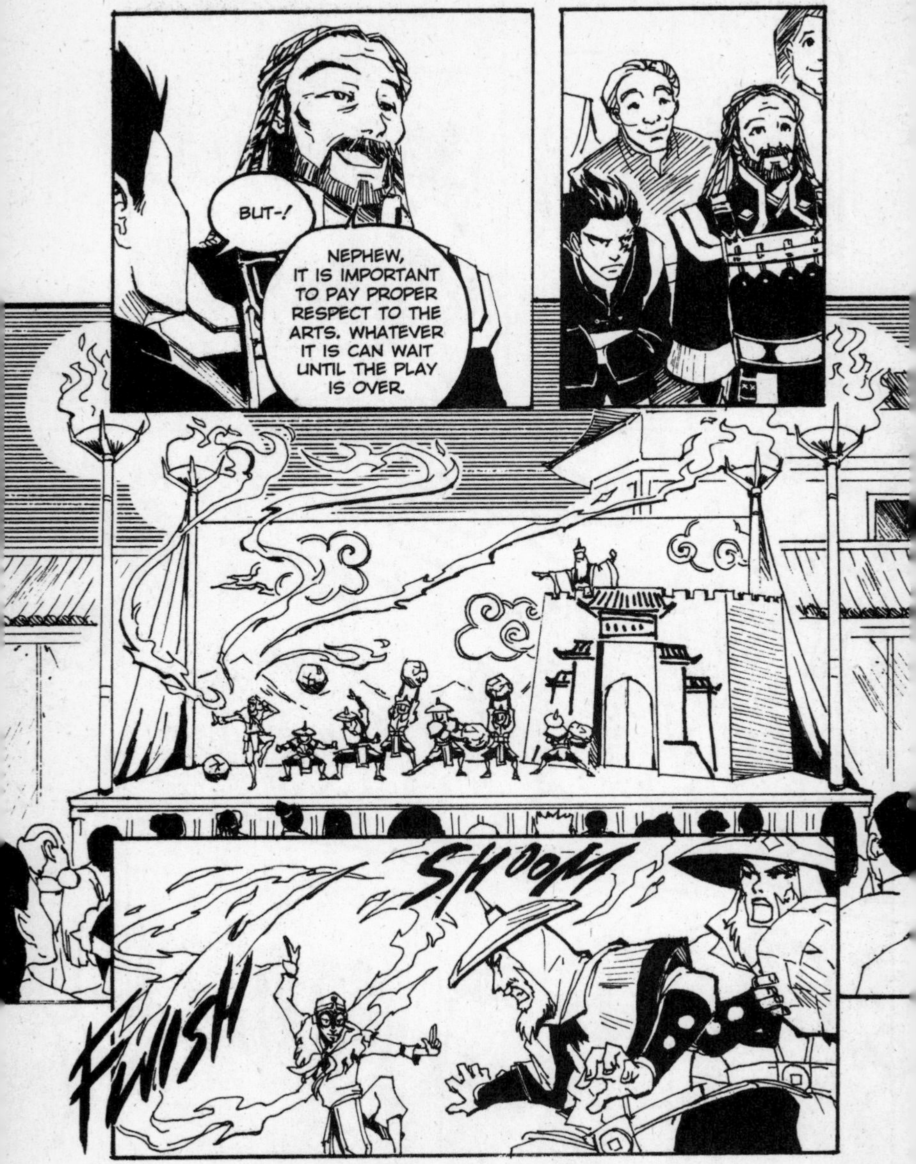
BUT-!
NEPHEW, IT IS IMPORTANT TO PAY PROPER RESPECT TO THE ARTS. WHATEVER IT IS CAN WAIT UNTIL THE PLAY IS OVER.
SHOOM
FWISH

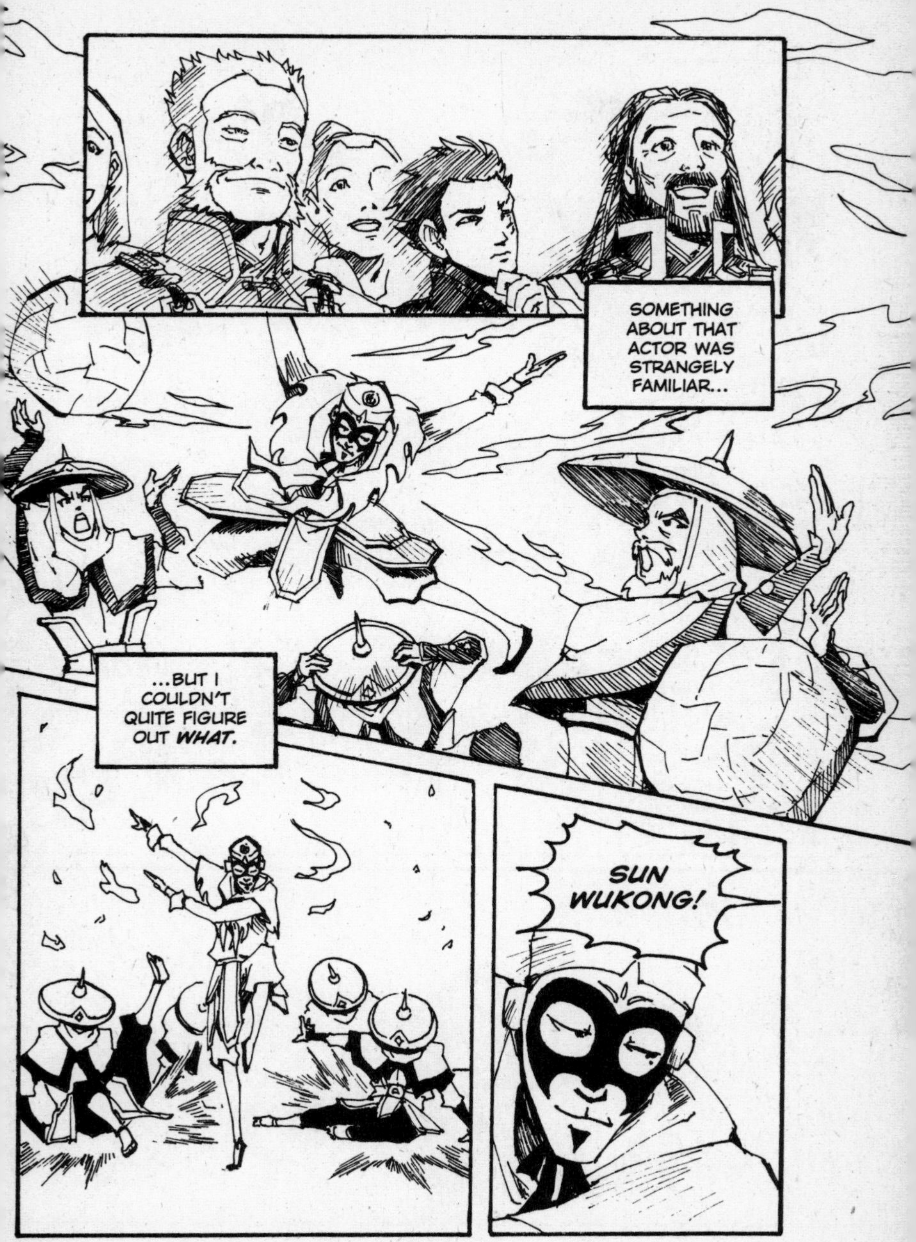
SOMETHING ABOUT THAT ACTOR WAS STRANGELY FAMILIAR...
...BUT I COULDN'T QUITE FIGURE OUT *WHAT*.
SUN WUKONG!

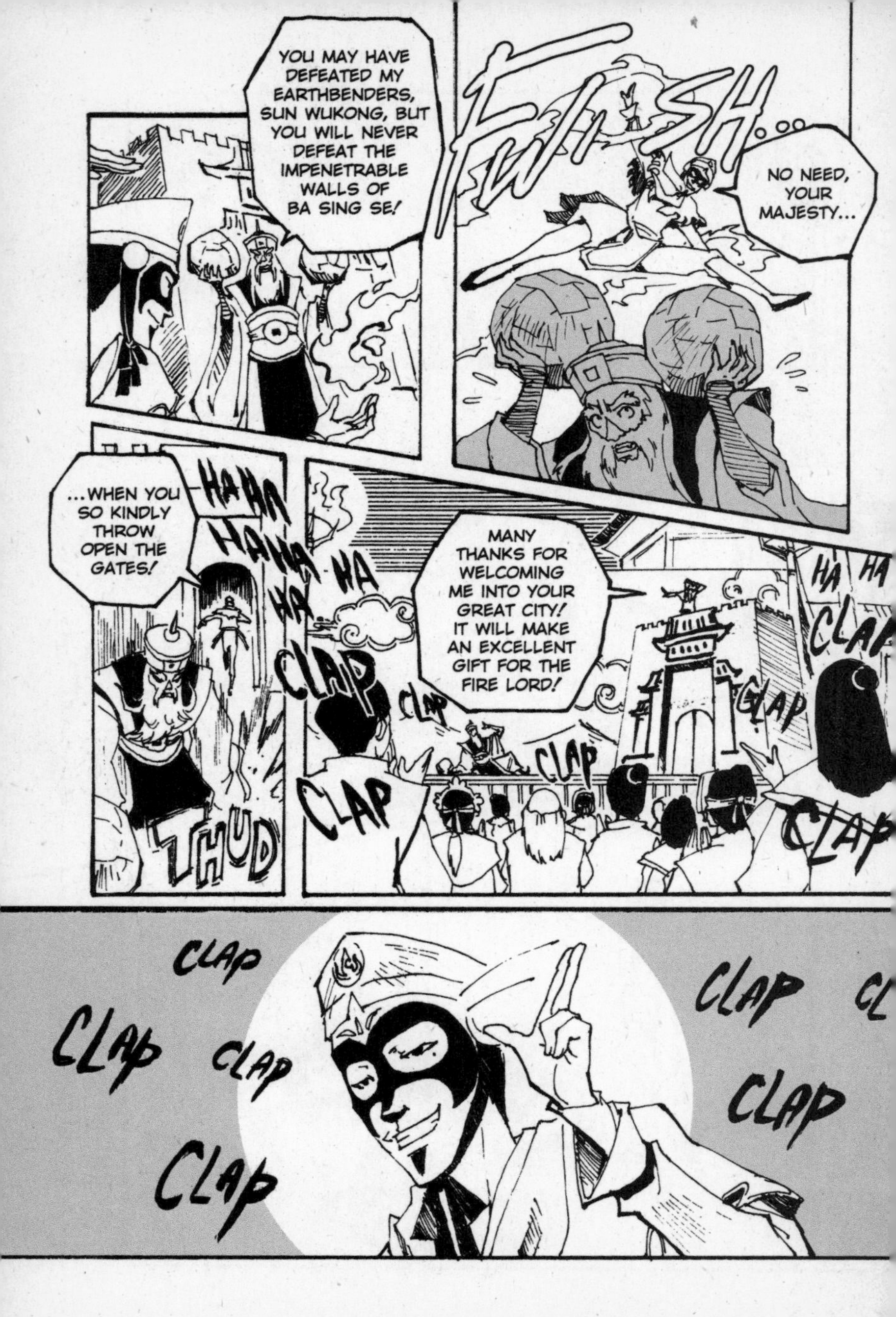
YOU MAY HAVE DEFEATED MY EARTHBENDERS, SUN WUKONG, BUT YOU WILL NEVER DEFEAT THE IMPENETRABLE WALLS OF BA SING SE!
FWOOSH...
NO NEED, YOUR MAJESTY...
...WHEN YOU SO KINDLY THROW OPEN THE GATES!
HA HA HA HA HA
THUD
HA
MANY THANKS FOR WELCOMING ME INTO YOUR GREAT CITY! IT WILL MAKE AN EXCELLENT GIFT FOR THE FIRE LORD!
HA HA
CLAP
CLAP
CLAP
CLAP
CLAP
CLAP
CLAP
CLAP
CLAP
CLAP
CLAP
CLAP
CLAP

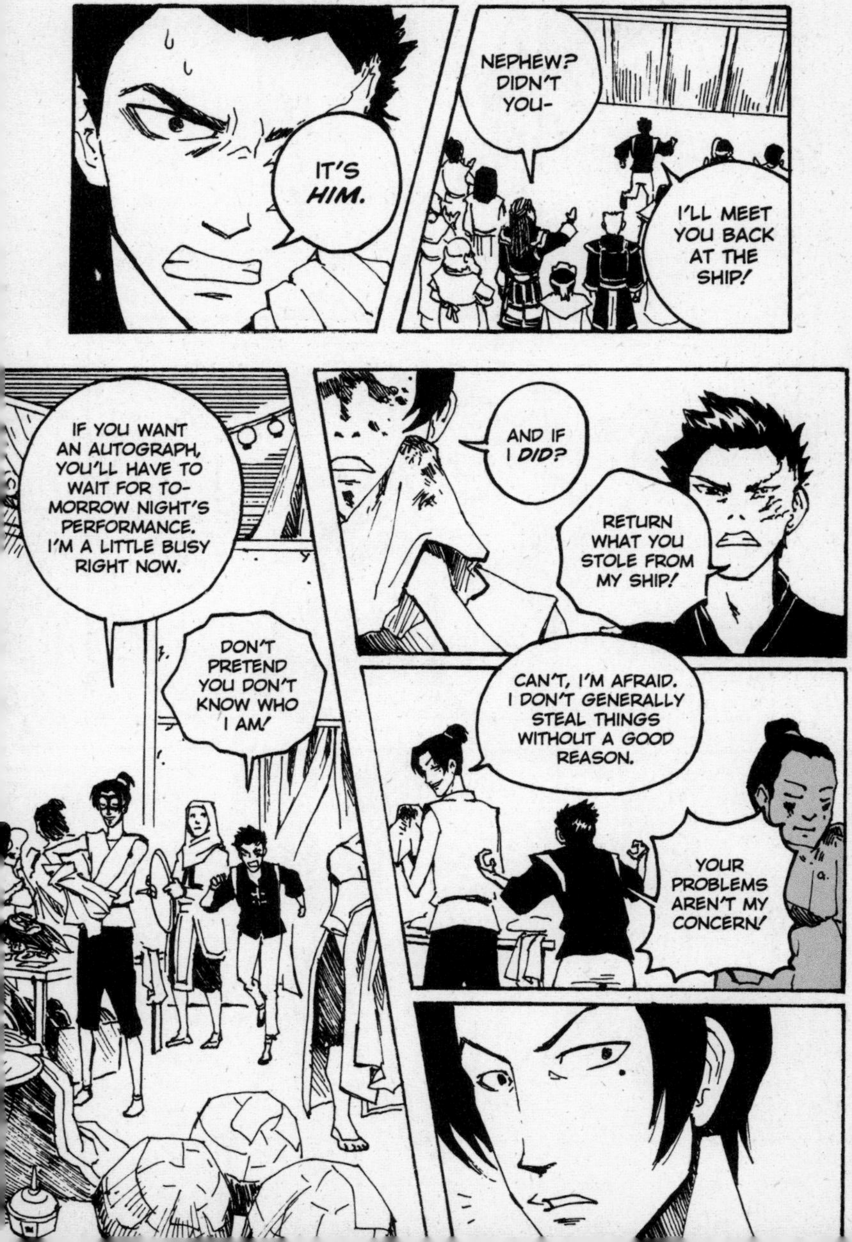
IT'S *HIM.*
NEPHEW? DIDN'T YOU-
I'LL MEET YOU BACK AT THE SHIP!
IF YOU WANT AN AUTOGRAPH, YOU'LL HAVE TO WAIT FOR TO-MORROW NIGHT'S PERFORMANCE. I'M A LITTLE BUSY RIGHT NOW.
DON'T PRETEND YOU DON'T KNOW WHO I AM!
AND IF I *DID*?
RETURN WHAT YOU STOLE FROM MY SHIP!
CAN'T, I'M AFRAID. I DON'T GENERALLY STEAL THINGS WITHOUT A GOOD REASON.
YOUR PROBLEMS AREN'T MY CONCERN!

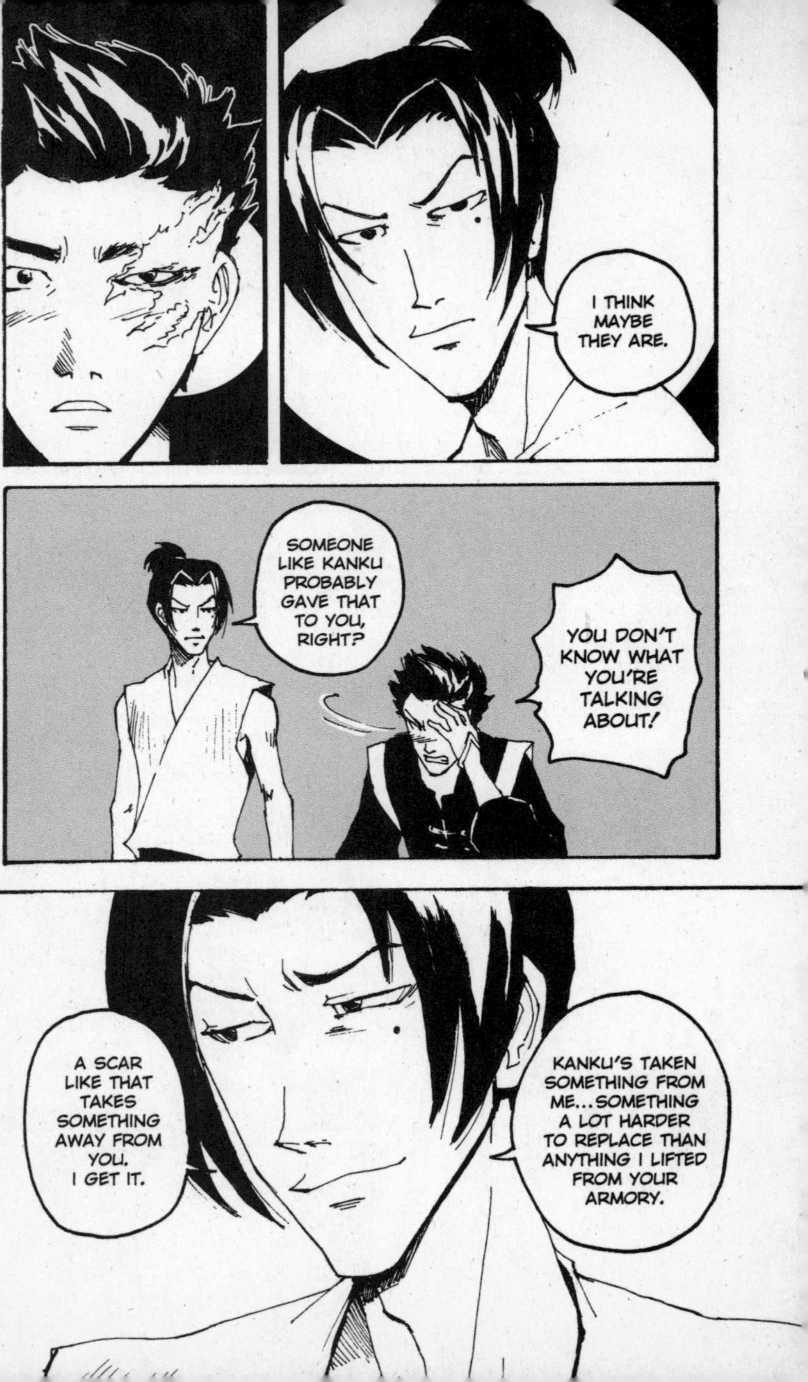
I THINK MAYBE THEY ARE.
SOMEONE LIKE KANKU PROBABLY GAVE THAT TO YOU, RIGHT?
YOU DON'T KNOW WHAT YOU'RE TALKING ABOUT!
A SCAR LIKE THAT TAKES SOMETHING AWAY FROM YOU. I GET IT.
KANKU'S TAKEN SOMETHING FROM ME...SOMETHING A LOT HARDER TO REPLACE THAN ANYTHING I LIFTED FROM YOUR ARMORY.

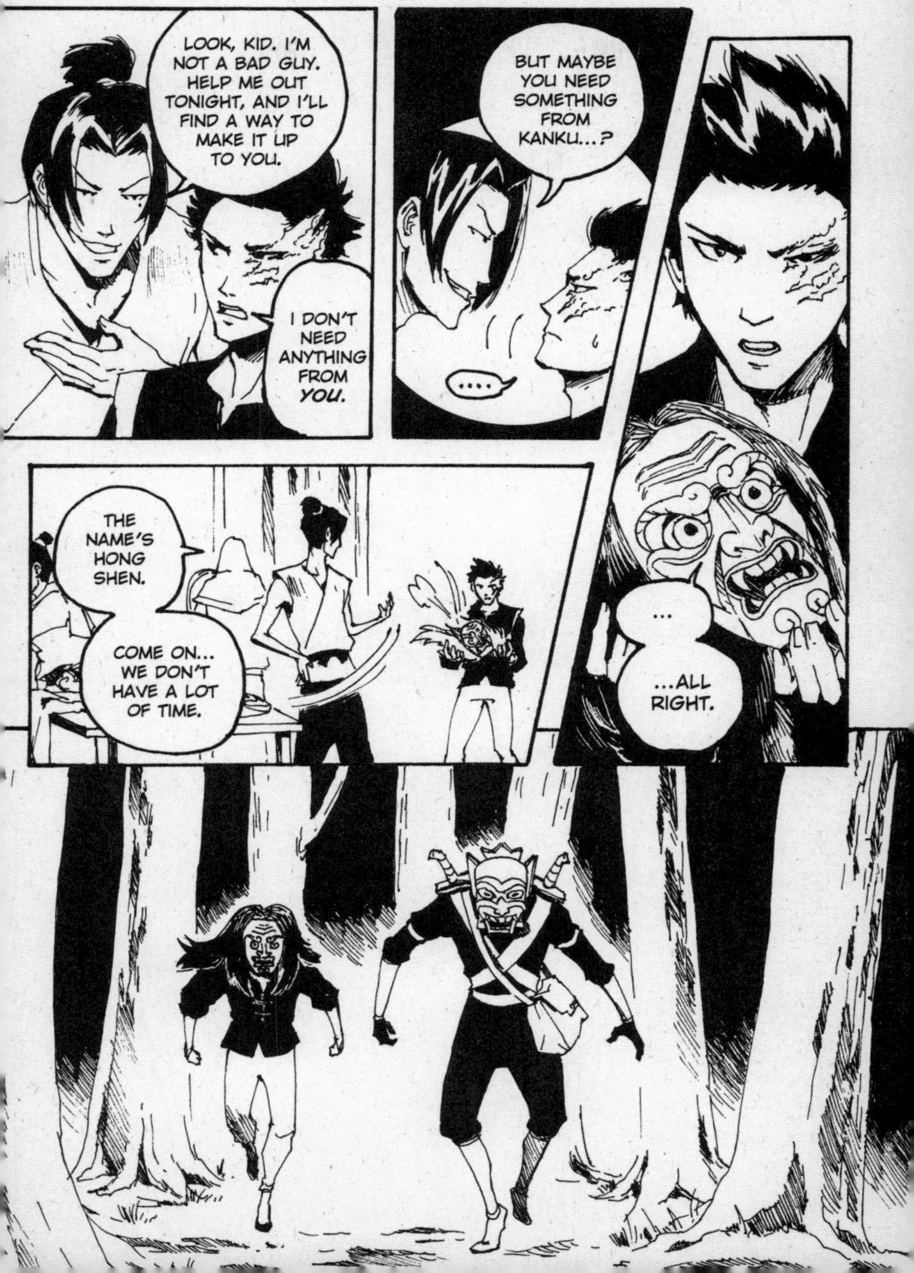
LOOK, KID. I'M NOT A BAD GUY. HELP ME OUT TONIGHT, AND I'LL FIND A WAY TO MAKE IT UP TO YOU.
I DON'T NEED ANYTHING FROM *YOU*.
BUT MAYBE YOU NEED SOMETHING FROM KANKU...?
....
THE NAME'S HONG SHEN.
COME ON... WE DON'T HAVE A LOT OF TIME.
...
...ALL RIGHT.

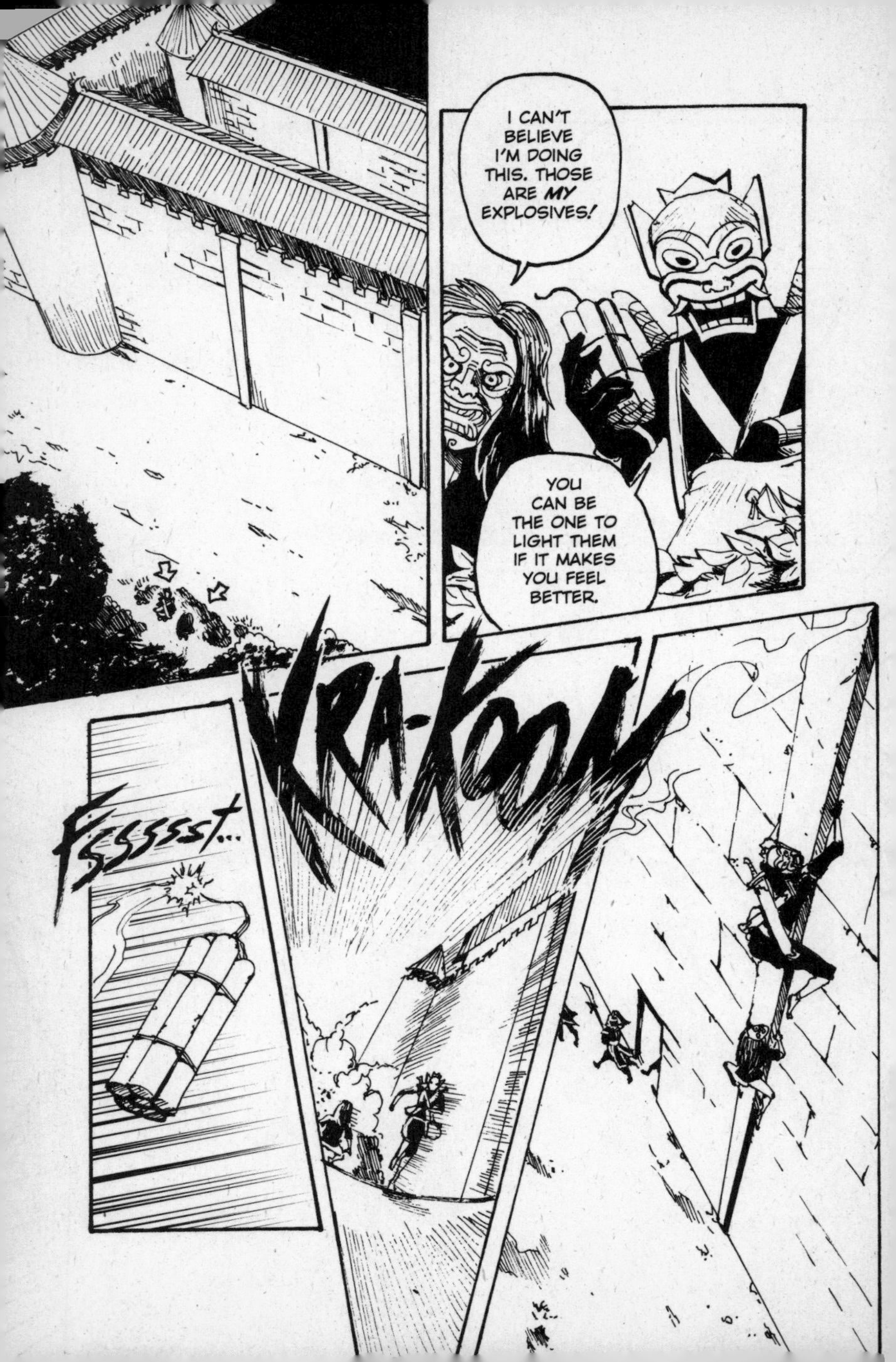
I CAN'T BELIEVE I'M DOING THIS. THOSE ARE MY EXPLOSIVES!
YOU CAN BE THE ONE TO LIGHT THEM IF IT MAKES YOU FEEL BETTER.
FSSSSST...
KRA-KOOM

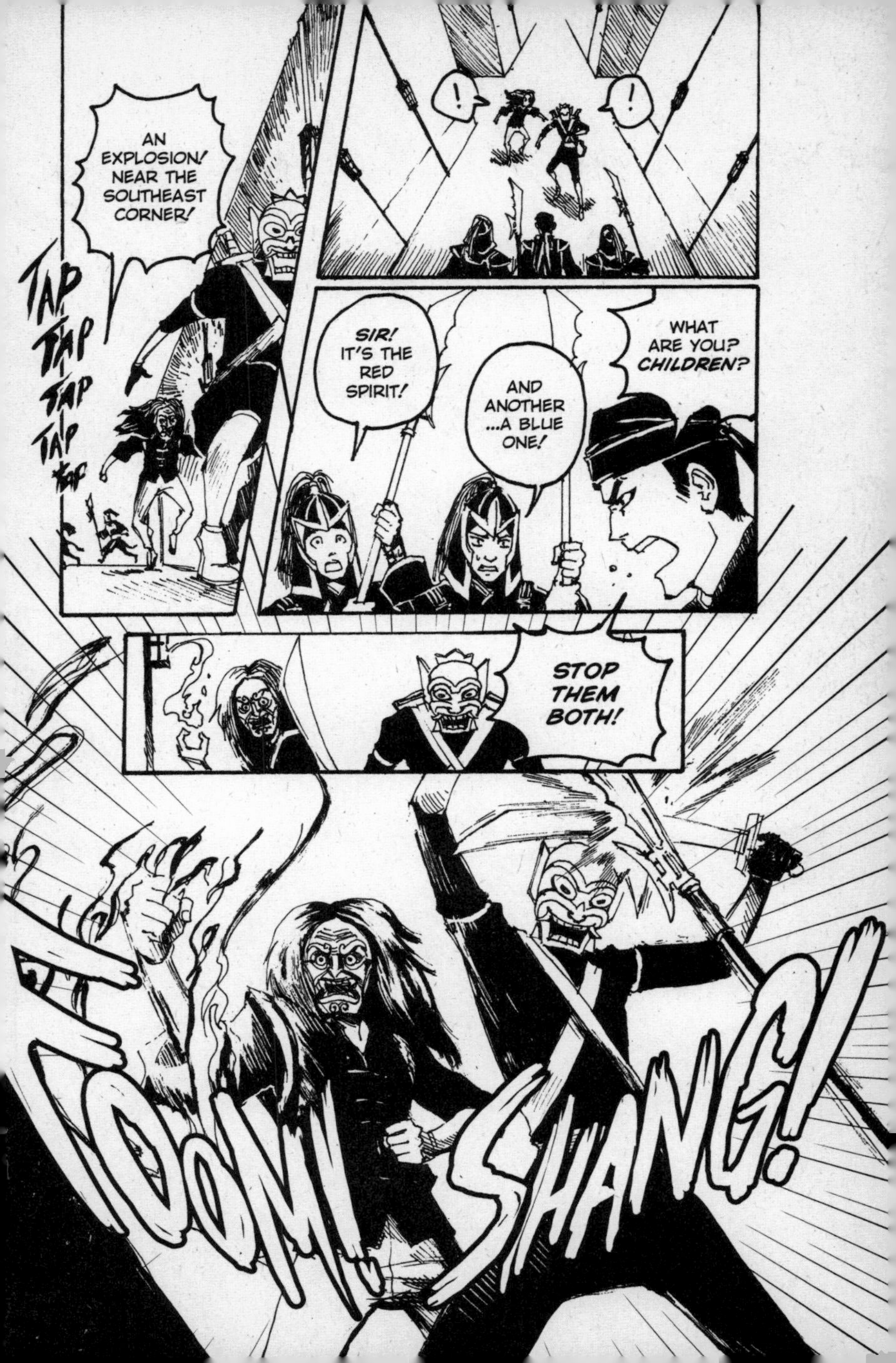
AN EXPLOSION! NEAR THE SOUTHEAST CORNER!
TAP TAP TAP TAP TAP
!
!
SIR! IT'S THE RED SPIRIT!
AND ANOTHER ...A BLUE ONE!
WHAT ARE YOU? CHILDREN?
STOP THEM BOTH!
FOOM
SHANG!

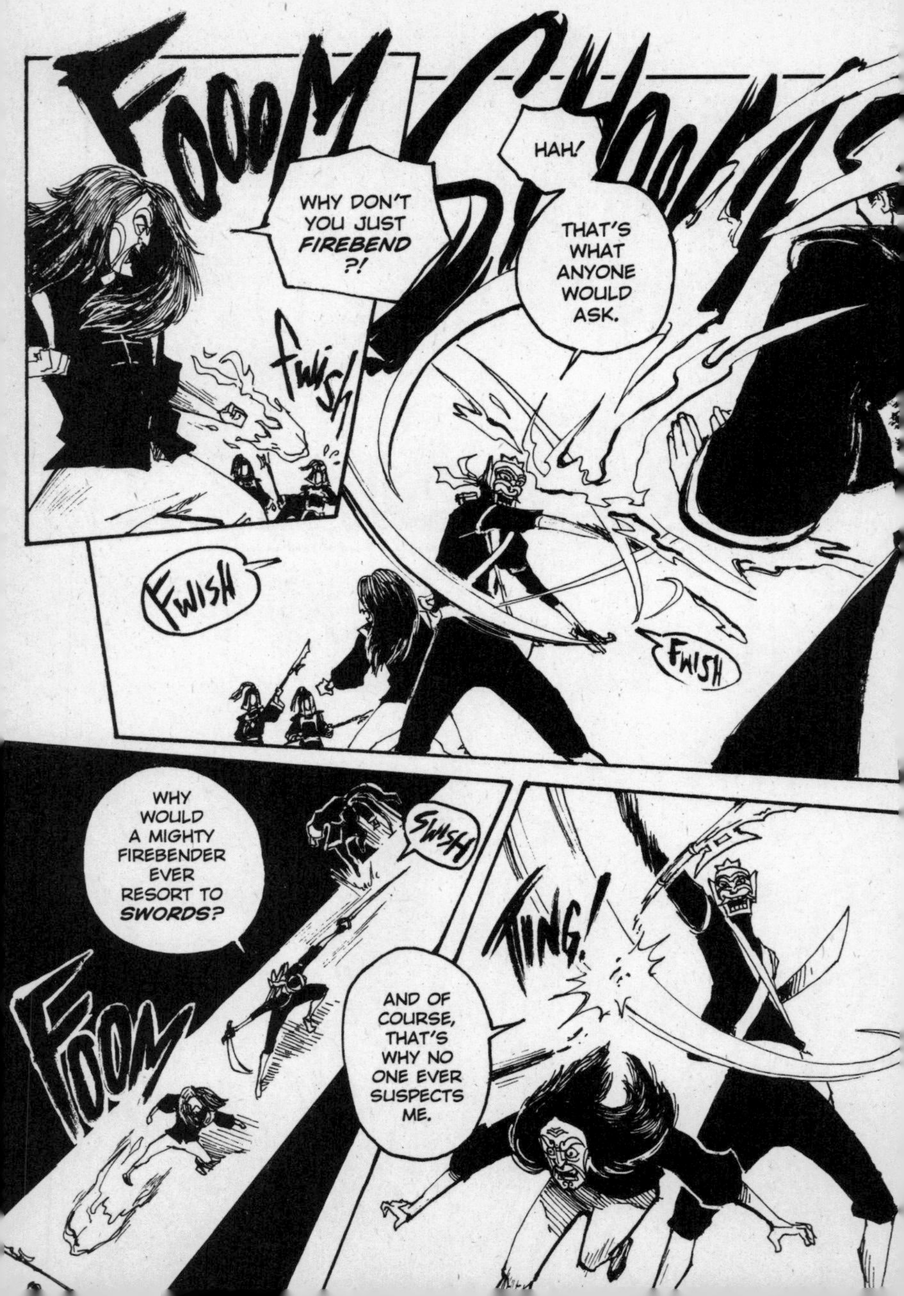
FOOOM
WHY DON'T YOU JUST *FIREBEND* ?!
FWISH
HAH!
THAT'S WHAT ANYONE WOULD ASK.
FWISH
FWISH
WHY WOULD A MIGHTY FIREBENDER EVER RESORT TO *SWORDS?*
SWISH
FOOM
AND OF COURSE, THAT'S WHY NO ONE EVER SUSPECTS ME.

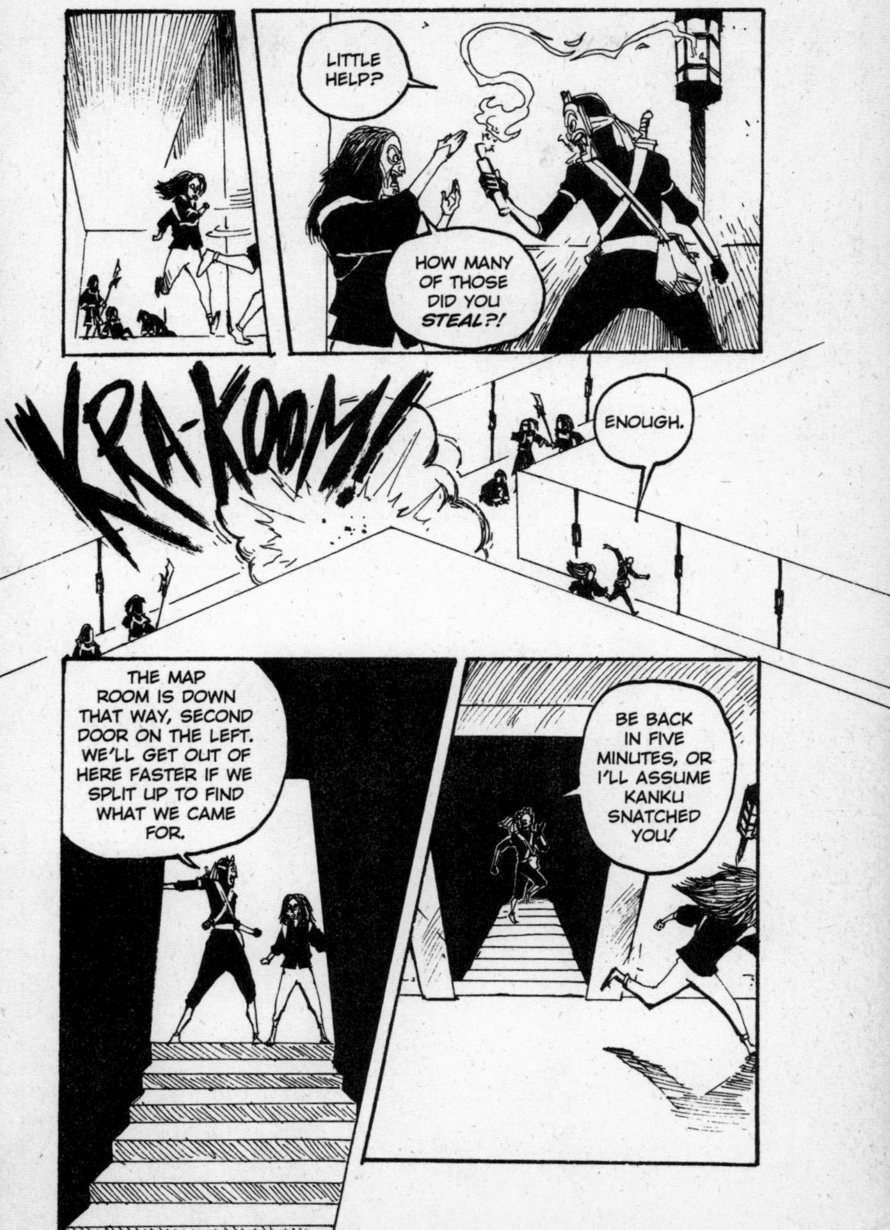
LITTLE HELP?
HOW MANY OF THOSE DID YOU *STEAL*?!
KRA-KOOM!!
ENOUGH.
THE MAP ROOM IS DOWN THAT WAY, SECOND DOOR ON THE LEFT. WE'LL GET OUT OF HERE FASTER IF WE SPLIT UP TO FIND WHAT WE CAME FOR.
BE BACK IN FIVE MINUTES, OR I'LL ASSUME KANKU SNATCHED YOU!

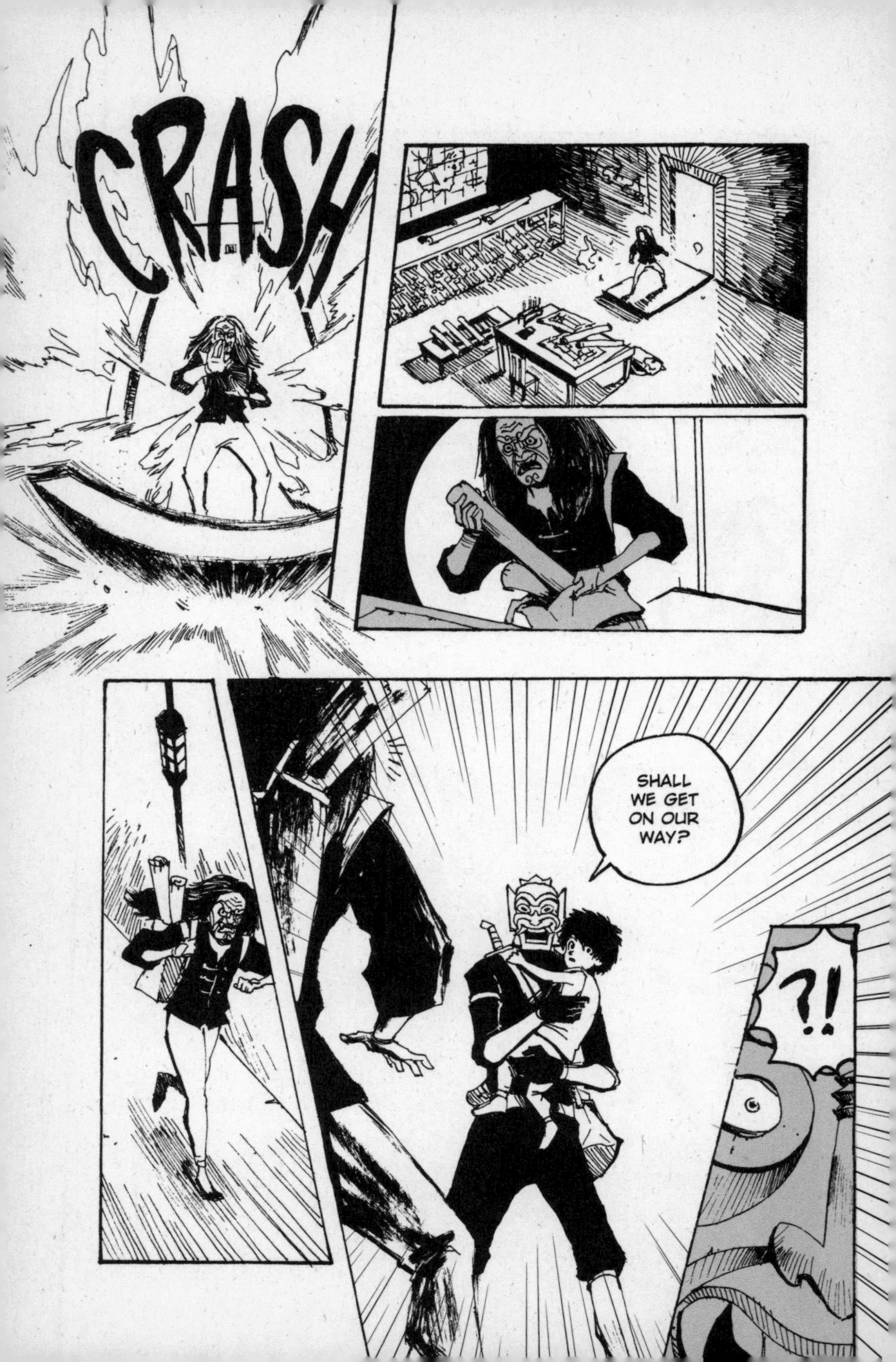
CRASH
SHALL WE GET ON OUR WAY?
?!

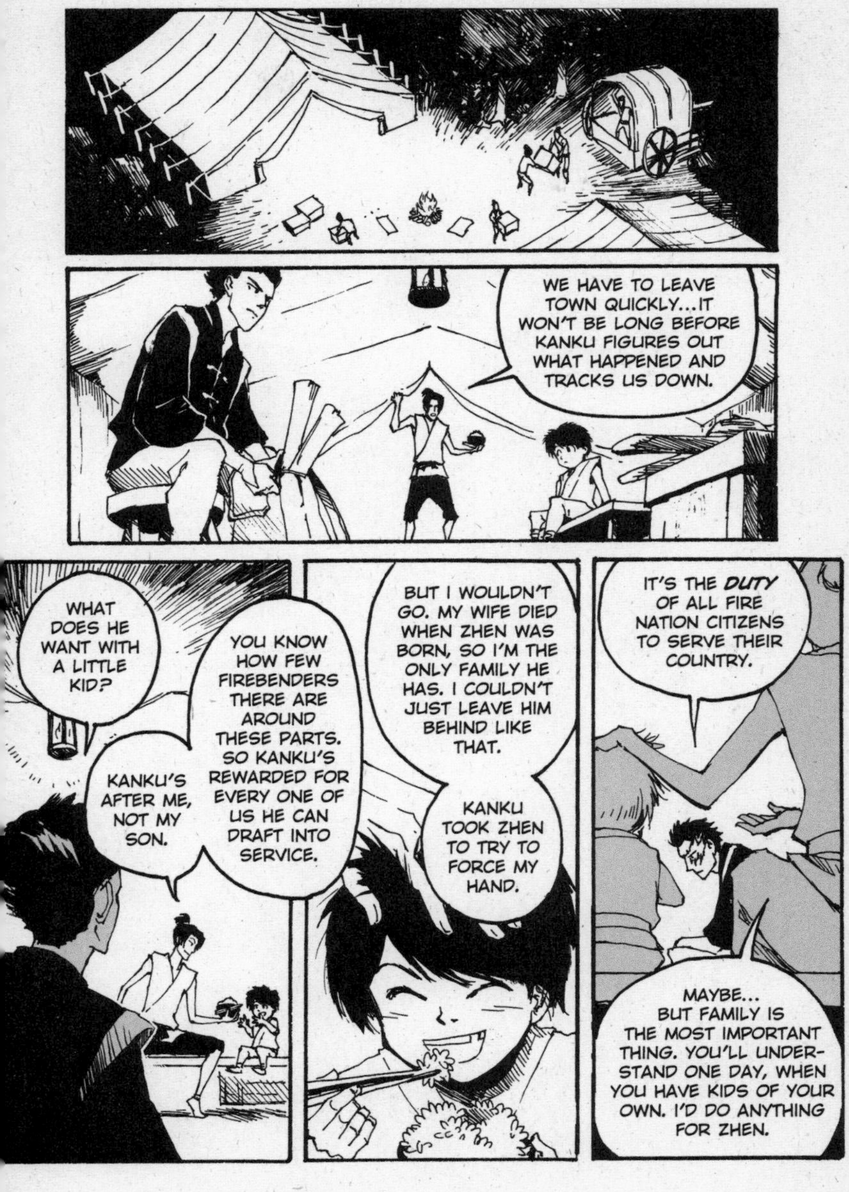
WE HAVE TO LEAVE TOWN QUICKLY...IT WON'T BE LONG BEFORE KANKU FIGURES OUT WHAT HAPPENED AND TRACKS US DOWN.
WHAT DOES HE WANT WITH A LITTLE KID?
KANKU'S AFTER ME, NOT MY SON.
YOU KNOW HOW FEW FIREBENDERS THERE ARE AROUND THESE PARTS. SO KANKU'S REWARDED FOR EVERY ONE OF US HE CAN DRAFT INTO SERVICE.
BUT I WOULDN'T GO. MY WIFE DIED WHEN ZHEN WAS BORN, SO I'M THE ONLY FAMILY HE HAS. I COULDN'T JUST LEAVE HIM BEHIND LIKE THAT.
KANKU TOOK ZHEN TO TRY TO FORCE MY HAND.
IT'S THE *DUTY* OF ALL FIRE NATION CITIZENS TO SERVE THEIR COUNTRY.
MAYBE... BUT FAMILY IS THE MOST IMPORTANT THING. YOU'LL UNDERSTAND ONE DAY, WHEN YOU HAVE KIDS OF YOUR OWN. I'D DO ANYTHING FOR ZHEN.

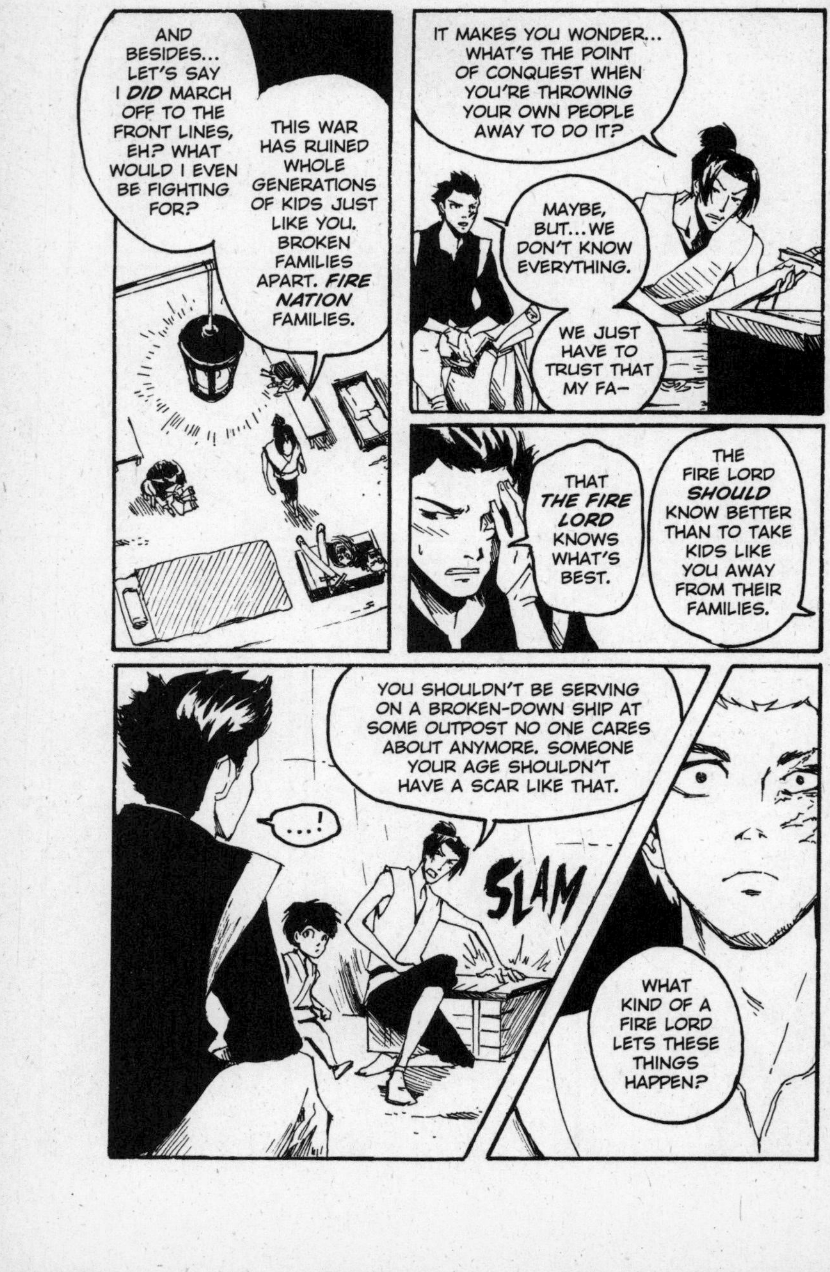
AND BESIDES... LET'S SAY I *DID* MARCH OFF TO THE FRONT LINES, EH? WHAT WOULD I EVEN BE FIGHTING FOR?
THIS WAR HAS RUINED WHOLE GENERATIONS OF KIDS JUST LIKE YOU. BROKEN FAMILIES APART. *FIRE NATION* FAMILIES.
IT MAKES YOU WONDER... WHAT'S THE POINT OF CONQUEST WHEN YOU'RE THROWING YOUR OWN PEOPLE AWAY TO DO IT?
MAYBE, BUT... WE DON'T KNOW EVERYTHING.
WE JUST HAVE TO TRUST THAT MY FA–
THAT *THE FIRE LORD* KNOWS WHAT'S BEST.
THE FIRE LORD *SHOULD* KNOW BETTER THAN TO TAKE KIDS LIKE YOU AWAY FROM THEIR FAMILIES.
YOU SHOULDN'T BE SERVING ON A BROKEN-DOWN SHIP AT SOME OUTPOST NO ONE CARES ABOUT ANYMORE. SOMEONE YOUR AGE SHOULDN'T HAVE A SCAR LIKE THAT.
...!
SLAM
WHAT KIND OF A FIRE LORD LETS THESE THINGS HAPPEN?

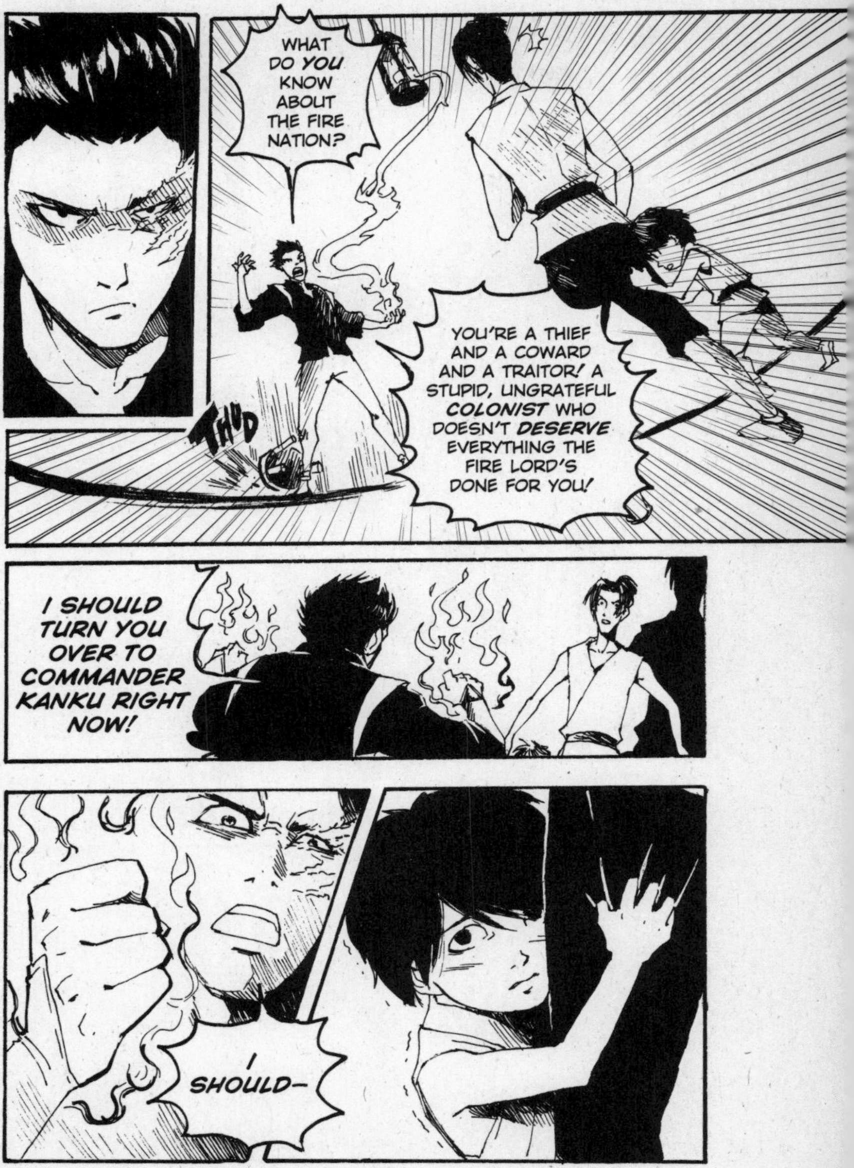
WHAT DO YOU KNOW ABOUT THE FIRE NATION?
THUD
YOU'RE A THIEF AND A COWARD AND A TRAITOR! A STUPID, UNGRATEFUL COLONIST WHO DOESN'T DESERVE EVERYTHING THE FIRE LORD'S DONE FOR YOU!
I SHOULD TURN YOU OVER TO COMMANDER KANKU RIGHT NOW!
I SHOULD-

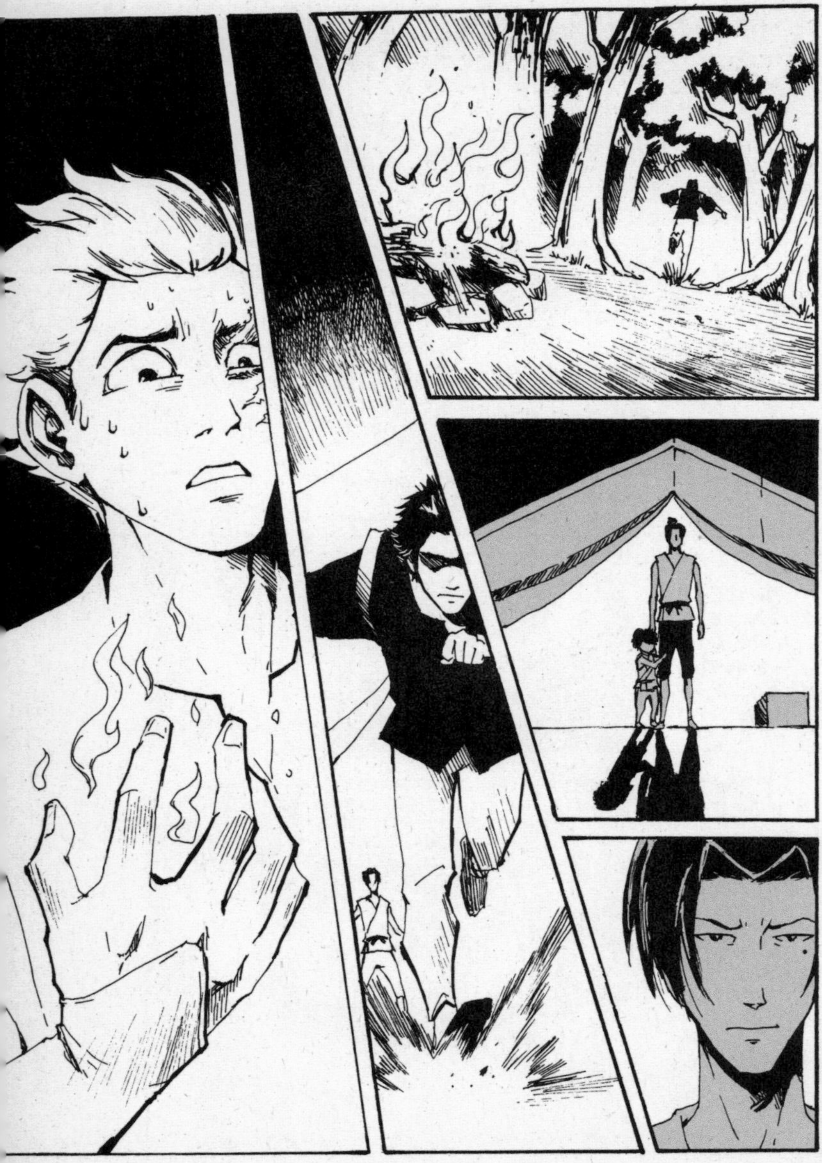

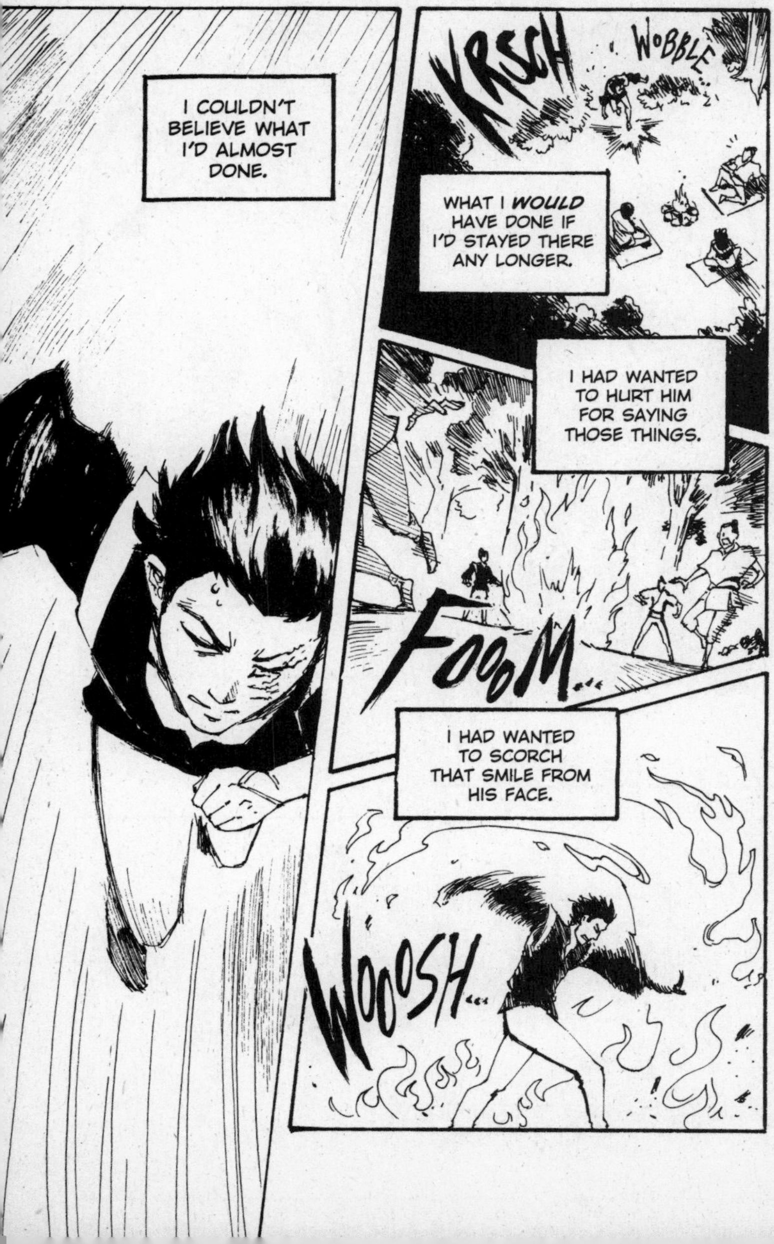
I COULDN'T BELIEVE WHAT I'D ALMOST DONE.
KRSCH
WOBBLE
WHAT I *WOULD* HAVE DONE IF I'D STAYED THERE ANY LONGER.
I HAD WANTED TO HURT HIM FOR SAYING THOSE THINGS.
FOOOM...
I HAD WANTED TO SCORCH THAT SMILE FROM HIS FACE.
WOOOSH...

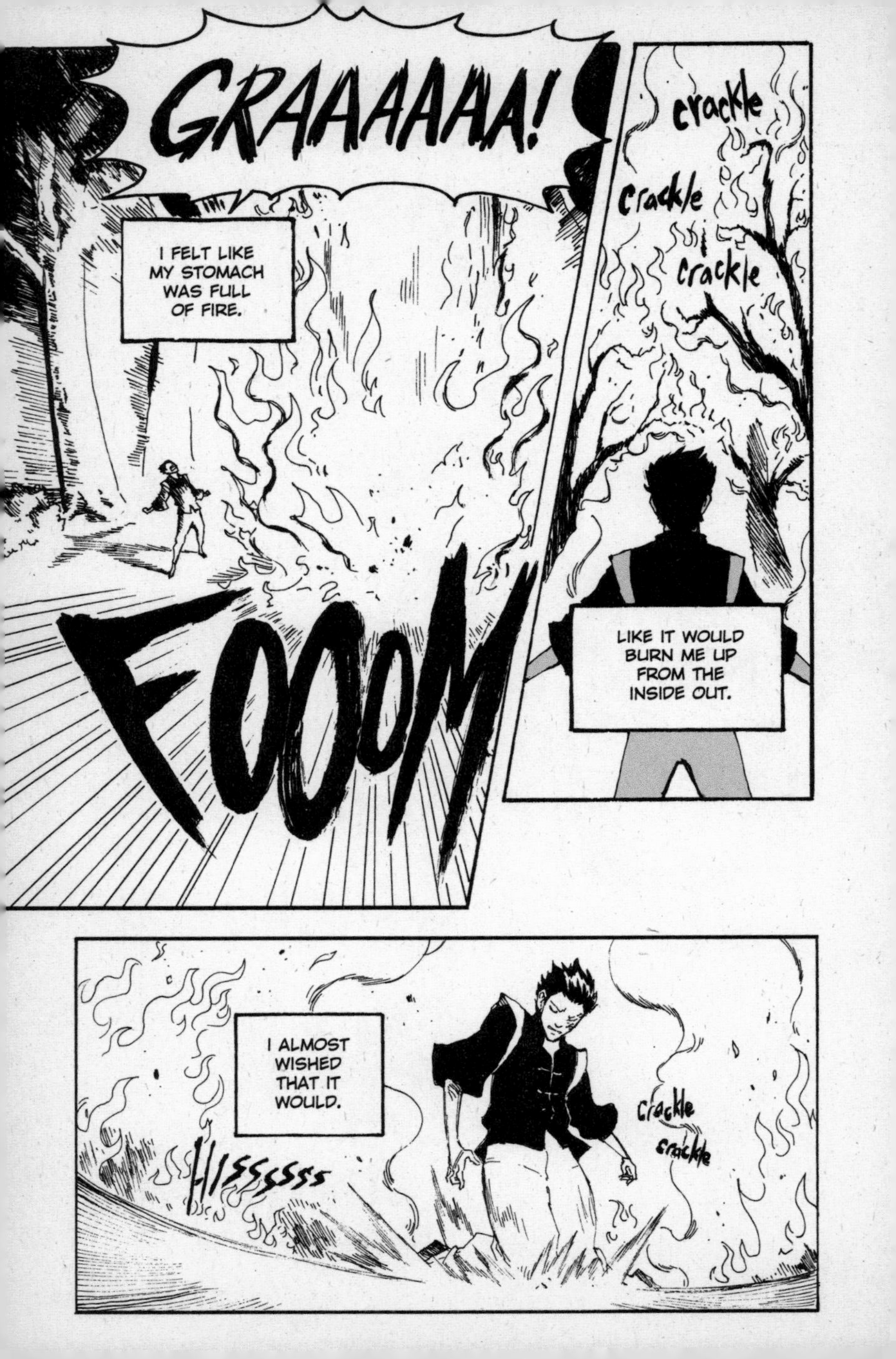
GRAAAAAA!
I FELT LIKE MY STOMACH WAS FULL OF FIRE.
FOOOM
crackle
crackle
crackle
LIKE IT WOULD BURN ME UP FROM THE INSIDE OUT.
I ALMOST WISHED THAT IT WOULD.
HISSSSSS
crackle
crackle

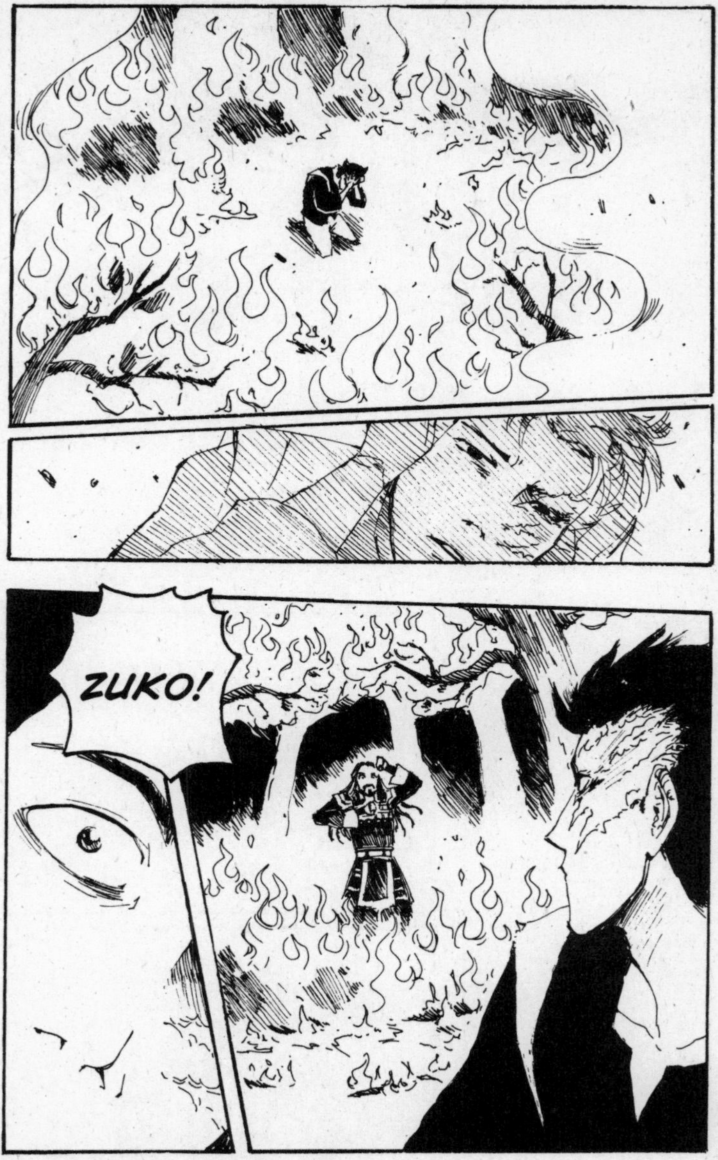
ZUKO!

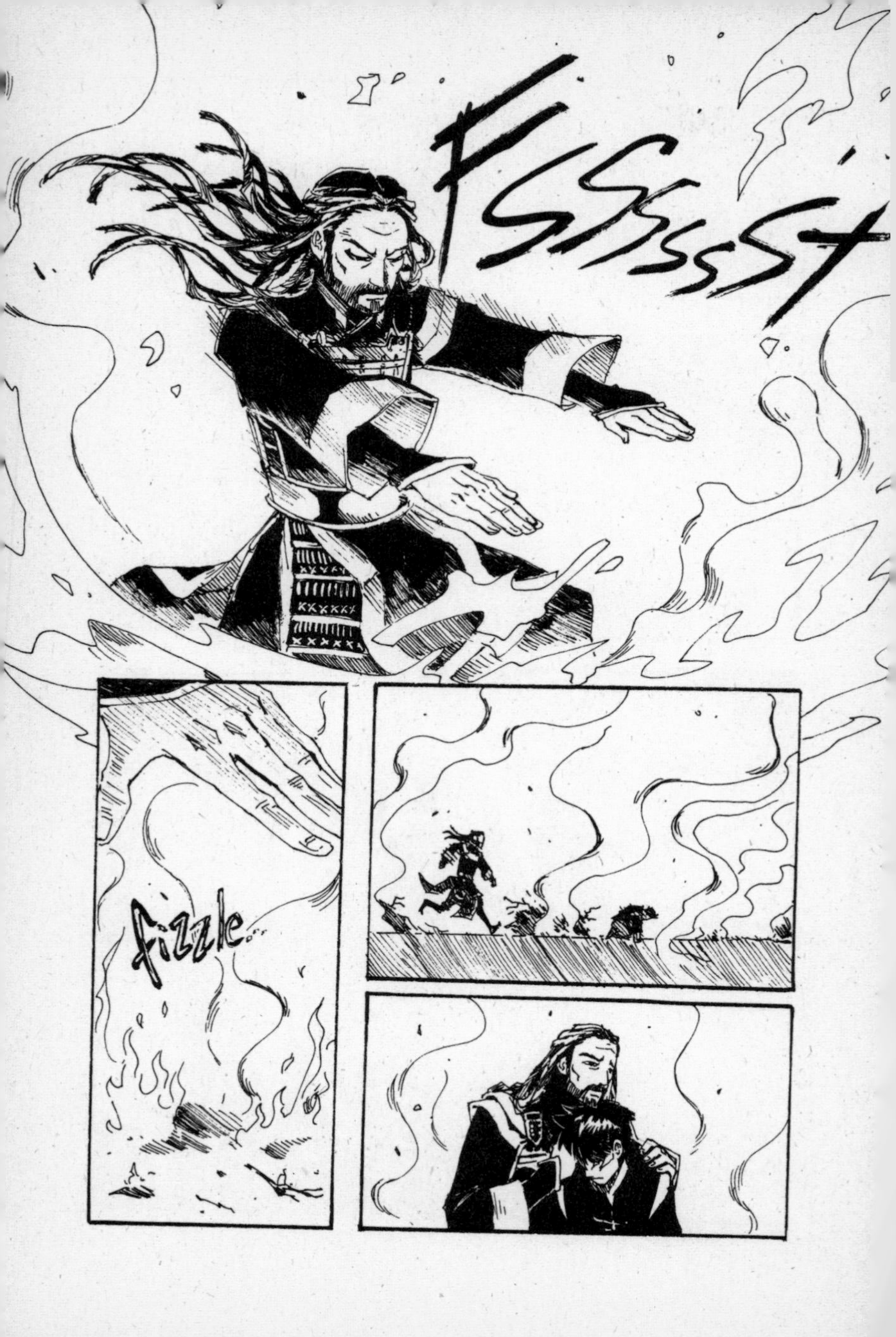
FSSSSST
fizzle...

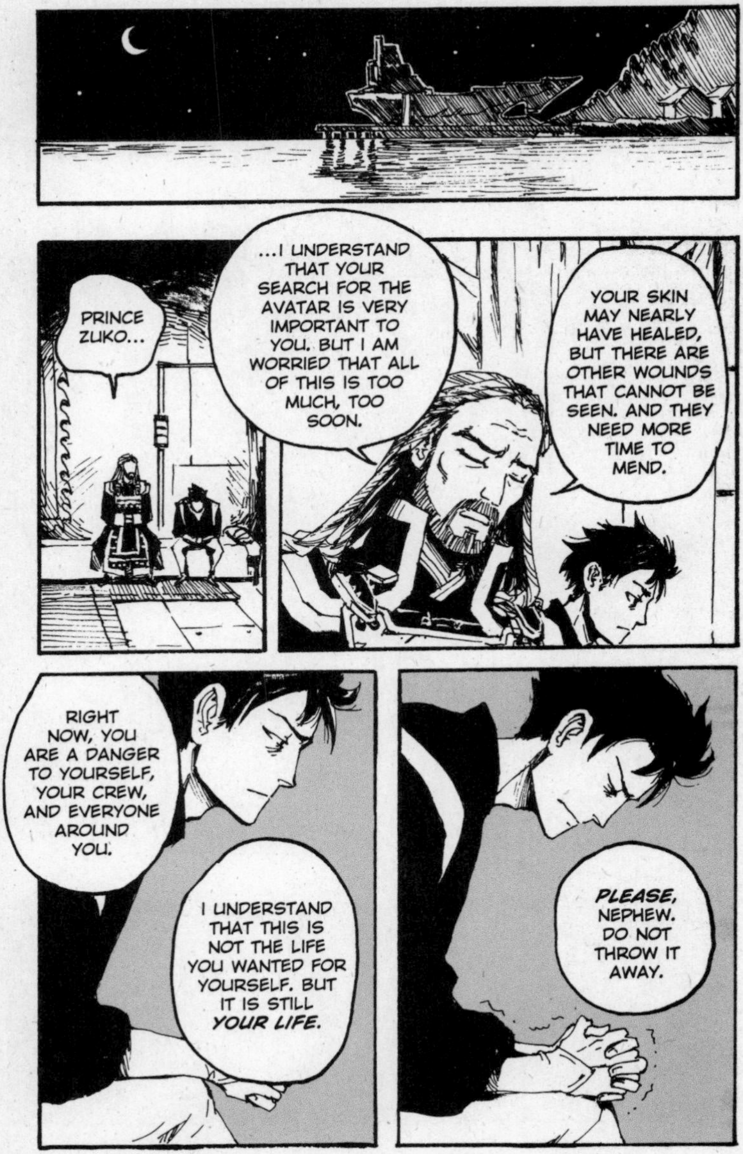
PRINCE ZUKO...
...I UNDERSTAND THAT YOUR SEARCH FOR THE AVATAR IS VERY IMPORTANT TO YOU. BUT I AM WORRIED THAT ALL OF THIS IS TOO MUCH, TOO SOON.
YOUR SKIN MAY NEARLY HAVE HEALED, BUT THERE ARE OTHER WOUNDS THAT CANNOT BE SEEN. AND THEY NEED MORE TIME TO MEND.
RIGHT NOW, YOU ARE A DANGER TO YOURSELF, YOUR CREW, AND EVERYONE AROUND YOU.
I UNDERSTAND THAT THIS IS NOT THE LIFE YOU WANTED FOR YOURSELF. BUT IT IS STILL ***YOUR LIFE***.
PLEASE, NEPHEW. DO NOT THROW IT AWAY.

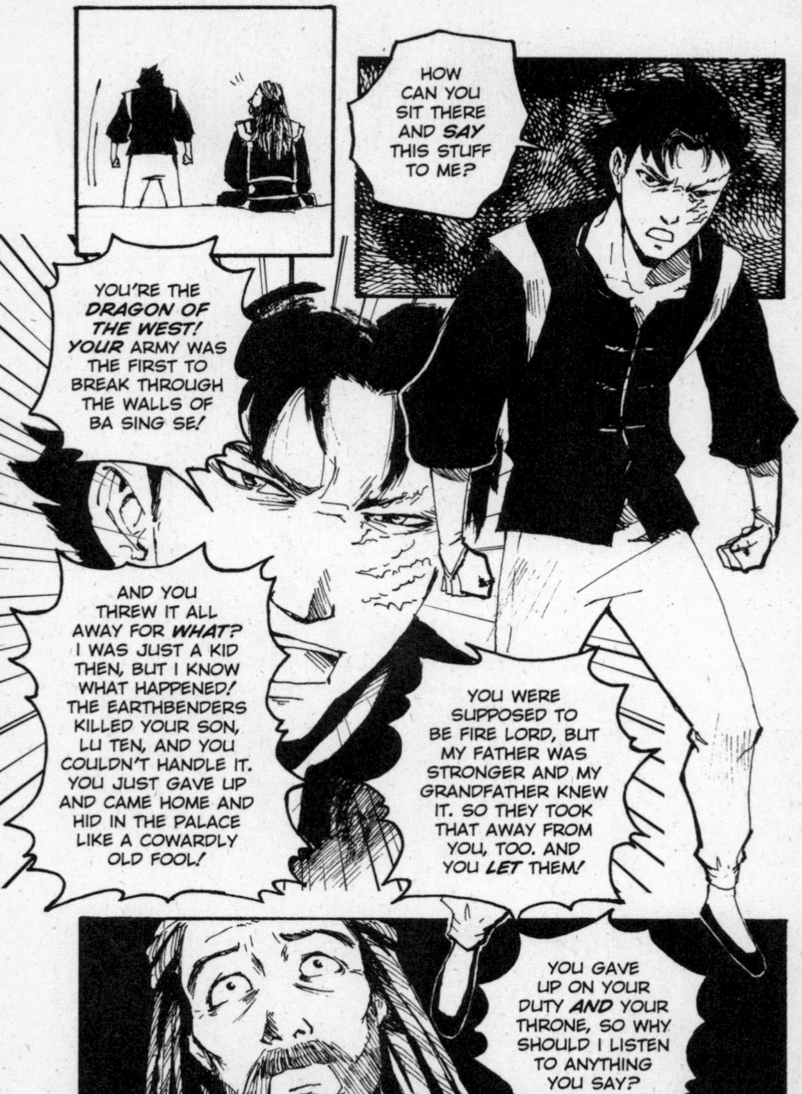
HOW CAN YOU SIT THERE AND SAY THIS STUFF TO ME?
YOU'RE THE DRAGON OF THE WEST! YOUR ARMY WAS THE FIRST TO BREAK THROUGH THE WALLS OF BA SING SE!
AND YOU THREW IT ALL AWAY FOR WHAT? I WAS JUST A KID THEN, BUT I KNOW WHAT HAPPENED! THE EARTHBENDERS KILLED YOUR SON, LU TEN, AND YOU COULDN'T HANDLE IT. YOU JUST GAVE UP AND CAME HOME AND HID IN THE PALACE LIKE A COWARDLY OLD FOOL!
YOU WERE SUPPOSED TO BE FIRE LORD, BUT MY FATHER WAS STRONGER AND MY GRANDFATHER KNEW IT. SO THEY TOOK THAT AWAY FROM YOU, TOO. AND YOU LET THEM!
YOU GAVE UP ON YOUR DUTY AND YOUR THRONE, SO WHY SHOULD I LISTEN TO ANYTHING YOU SAY?

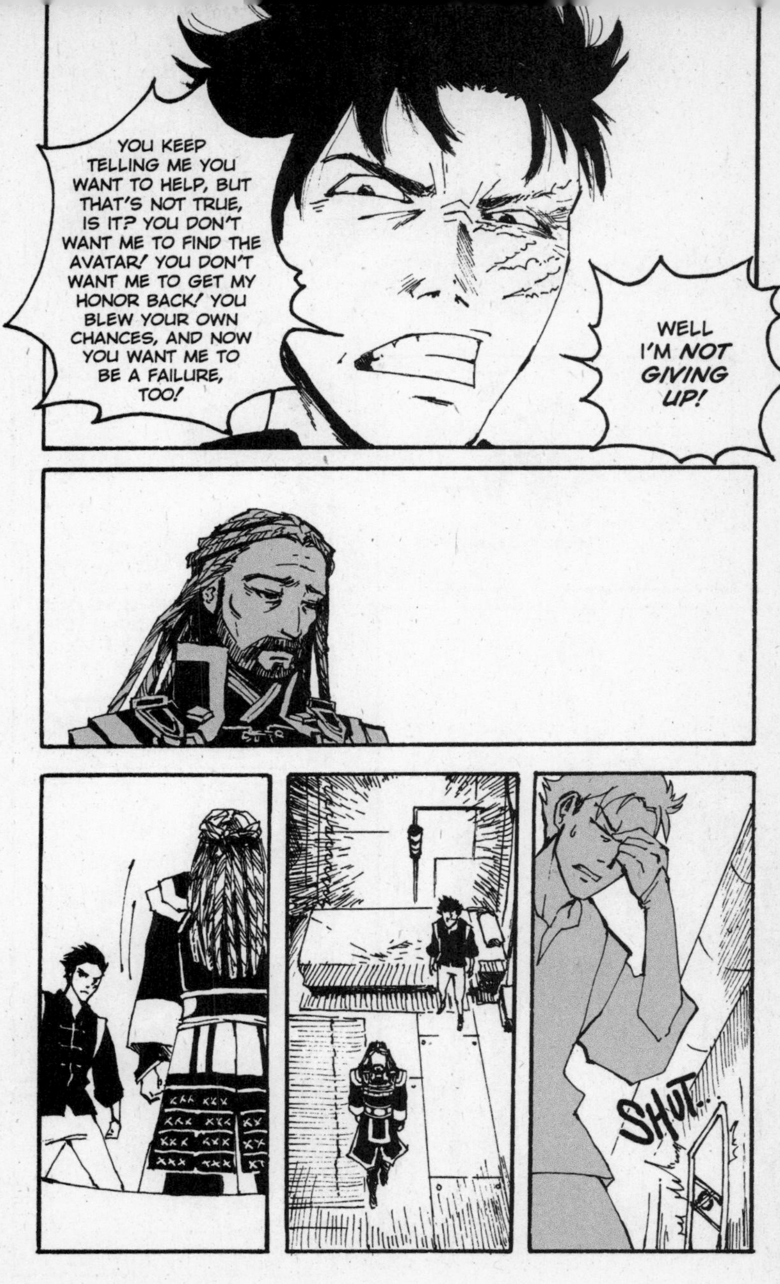
YOU KEEP TELLING ME YOU WANT TO HELP, BUT THAT'S NOT TRUE, IS IT? YOU DON'T WANT ME TO FIND THE AVATAR! YOU DON'T WANT ME TO GET MY HONOR BACK! YOU BLEW YOUR OWN CHANCES, AND NOW YOU WANT ME TO BE A FAILURE, TOO!
WELL I'M *NOT GIVING UP!*
SHUT...

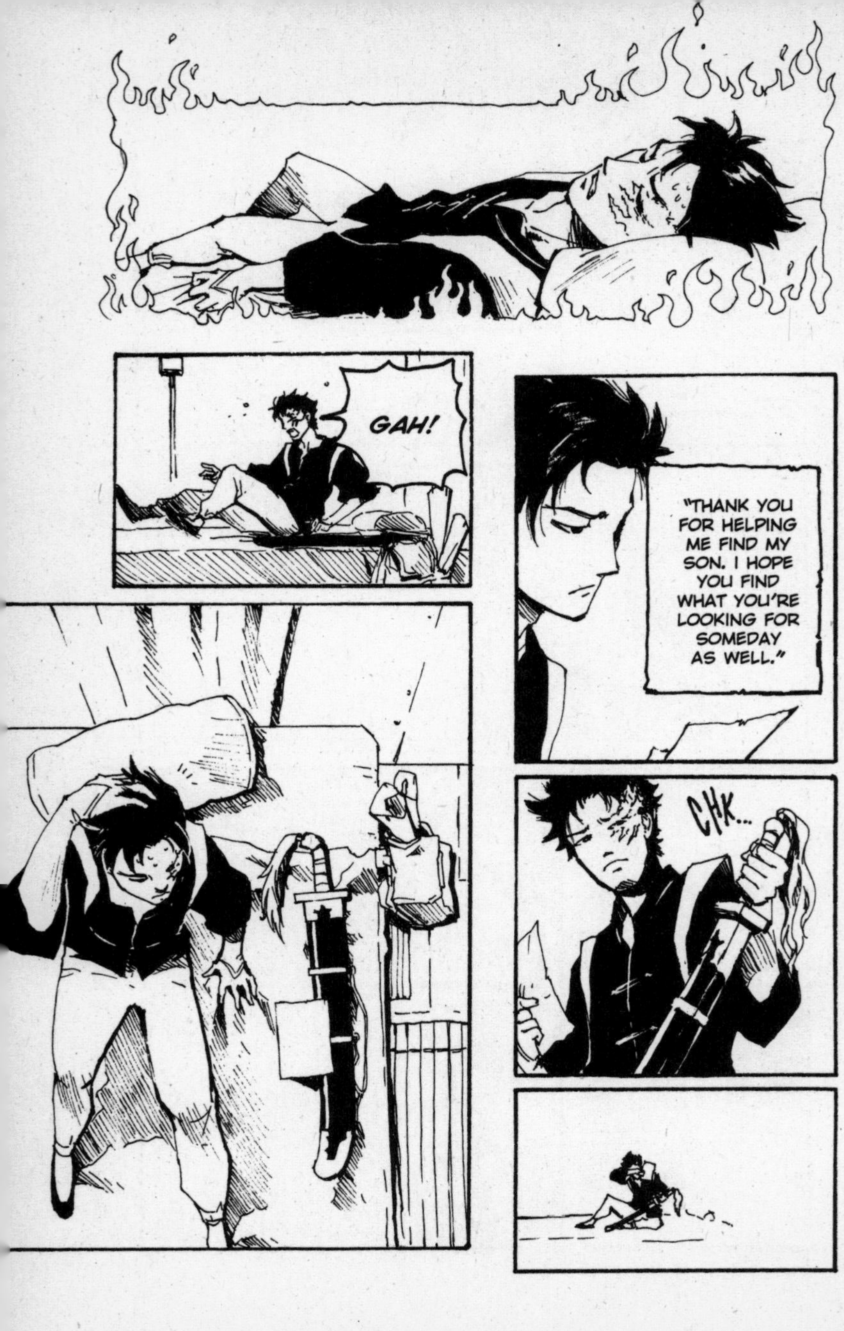
GAH!
"THANK YOU FOR HELPING ME FIND MY SON. I HOPE YOU FIND WHAT YOU'RE LOOKING FOR SOMEDAY AS WELL."
CHK...

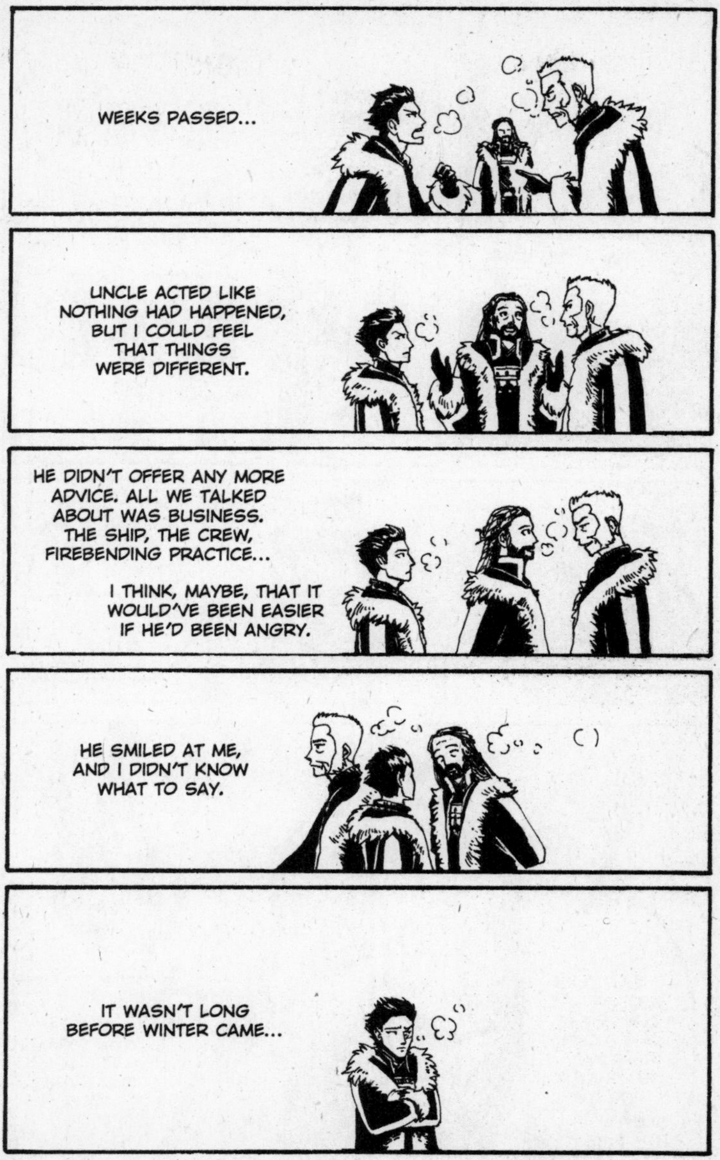
WEEKS PASSED...
UNCLE ACTED LIKE NOTHING HAD HAPPENED, BUT I COULD FEEL THAT THINGS WERE DIFFERENT.
HE DIDN'T OFFER ANY MORE ADVICE. ALL WE TALKED ABOUT WAS BUSINESS. THE SHIP, THE CREW, FIREBENDING PRACTICE...
I THINK, MAYBE, THAT IT WOULD'VE BEEN EASIER IF HE'D BEEN ANGRY.
HE SMILED AT ME, AND I DIDN'T KNOW WHAT TO SAY.
IT WASN'T LONG BEFORE WINTER CAME...

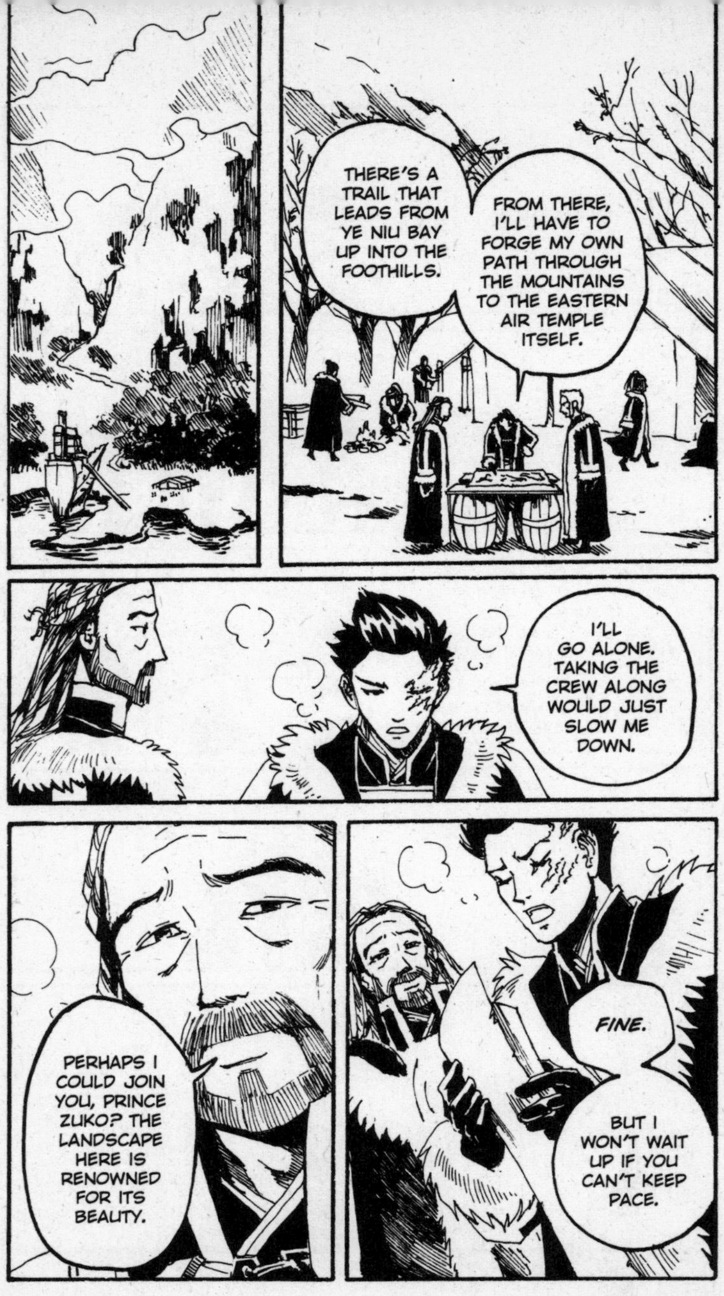
THERE'S A TRAIL THAT LEADS FROM YE NIU BAY UP INTO THE FOOTHILLS.
FROM THERE, I'LL HAVE TO FORGE MY OWN PATH THROUGH THE MOUNTAINS TO THE EASTERN AIR TEMPLE ITSELF.
I'LL GO ALONE. TAKING THE CREW ALONG WOULD JUST SLOW ME DOWN.
PERHAPS I COULD JOIN YOU, PRINCE ZUKO? THE LANDSCAPE HERE IS RENOWNED FOR ITS BEAUTY.
FINE.
BUT I WON'T WAIT UP IF YOU CAN'T KEEP PACE.

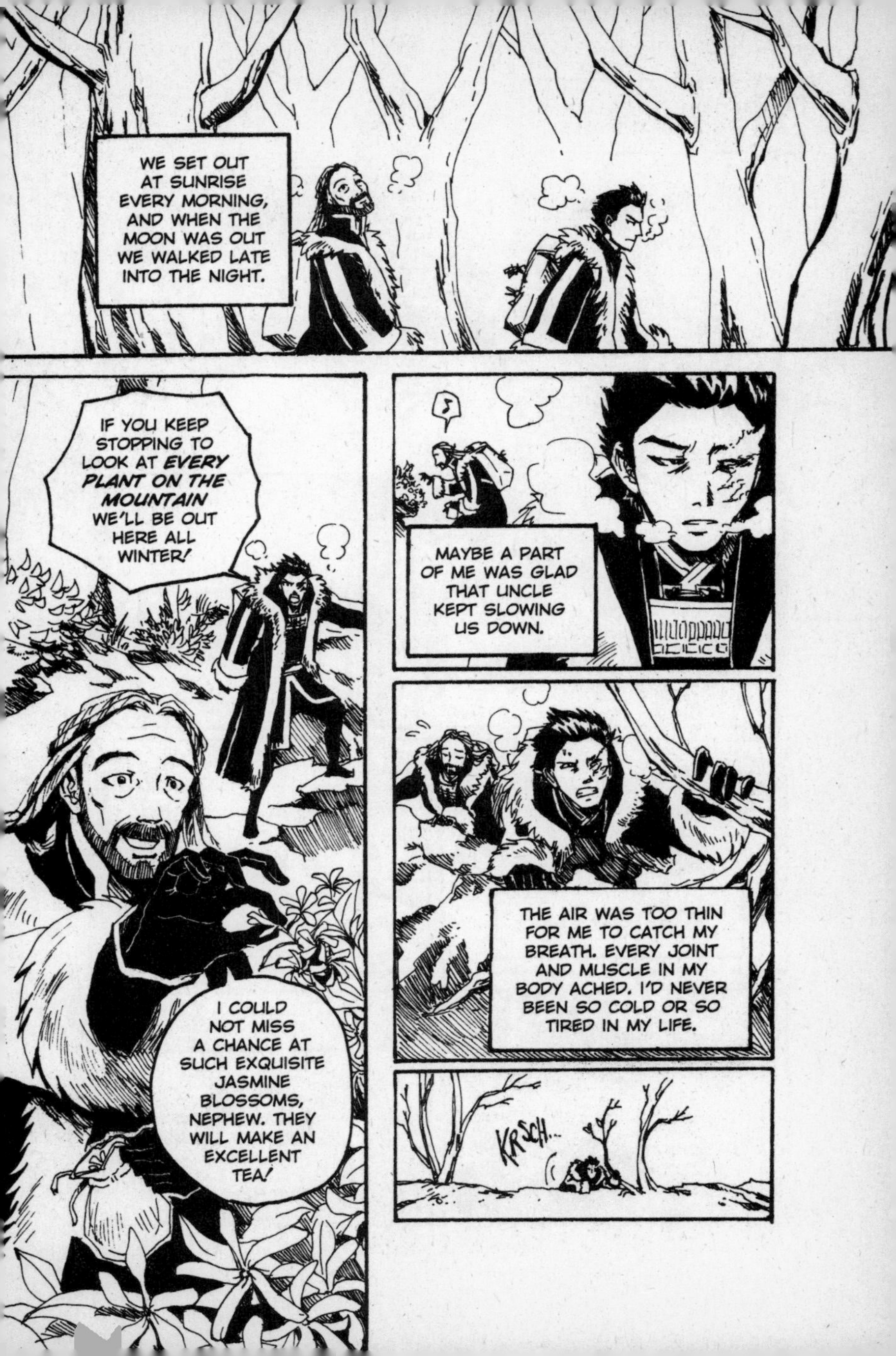
WE SET OUT AT SUNRISE EVERY MORNING, AND WHEN THE MOON WAS OUT WE WALKED LATE INTO THE NIGHT.
IF YOU KEEP STOPPING TO LOOK AT *EVERY PLANT ON THE MOUNTAIN* WE'LL BE OUT HERE ALL WINTER!
I COULD NOT MISS A CHANCE AT SUCH EXQUISITE JASMINE BLOSSOMS, NEPHEW. THEY WILL MAKE AN EXCELLENT TEA!
MAYBE A PART OF ME WAS GLAD THAT UNCLE KEPT SLOWING US DOWN.
THE AIR WAS TOO THIN FOR ME TO CATCH MY BREATH. EVERY JOINT AND MUSCLE IN MY BODY ACHED. I'D NEVER BEEN SO COLD OR SO TIRED IN MY LIFE.
KRSCH...

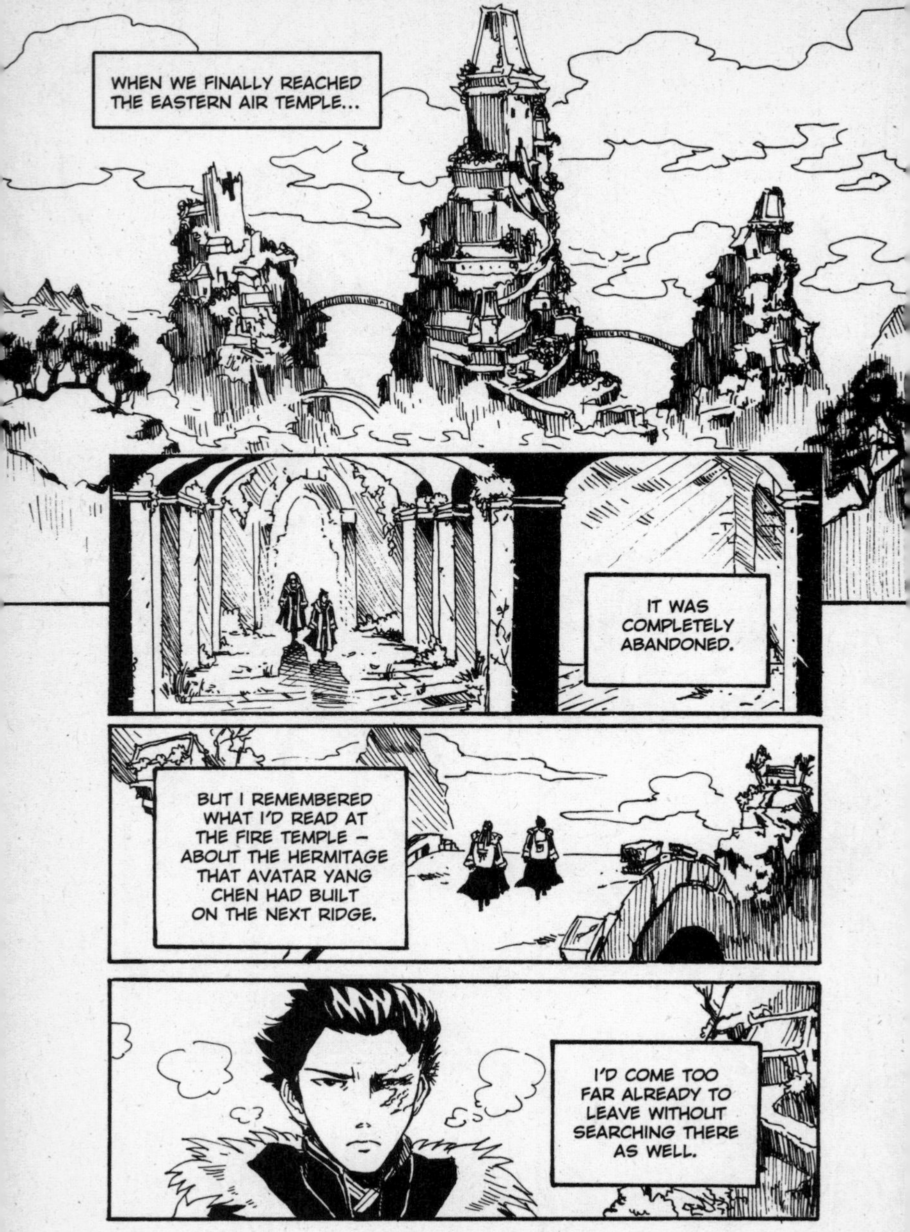
WHEN WE FINALLY REACHED THE EASTERN AIR TEMPLE...
IT WAS COMPLETELY ABANDONED.
BUT I REMEMBERED WHAT I'D READ AT THE FIRE TEMPLE – ABOUT THE HERMITAGE THAT AVATAR YANG CHEN HAD BUILT ON THE NEXT RIDGE.
I'D COME TOO FAR ALREADY TO LEAVE WITHOUT SEARCHING THERE AS WELL.

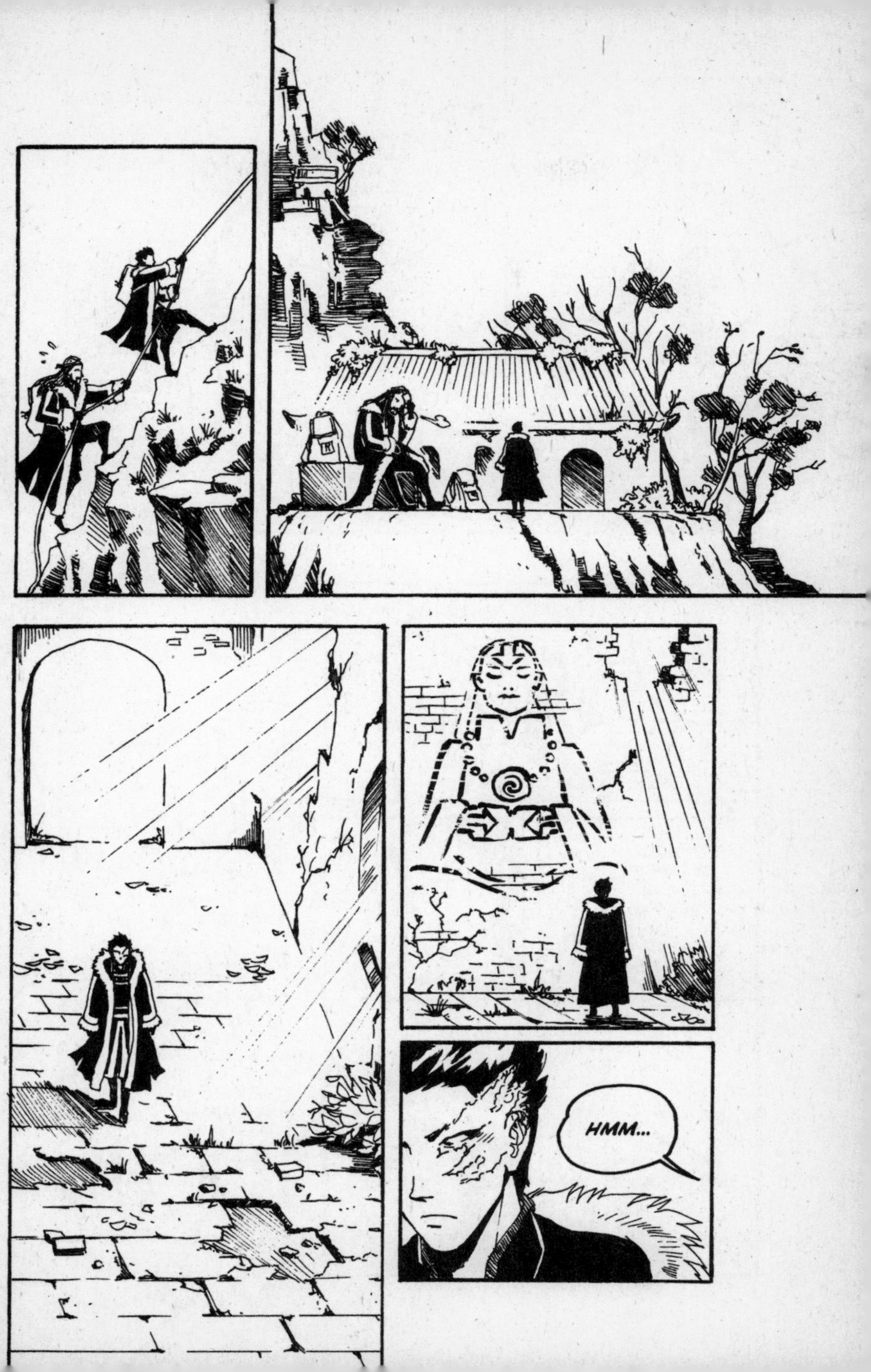
HMM...

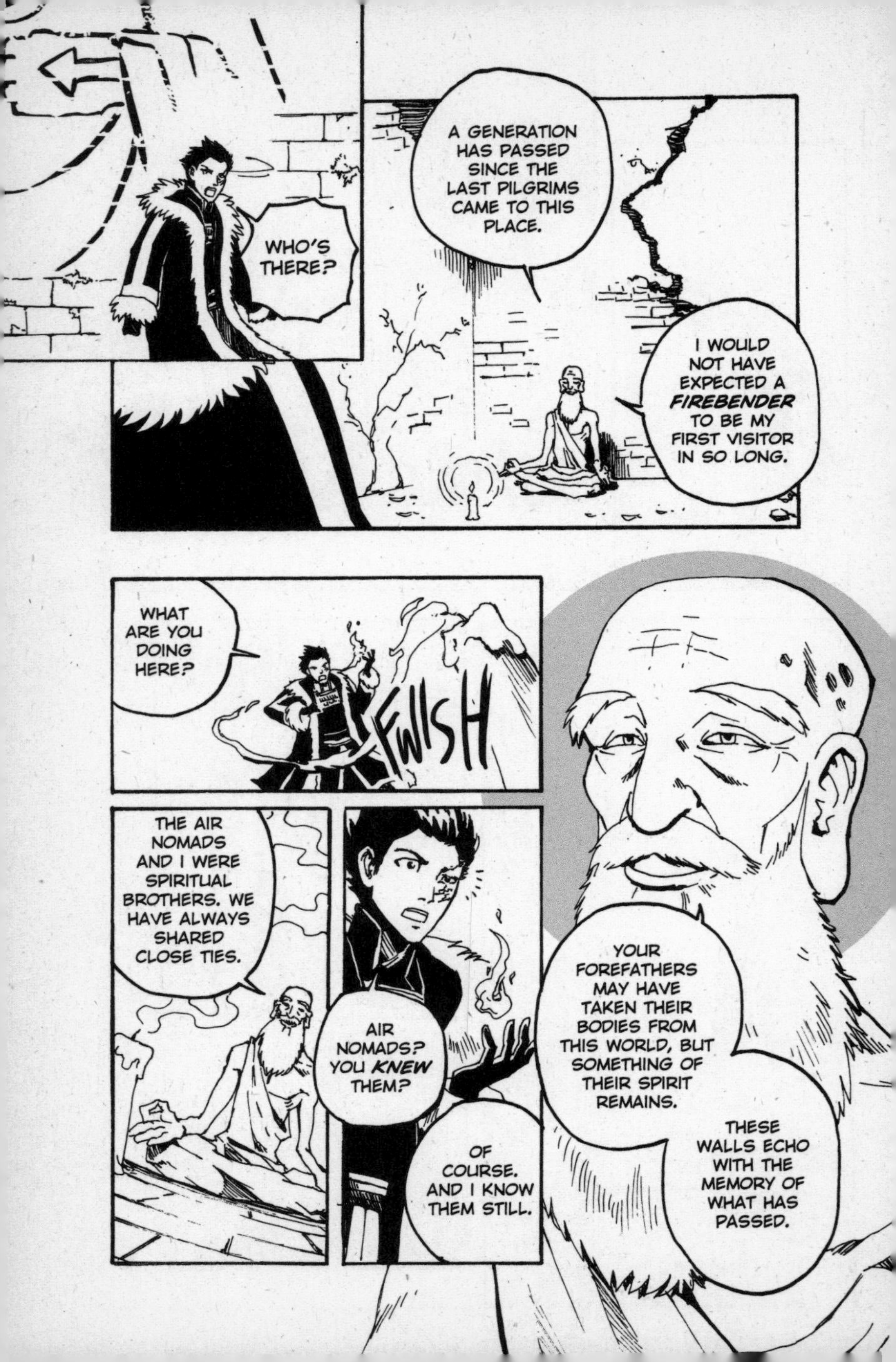
WHO'S THERE?
A GENERATION HAS PASSED SINCE THE LAST PILGRIMS CAME TO THIS PLACE.
I WOULD NOT HAVE EXPECTED A *FIREBENDER* TO BE MY FIRST VISITOR IN SO LONG.
WHAT ARE YOU DOING HERE?
FWISH
THE AIR NOMADS AND I WERE SPIRITUAL BROTHERS. WE HAVE ALWAYS SHARED CLOSE TIES.
AIR NOMADS? YOU *KNEW* THEM?
OF COURSE. AND I KNOW THEM STILL.
YOUR FOREFATHERS MAY HAVE TAKEN THEIR BODIES FROM THIS WORLD, BUT SOMETHING OF THEIR SPIRIT REMAINS.
THESE WALLS ECHO WITH THE MEMORY OF WHAT HAS PASSED.

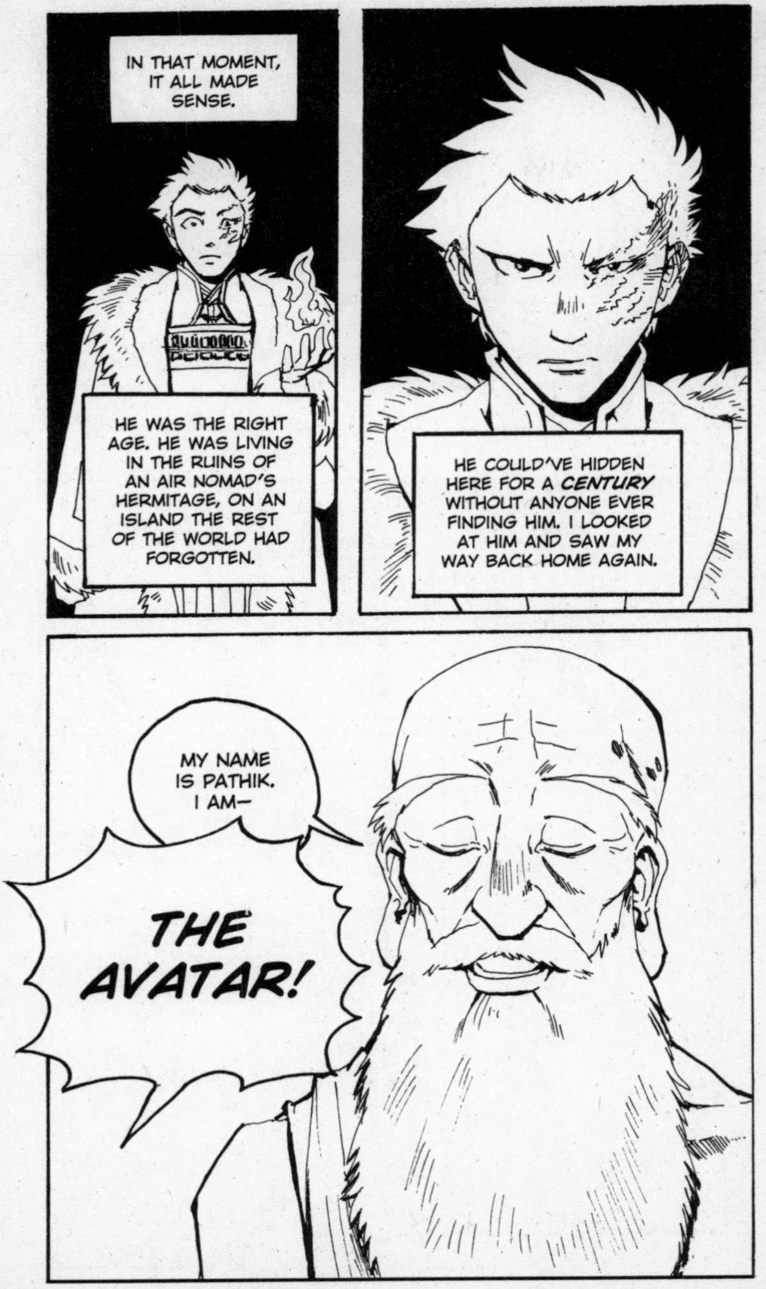
IN THAT MOMENT, IT ALL MADE SENSE.
HE WAS THE RIGHT AGE. HE WAS LIVING IN THE RUINS OF AN AIR NOMAD'S HERMITAGE, ON AN ISLAND THE REST OF THE WORLD HAD FORGOTTEN.
HE COULD'VE HIDDEN HERE FOR A *CENTURY* WITHOUT ANYONE EVER FINDING HIM. I LOOKED AT HIM AND SAW MY WAY BACK HOME AGAIN.
MY NAME IS PATHIK. I AM—
THE AVATAR!

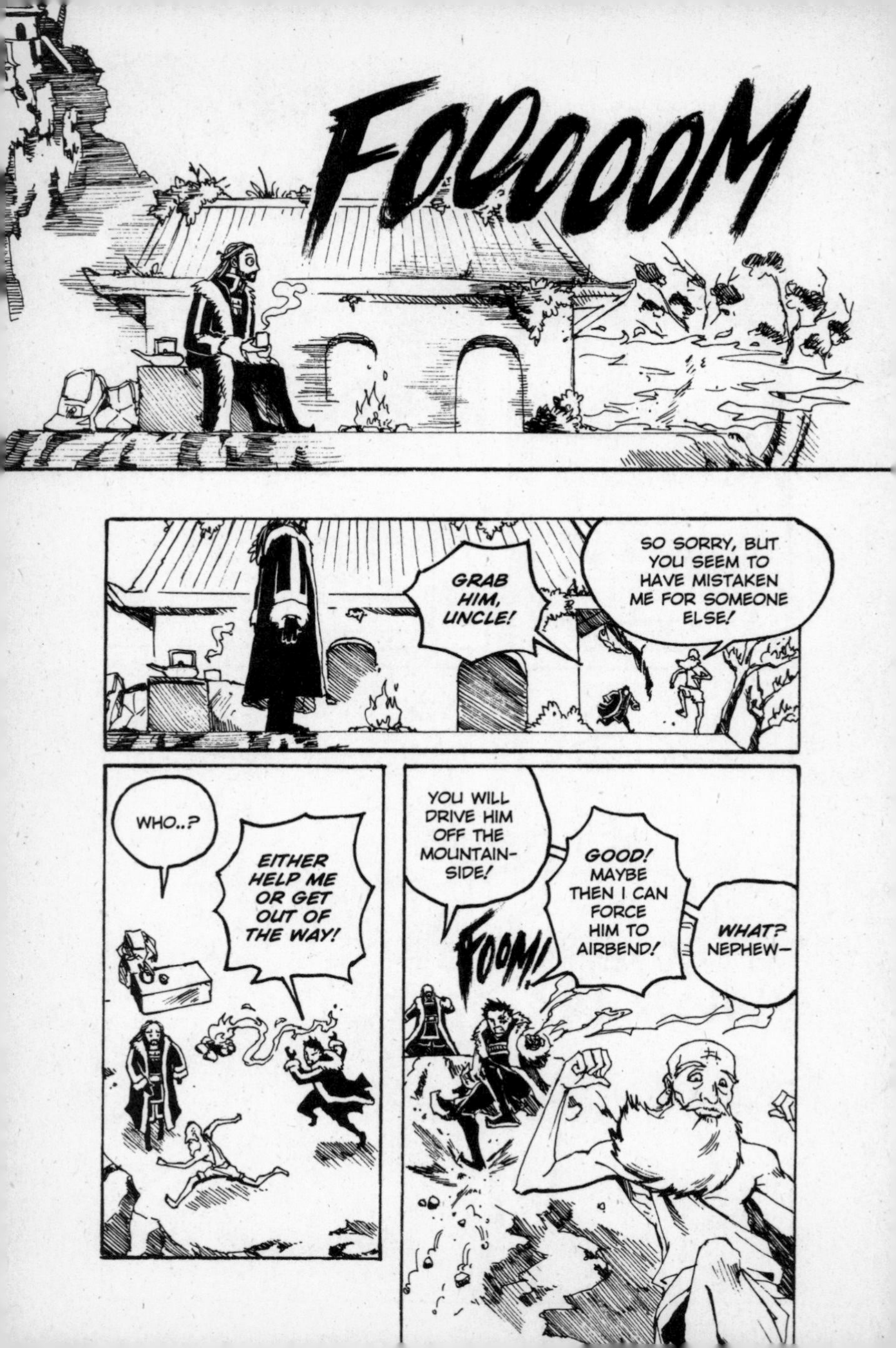
FOOOOOM
GRAB HIM, UNCLE!
SO SORRY, BUT YOU SEEM TO HAVE MISTAKEN ME FOR SOMEONE ELSE!
WHO..?
EITHER HELP ME OR GET OUT OF THE WAY!
YOU WILL DRIVE HIM OFF THE MOUNTAIN-SIDE!
FOOM!
GOOD! MAYBE THEN I CAN FORCE HIM TO AIRBEND!
WHAT? NEPHEW—

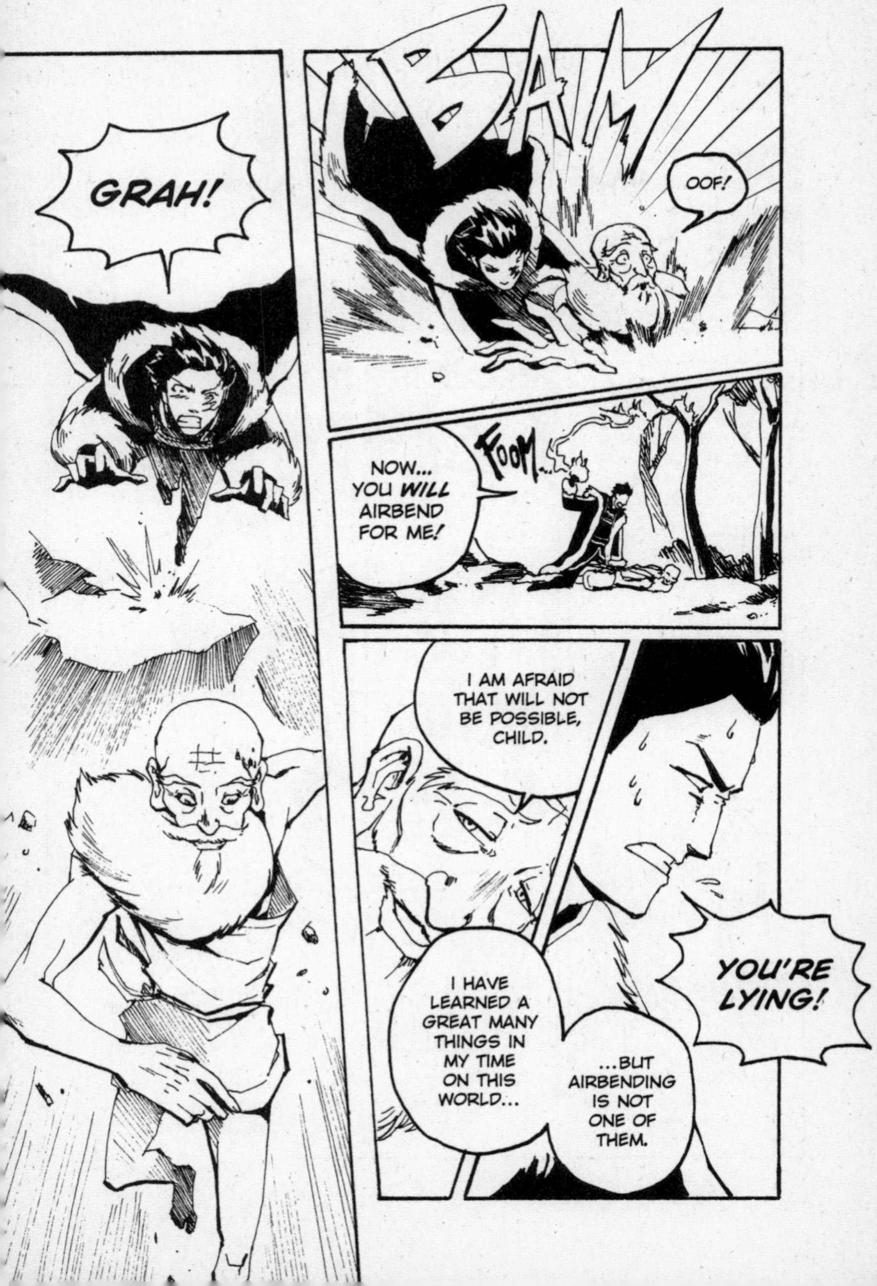
GRAH!
BAM
OOF!
NOW... YOU WILL AIRBEND FOR ME!
FOOM...
I AM AFRAID THAT WILL NOT BE POSSIBLE, CHILD.
YOU'RE LYING!
I HAVE LEARNED A GREAT MANY THINGS IN MY TIME ON THIS WORLD...
...BUT AIRBENDING IS NOT ONE OF THEM.

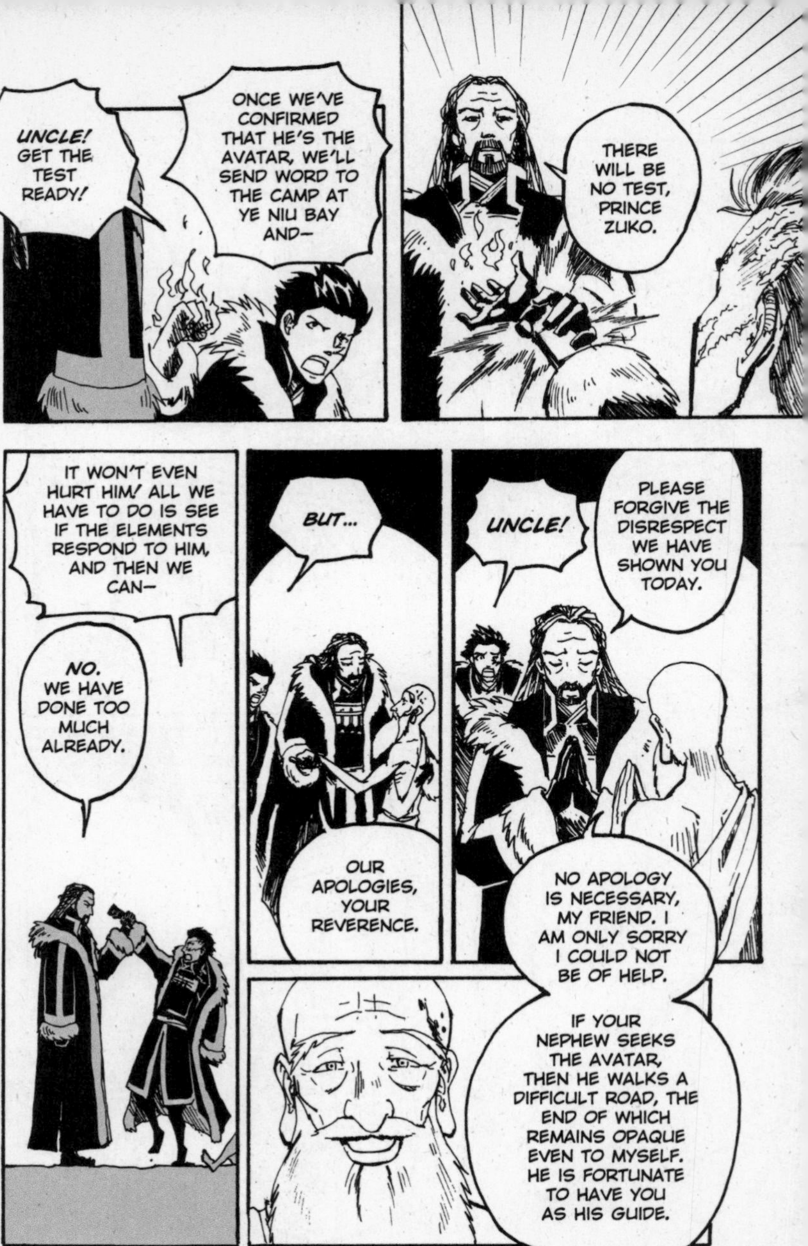
UNCLE! GET THE TEST READY!
ONCE WE'VE CONFIRMED THAT HE'S THE AVATAR, WE'LL SEND WORD TO THE CAMP AT YE NIU BAY AND—
THERE WILL BE NO TEST, PRINCE ZUKO.
IT WON'T EVEN HURT HIM! ALL WE HAVE TO DO IS SEE IF THE ELEMENTS RESPOND TO HIM, AND THEN WE CAN—
NO. WE HAVE DONE TOO MUCH ALREADY.
BUT...
OUR APOLOGIES, YOUR REVERENCE.
UNCLE!
PLEASE FORGIVE THE DISRESPECT WE HAVE SHOWN YOU TODAY.
NO APOLOGY IS NECESSARY, MY FRIEND. I AM ONLY SORRY I COULD NOT BE OF HELP.
IF YOUR NEPHEW SEEKS THE AVATAR, THEN HE WALKS A DIFFICULT ROAD, THE END OF WHICH REMAINS OPAQUE EVEN TO MYSELF. HE IS FORTUNATE TO HAVE YOU AS HIS GUIDE.

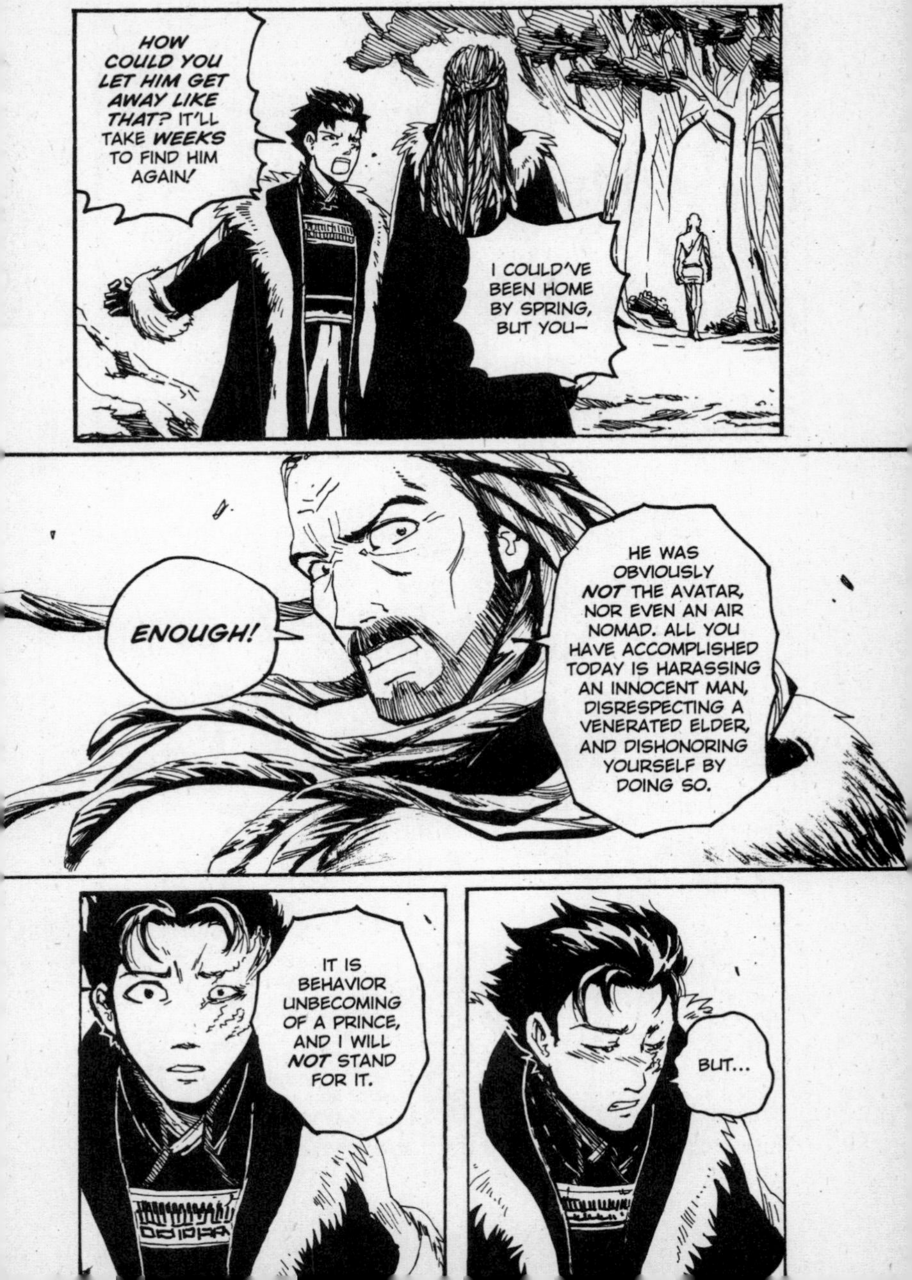
HOW COULD YOU LET HIM GET AWAY LIKE THAT? IT'LL TAKE WEEKS TO FIND HIM AGAIN!
I COULD'VE BEEN HOME BY SPRING, BUT YOU–
ENOUGH!
HE WAS OBVIOUSLY NOT THE AVATAR, NOR EVEN AN AIR NOMAD. ALL YOU HAVE ACCOMPLISHED TODAY IS HARASSING AN INNOCENT MAN, DISRESPECTING A VENERATED ELDER, AND DISHONORING YOURSELF BY DOING SO.
IT IS BEHAVIOR UNBECOMING OF A PRINCE, AND I WILL NOT STAND FOR IT.
BUT...

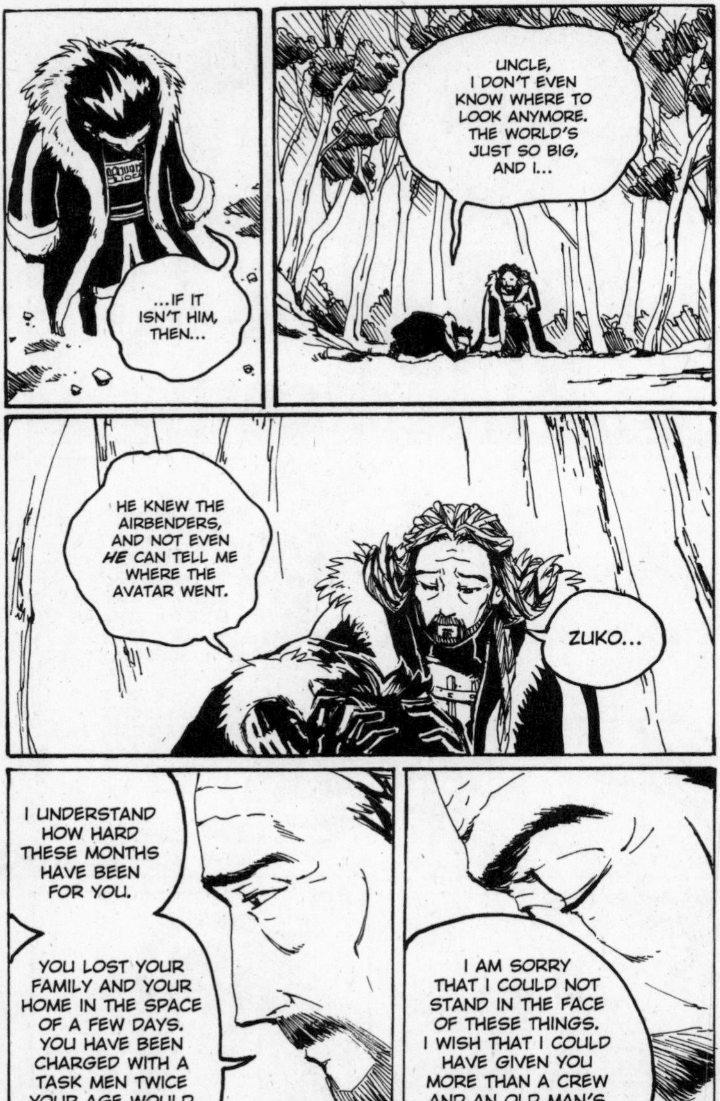
...IF IT ISN'T HIM, THEN...
UNCLE, I DON'T EVEN KNOW WHERE TO LOOK ANYMORE. THE WORLD'S JUST SO BIG, AND I...
HE KNEW THE AIRBENDERS, AND NOT EVEN *HE* CAN TELL ME WHERE THE AVATAR WENT.
ZUKO...
I UNDERSTAND HOW HARD THESE MONTHS HAVE BEEN FOR YOU.
YOU LOST YOUR FAMILY AND YOUR HOME IN THE SPACE OF A FEW DAYS. YOU HAVE BEEN CHARGED WITH A TASK MEN TWICE YOUR AGE WOULD COWER FROM.
I AM SORRY THAT I COULD NOT STAND IN THE FACE OF THESE THINGS. I WISH THAT I COULD HAVE GIVEN YOU MORE THAN A CREW AND AN OLD MAN'S COMPANIONSHIP.

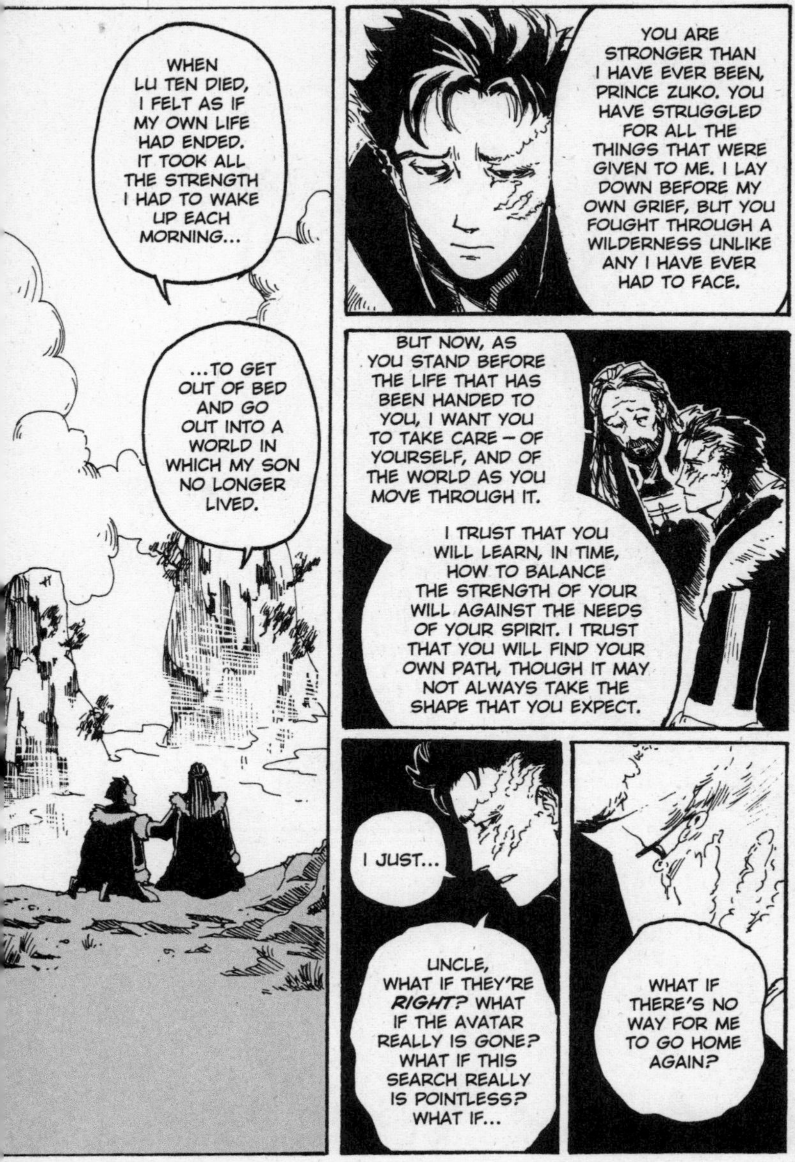
WHEN LU TEN DIED, I FELT AS IF MY OWN LIFE HAD ENDED. IT TOOK ALL THE STRENGTH I HAD TO WAKE UP EACH MORNING...
...TO GET OUT OF BED AND GO OUT INTO A WORLD IN WHICH MY SON NO LONGER LIVED.
YOU ARE STRONGER THAN I HAVE EVER BEEN, PRINCE ZUKO. YOU HAVE STRUGGLED FOR ALL THE THINGS THAT WERE GIVEN TO ME. I LAY DOWN BEFORE MY OWN GRIEF, BUT YOU FOUGHT THROUGH A WILDERNESS UNLIKE ANY I HAVE EVER HAD TO FACE.
BUT NOW, AS YOU STAND BEFORE THE LIFE THAT HAS BEEN HANDED TO YOU, I WANT YOU TO TAKE CARE — OF YOURSELF, AND OF THE WORLD AS YOU MOVE THROUGH IT.
I TRUST THAT YOU WILL LEARN, IN TIME, HOW TO BALANCE THE STRENGTH OF YOUR WILL AGAINST THE NEEDS OF YOUR SPIRIT. I TRUST THAT YOU WILL FIND YOUR OWN PATH, THOUGH IT MAY NOT ALWAYS TAKE THE SHAPE THAT YOU EXPECT.
I JUST...
UNCLE, WHAT IF THEY'RE *RIGHT?* WHAT IF THE AVATAR REALLY IS GONE? WHAT IF THIS SEARCH REALLY IS POINTLESS? WHAT IF...
WHAT IF THERE'S NO WAY FOR ME TO GO HOME AGAIN?

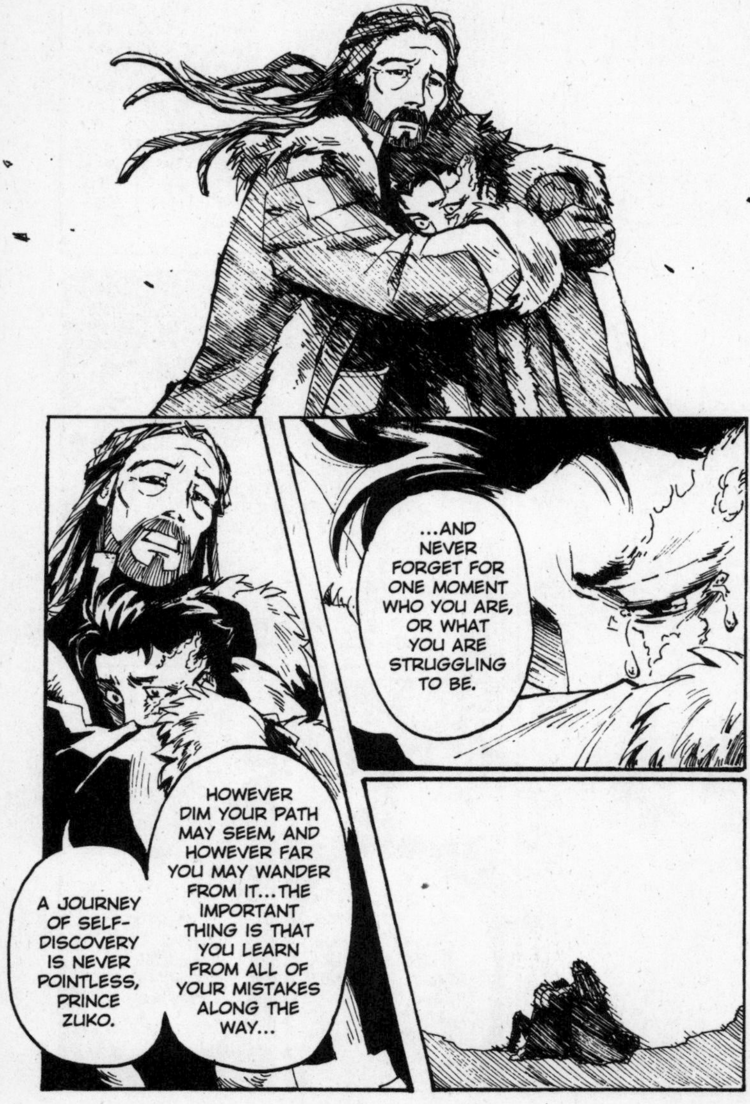
A JOURNEY OF SELF-DISCOVERY IS NEVER POINTLESS, PRINCE ZUKO.
HOWEVER DIM YOUR PATH MAY SEEM, AND HOWEVER FAR YOU MAY WANDER FROM IT... THE IMPORTANT THING IS THAT YOU LEARN FROM ALL OF YOUR MISTAKES ALONG THE WAY...
...AND NEVER FORGET FOR ONE MOMENT WHO YOU ARE, OR WHAT YOU ARE STRUGGLING TO BE.

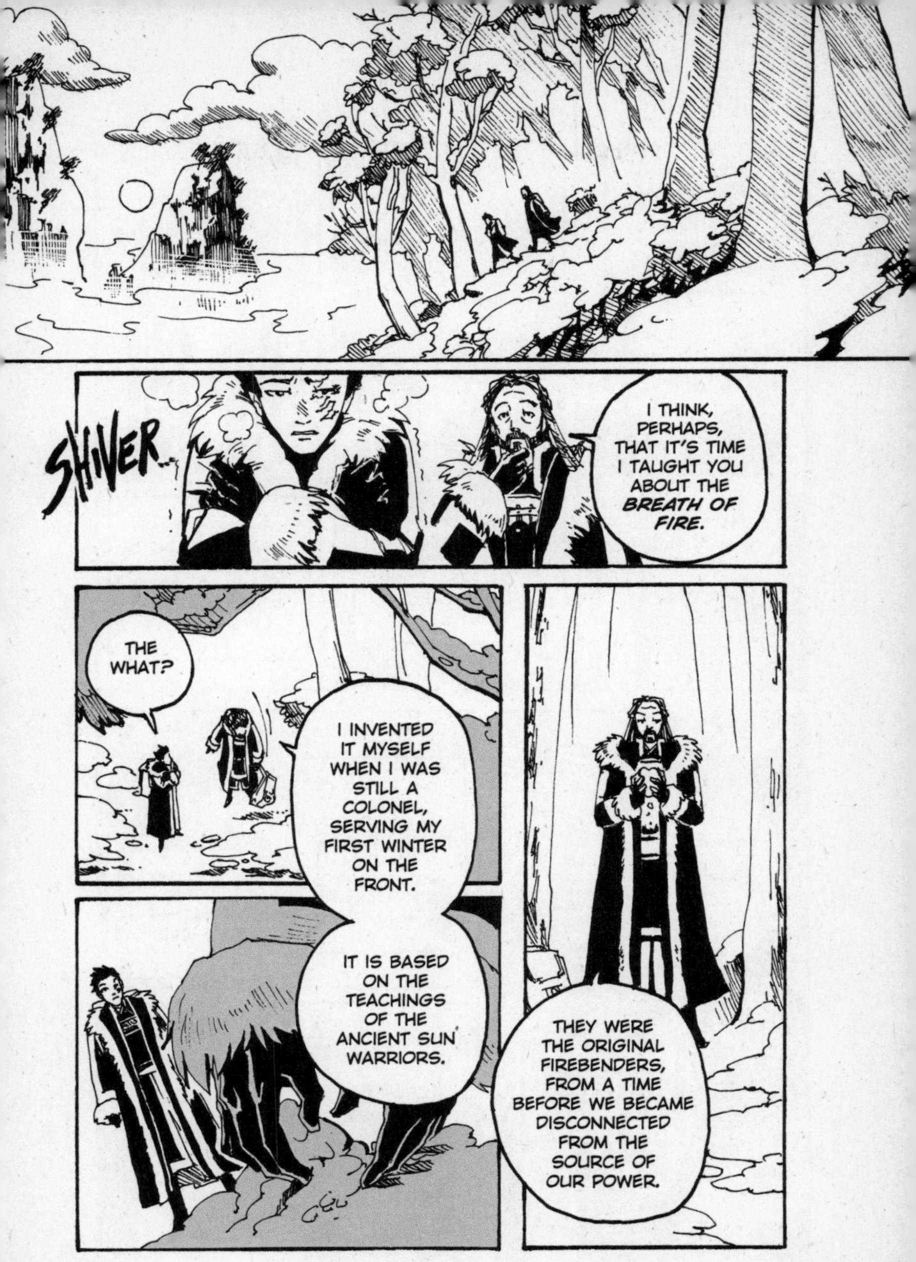
SHIVER
I THINK, PERHAPS, THAT IT'S TIME I TAUGHT YOU ABOUT THE *BREATH OF FIRE*.
THE WHAT?
I INVENTED IT MYSELF WHEN I WAS STILL A COLONEL, SERVING MY FIRST WINTER ON THE FRONT.
IT IS BASED ON THE TEACHINGS OF THE ANCIENT SUN WARRIORS.
THEY WERE THE ORIGINAL FIREBENDERS, FROM A TIME BEFORE WE BECAME DISCONNECTED FROM THE SOURCE OF OUR POWER.

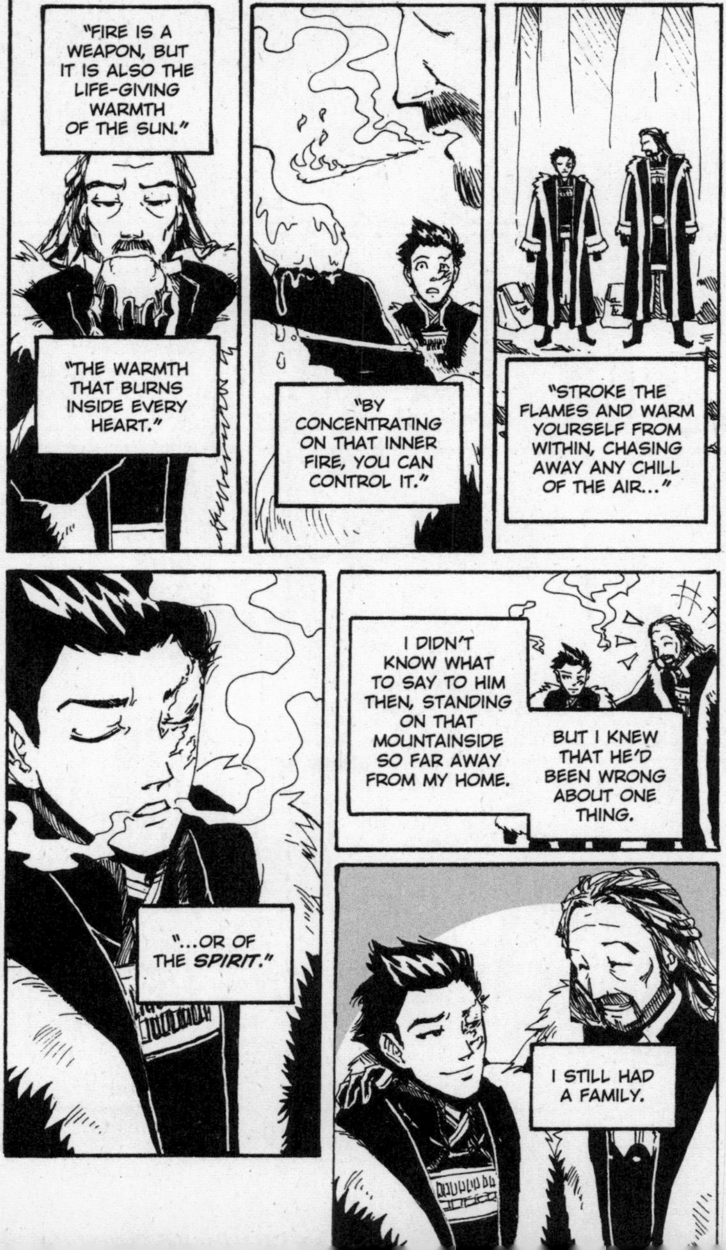
"FIRE IS A WEAPON, BUT IT IS ALSO THE LIFE-GIVING WARMTH OF THE SUN."
"THE WARMTH THAT BURNS INSIDE EVERY HEART."
"BY CONCENTRATING ON THAT INNER FIRE, YOU CAN CONTROL IT."
"STROKE THE FLAMES AND WARM YOURSELF FROM WITHIN, CHASING AWAY ANY CHILL OF THE AIR..."
"...OR OF THE *SPIRIT*."
I DIDN'T KNOW WHAT TO SAY TO HIM THEN, STANDING ON THAT MOUNTAINSIDE SO FAR AWAY FROM MY HOME.
BUT I KNEW THAT HE'D BEEN WRONG ABOUT ONE THING.
I STILL HAD A FAMILY.

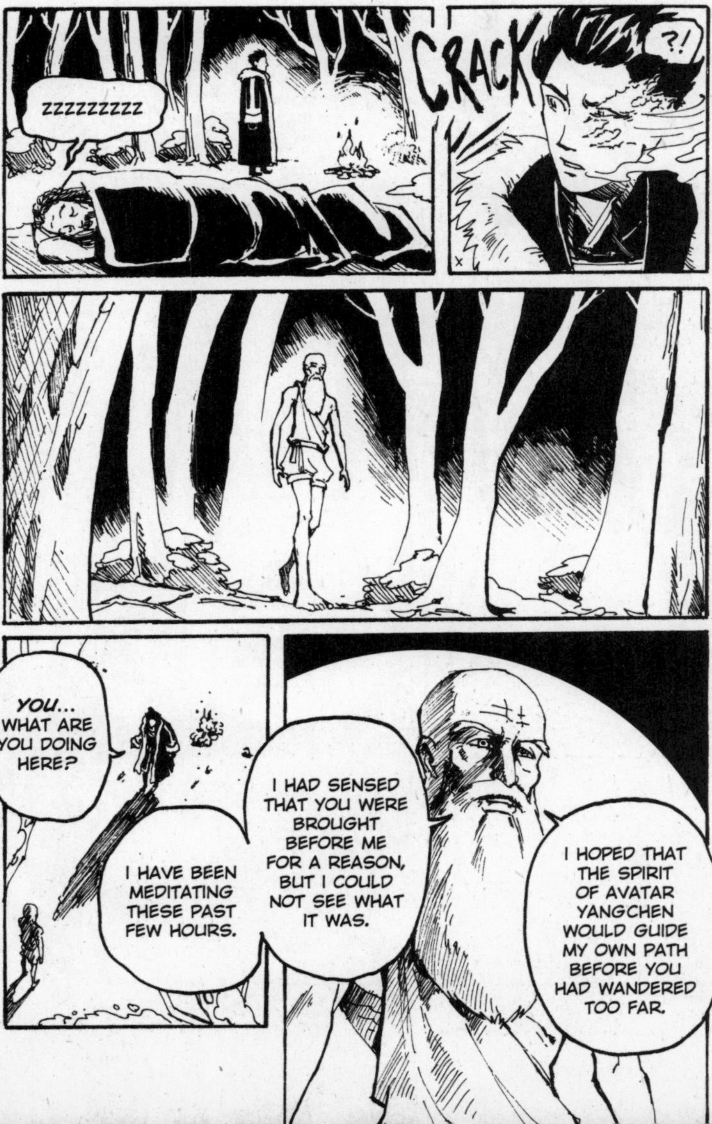
ZZZZZZZZZ
CRACK
?!
YOU... WHAT ARE YOU DOING HERE?
I HAVE BEEN MEDITATING THESE PAST FEW HOURS.
I HAD SENSED THAT YOU WERE BROUGHT BEFORE ME FOR A REASON, BUT I COULD NOT SEE WHAT IT WAS.
I HOPED THAT THE SPIRIT OF AVATAR YANGCHEN WOULD GUIDE MY OWN PATH BEFORE YOU HAD WANDERED TOO FAR.

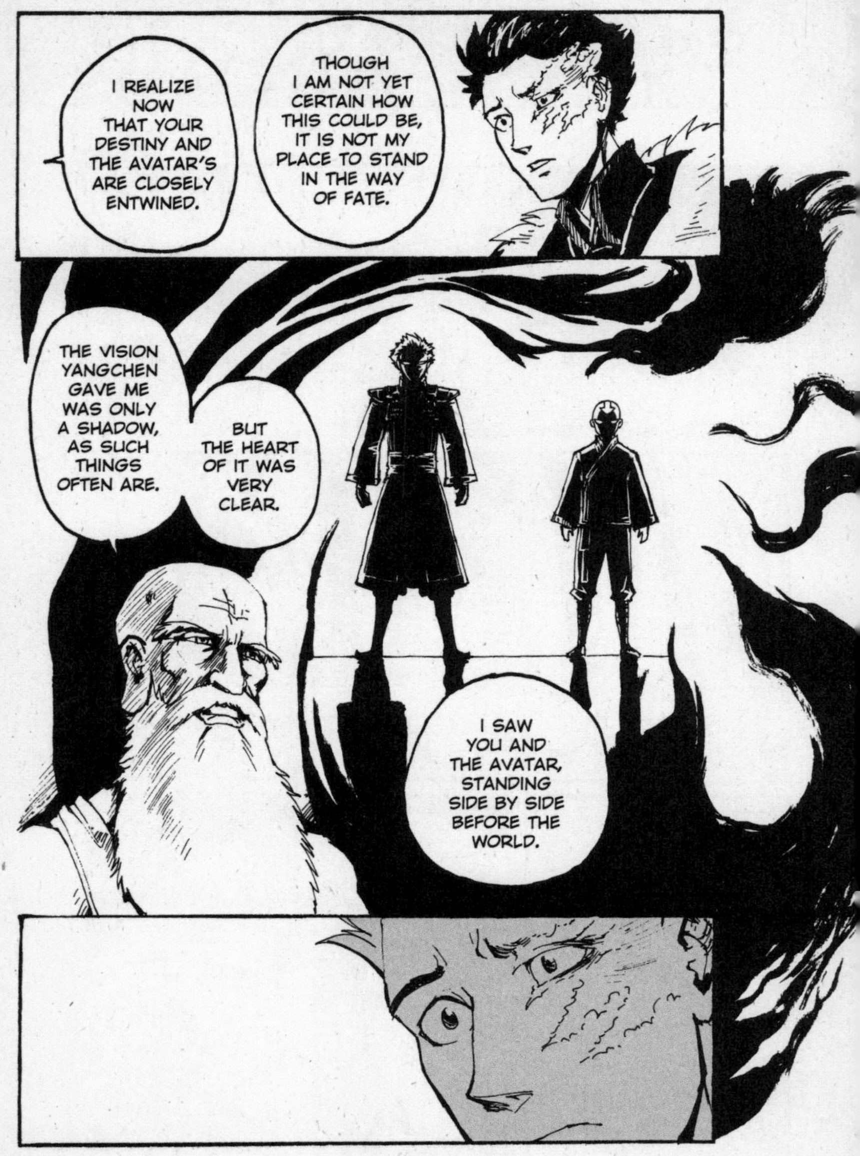
I REALIZE NOW THAT YOUR DESTINY AND THE AVATAR'S ARE CLOSELY ENTWINED.
THOUGH I AM NOT YET CERTAIN HOW THIS COULD BE, IT IS NOT MY PLACE TO STAND IN THE WAY OF FATE.
THE VISION YANGCHEN GAVE ME WAS ONLY A SHADOW, AS SUCH THINGS OFTEN ARE.
BUT THE HEART OF IT WAS VERY CLEAR.
I SAW YOU AND THE AVATAR, STANDING SIDE BY SIDE BEFORE THE WORLD.

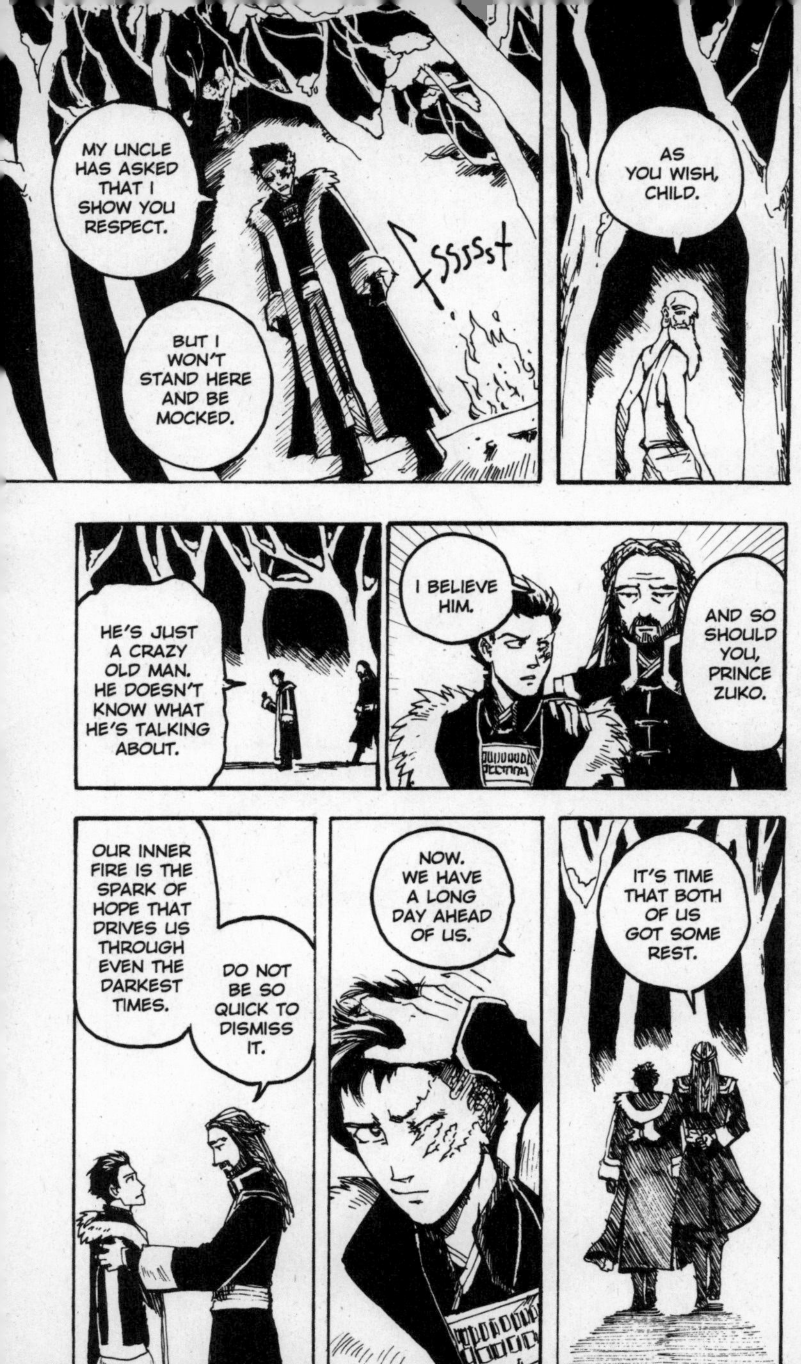
MY UNCLE HAS ASKED THAT I SHOW YOU RESPECT.
BUT I WON'T STAND HERE AND BE MOCKED.
FSSSSST
AS YOU WISH, CHILD.
HE'S JUST A CRAZY OLD MAN. HE DOESN'T KNOW WHAT HE'S TALKING ABOUT.
I BELIEVE HIM.
AND SO SHOULD YOU, PRINCE ZUKO.
OUR INNER FIRE IS THE SPARK OF HOPE THAT DRIVES US THROUGH EVEN THE DARKEST TIMES.
DO NOT BE SO QUICK TO DISMISS IT.
NOW. WE HAVE A LONG DAY AHEAD OF US.
IT'S TIME THAT BOTH OF US GOT SOME REST.

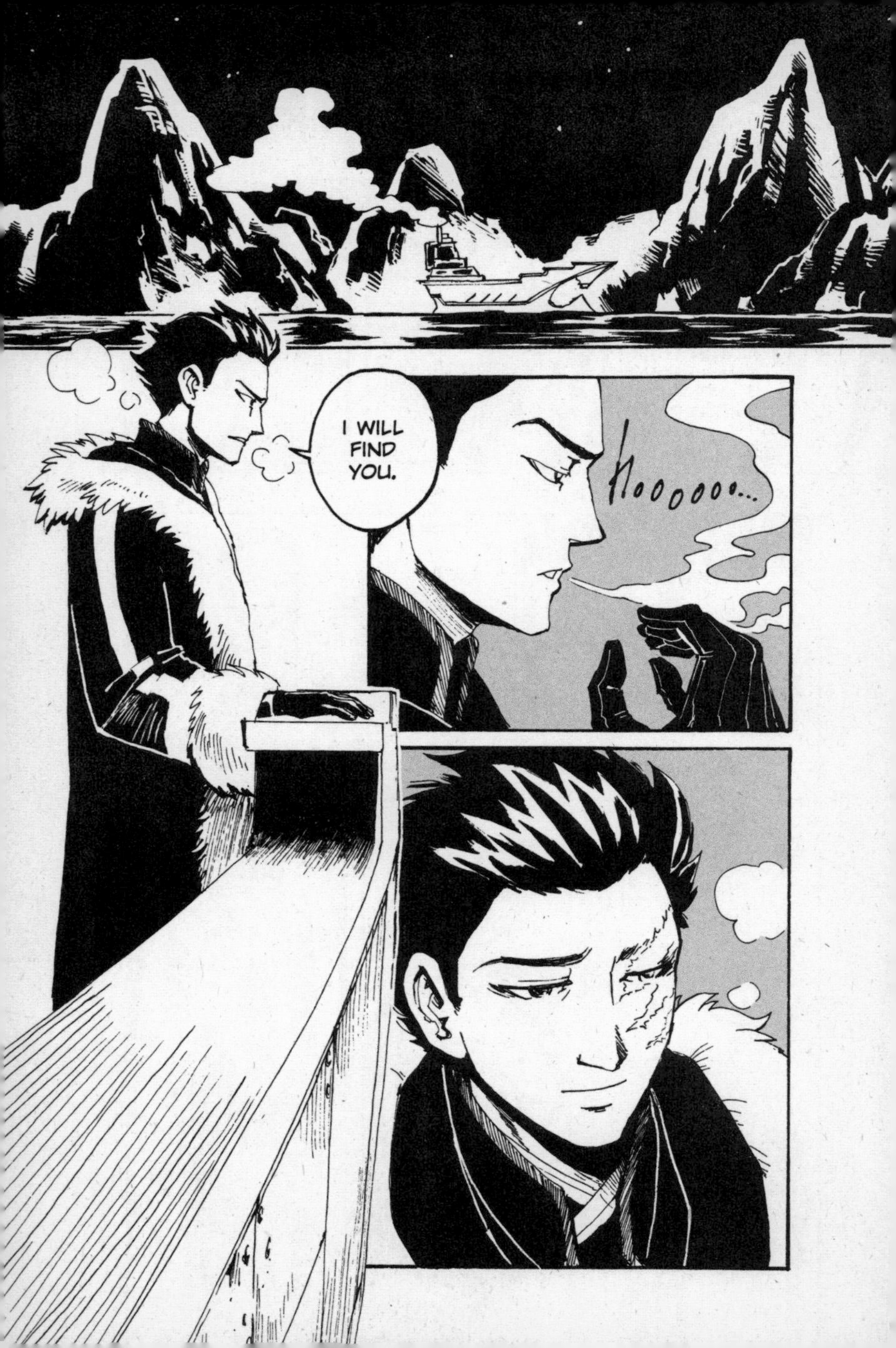
I WILL FIND YOU.
Hooooooo...

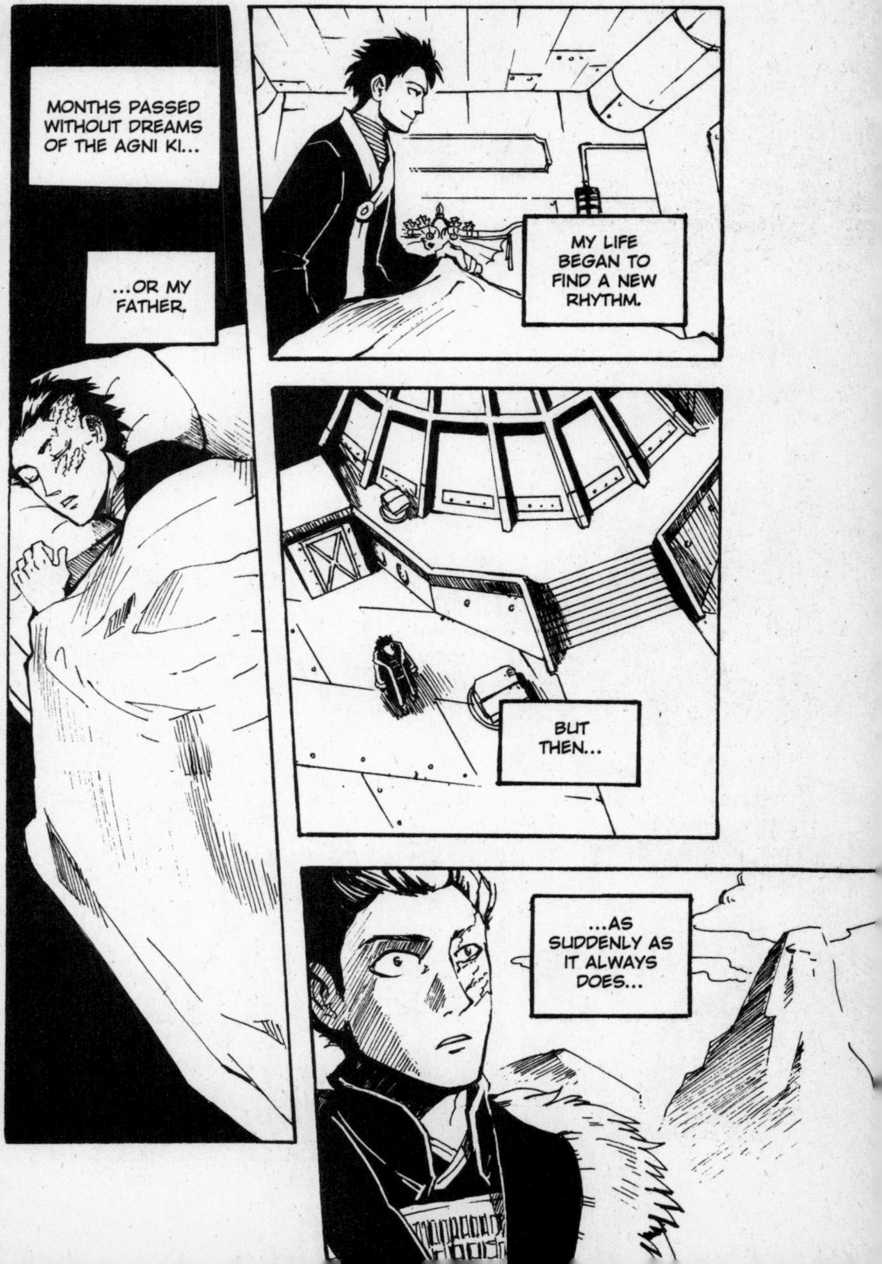
MONTHS PASSED WITHOUT DREAMS OF THE AGNI KI...
...OR MY FATHER.
MY LIFE BEGAN TO FIND A NEW RHYTHM.
BUT THEN...
...AS SUDDENLY AS IT ALWAYS DOES...

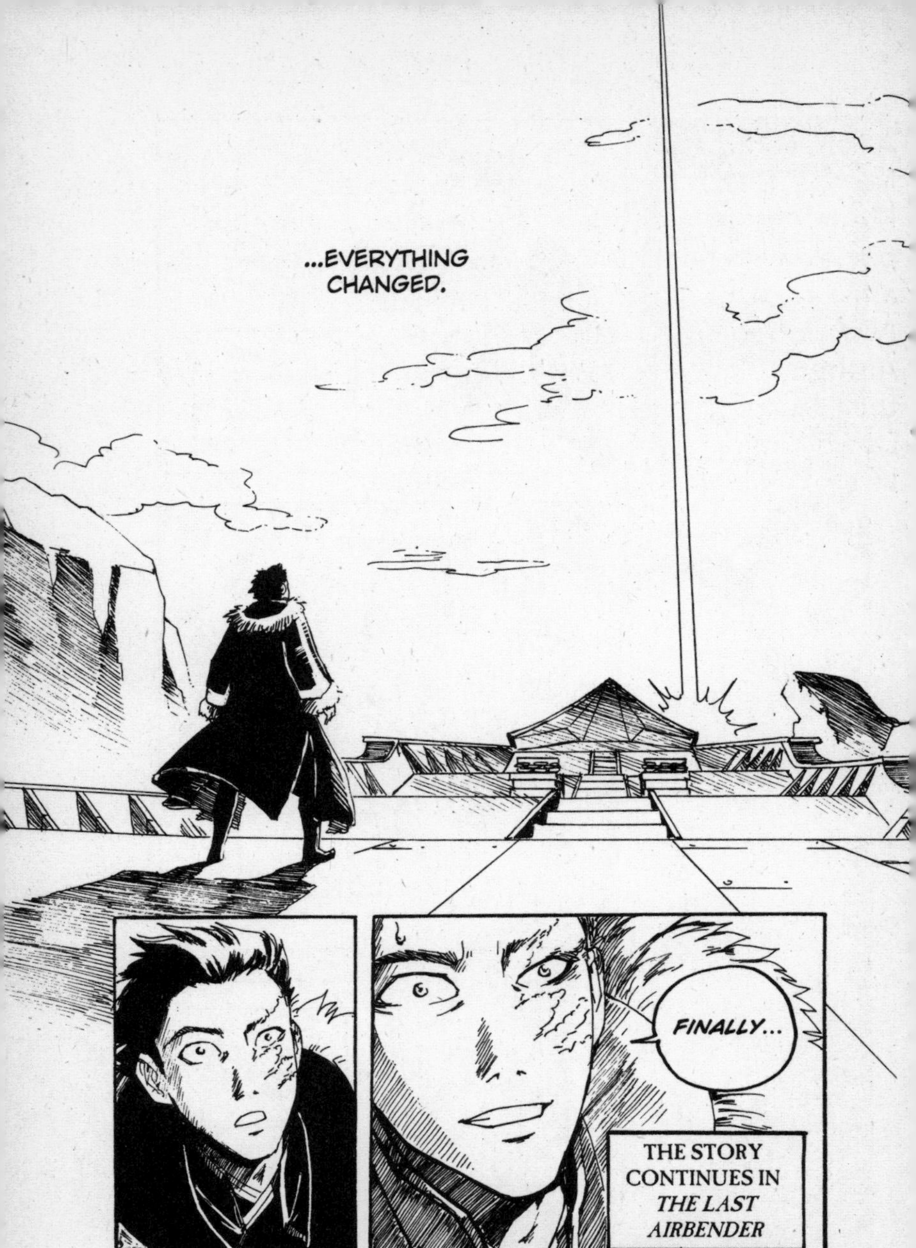
...EVERYTHING CHANGED.
FINALLY...
THE STORY CONTINUES IN *THE LAST AIRBENDER*

ACKNOWLEDGMENTS

Alison and Dave would like to give special thanks to Michael Dante DiMartino, Bryan Konietzko, Aaron Ehasz, Megan Casey, Ashley St. Sauveur, and all the amazing people who helped make *The Last Airbender* such an amazing experience. Extra thanks to everyone at *Nickelodeon Magazine*, Starlet Hawk, Jenifer Huitt, Anthony Nguyen, Johanne Matte, and Helen Ryan for all their support. And immense gratitude to Dallas Midaugh, David Yoo, everyone at Del Rey Manga, Paula Allen, Linda Lee, and the dazzlingly talented Nina Matsumoto!

THE MAKING OF *THE LAST AIRBENDER PREQUEL: ZUKO'S STORY*

M. NIGHT SHYAMALAN FILM

THE LAST AIRBENDER

PREQUEL

ZUKO'S STORY

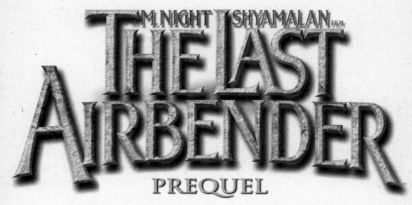

In a collaborative manga, when the artist and writer are not the same person, the writers write a script that has descriptive text. The artist must transform the script into artwork that captures the action, the emotion, the *scene* the writer is setting.

The following pages contain pages of the script that was written by Dave Roman and Alison Wilgus. The artist, Nina Matsumoto, worked from this script to create the manga you just read. It is quite interesting to see the images the artist created from the written direction of the writers. Each page is a journey in creative exercise, considering the artist must take paragraphs of descriptive text and create several panels of art that can also accommodate the included dialogue. We hope that seeing the script will provide a little behind-the-scenes insight into the making of this manga.

PAGE 1

Panel 1
It's nighttime on the frozen southern sea. We see a worn-down Fire Nation ship on the horizon, black smoke billowing from its engines into the otherwise clear and starry sky.

Panel 2
The camera zooms in closer, revealing the silhouette of a young man in armor. He stands alone on the deck of the ship, moonlight catching on the metal fastenings of his armor and his short, dark hair.

Panel 3
The frame tightens on Zuko's head and shoulders. His hands are clasped on the railing, his body stiff and his face scowling as he looks out over the water. The moonlight casts deep shadows, making his scar even more prominent than usual. He's sixteen years old, but his expression is anything but boyish—the years at sea have hardened him.

Panel 4
Zuko shivers in the cold, clouds of frozen breath curling from his mouth. [At this point in the story he has not yet learned to warm himself with his inner chi—which will become important later.]

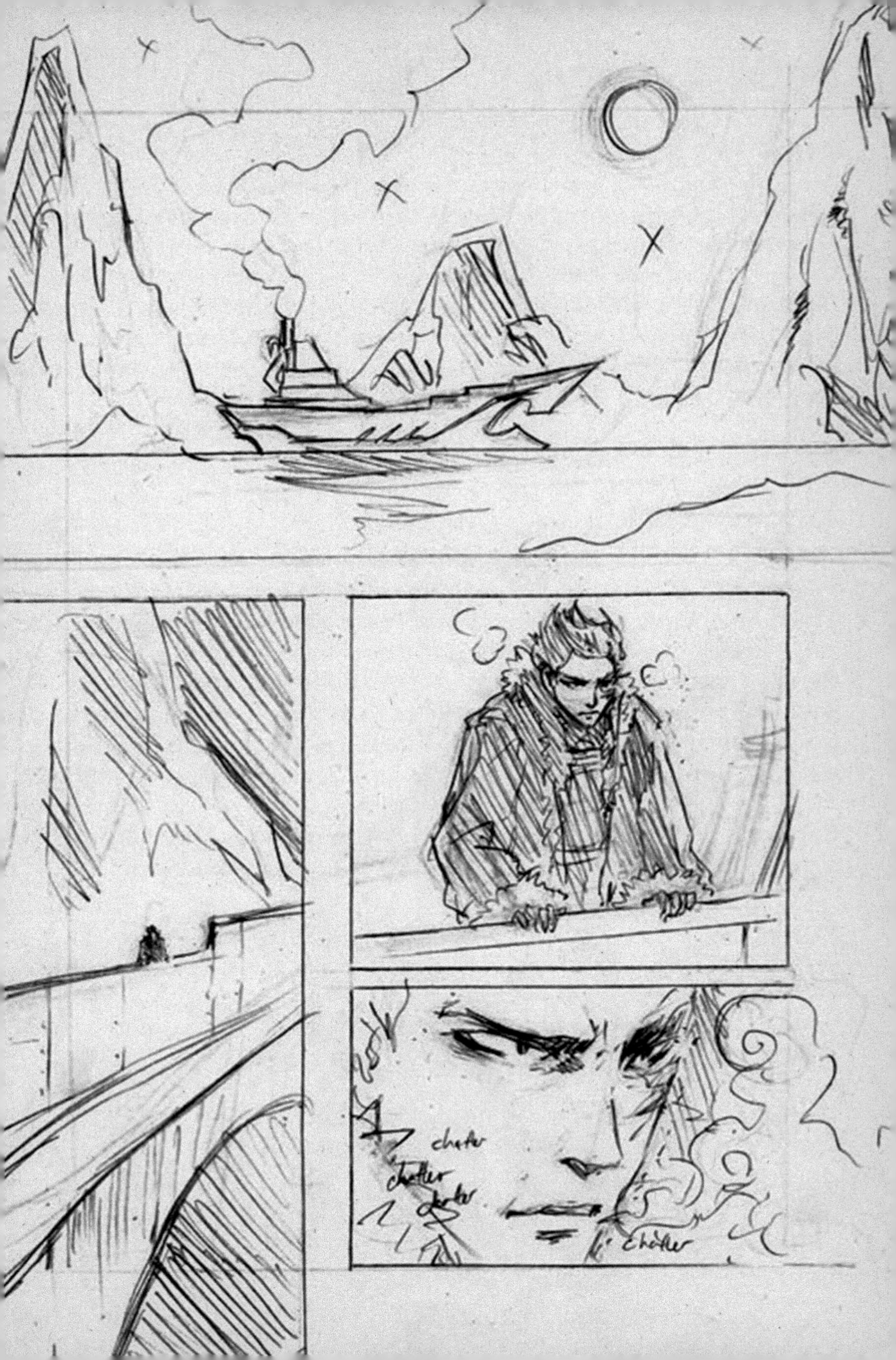
chatter
chatter
chatter
chatter

PAGE 2–3 spread

Panel 1
A splash image stretches across the top of both pages of a high-ceilinged corridor inside the Fire Nation Royal Palace. Prince Zuko, now only thirteen, storms out of the palace infirmary with several nurses and his uncle Iroh chasing after him. Barely an hour or so have passed since the Agni Ki with his father, Fire Lord Ozai, and his left eye is covered in fresh bandages. Around him, royal guards turn their heads, and servant stop whatever they're doing to stare. It's clear he feels the weight of all their eyes.

Iroh: Nephew! Please, you aren't well—

Zuko: I'll decide if I'm well or not!

Panel 2
This time, the panel only stretches across page 2. To the far right, Zuko storms away down the corridor, and we're close enough to see the details of his expression: his lips pressed tightly together, his good eye wide and shining with tears he refuses to let fall. To the far left, Iroh and the nurses watch him with worried faces—he shouldn't be up and about so soon.

Caption: "Prince Zuko, you have shown yourself to be unworthy of the crown and unfit to stand upon the land of our noble ancestors."

Panel 3
A similar panel on page 3, close in on Iroh's face. He can't bear to see his nephew like this, but what can he do? The damage has already been done. He doesn't want to push Zuko too hard, for fear of solidifying this new distance between them.

Caption: "You are therefore stripped of your birthright and banished from the Fire Nation until you can prove your worth."

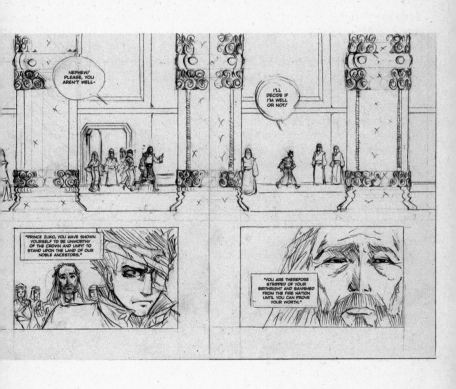

PAGE 4

Panel 1
A wide shot as Zuko continues down the hall, which has never seemed so long or so full of people. He tries to hold his head up high, but the pain is terrible and the shock of his injury has left him dizzy. It's all he can do to keep his stride even and his face dry. Behind him, two servants whisper behind their hands, both of them older women.

Servant 1 (whispering): An Agni Ki duel? You're sure? But he's barely more than a child—

Servant 2 (whispering): The Fire Lord challenged him. He couldn't very well refuse.

Panel 2
Close in on another group of servants, gossiping busily about their dishonored prince. These two are younger—the first wide-eyed and a little shocked, the second obviously reluctant to attract unwanted attention. We see the trailing edge of Zuko's clothes, enough to make it clear he's just walked by.

Servant 3 (whispering): Can you imagine? Disowned and shamed in front of the entire court. It seems so cruel…

Servant 4 (whispering): *Shh!* Don't let the guards hear you talking like that.

Panel 3
Close-up of Zuko, face twisted up with anger and pain and humiliation, his attempt at calm almost entirely failed. The whispers continue all around him, and it's clear that he can hear every word.

Servant 5 (whispering): Has he ever even *been* outside the Fire Nation? Or the capital?

Servant 6 (whispering): He won't last a month in the colonies.

Panel 4
More servants hover near the door to Zuko's room as he pushes it roughly open, now almost at a run in his eagerness to be alone.

Servant 7 (whispering): That poor boy…

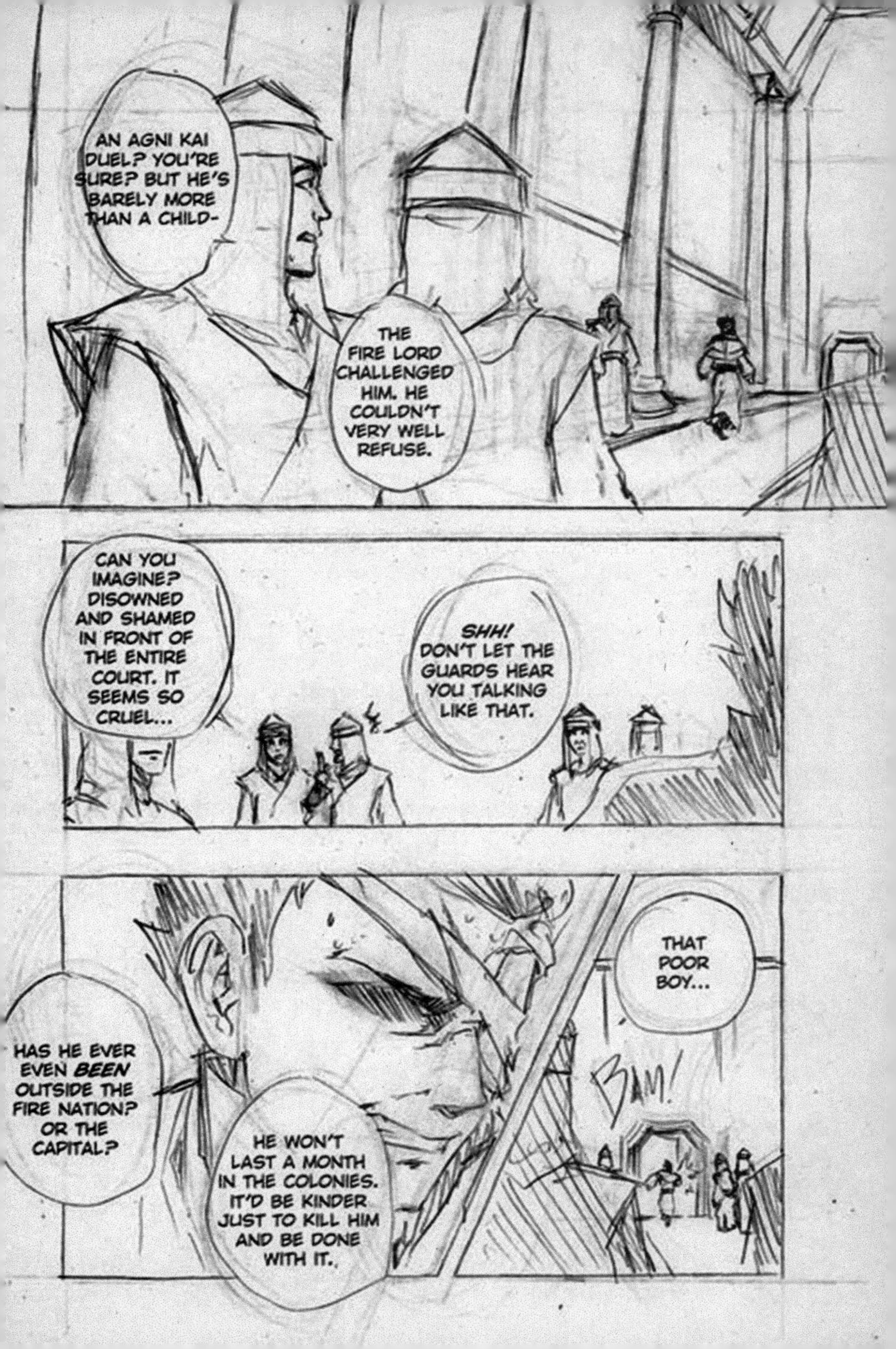
AN AGNI KAI DUEL? YOU'RE SURE? BUT HE'S BARELY MORE THAN A CHILD-
THE FIRE LORD CHALLENGED HIM. HE COULDN'T VERY WELL REFUSE.
CAN YOU IMAGINE? DISOWNED AND SHAMED IN FRONT OF THE ENTIRE COURT. IT SEEMS SO CRUEL...
SHH! DON'T LET THE GUARDS HEAR YOU TALKING LIKE THAT.
HAS HE EVER EVEN **BEEN** OUTSIDE THE FIRE NATION? OR THE CAPITAL?
HE WON'T LAST A MONTH IN THE COLONIES. IT'D BE KINDER JUST TO KILL HIM AND BE DONE WITH IT.
THAT POOR BOY...
BAM!

PAGE 5

Panel 1
Now inside his room at last, Zuko slams the door behind him and leans back against it.

Servant 7 (caption): ...I know we should trust in the Fire Lord's wisdom...

SFX: *SLAM*

Panel 2
Zuko slides down to the floor, tears escaping from his good eye even as he squeezes it shut, his bottom lip between his teeth. He can cry now that he's alone, but he can't let anyone hear him—the shame and dishonor are horrifying enough as it is.

Servant 7 (caption): ...But how could anyone do such a thing to his own son?

Panel 3
Zuko holds his head in his hands, fingers tangled in his hair and shoulders trembling with the force of his silent sobs.

Panel 4
A closer frame, angled so we can see Zuko's face. He presses his hand against his bandaged eye, the other still shut and his features twisted with pain. He's breathing hard as a wave of panic takes hold—now that he's alone, there's nothing to distract him from the memory of what happened.

PAGE 6

Panel 1
An even closer shot, Zuko curling in on himself as recollection over-whelms him. We begin to hear what he hears—the chant of a crowd that doesn't know what it's about to witness.

Crowd (as SFX): Agni Ki! Agni Ki!

Panel 2
As we enter Zuko's dream, everything is dark and a bit distorted. The camera is behind Zuko as he walks into the middle of the stadium, the crowd shouting enthusiastically. Great sconces of flame stand around the borders of the rectangular platform Zuko stands on. [See movie reference if available.]

Crowd (as SFX): Agni Ki! Agni Ki!

Panel 3
The frame shifts to Zuko, nervous as he waits for his opponent but not overwhelmingly so—he has all the easy confidence of youth.

Panel 4
A closer shot of his face, eyes widening in shock at the sight before him

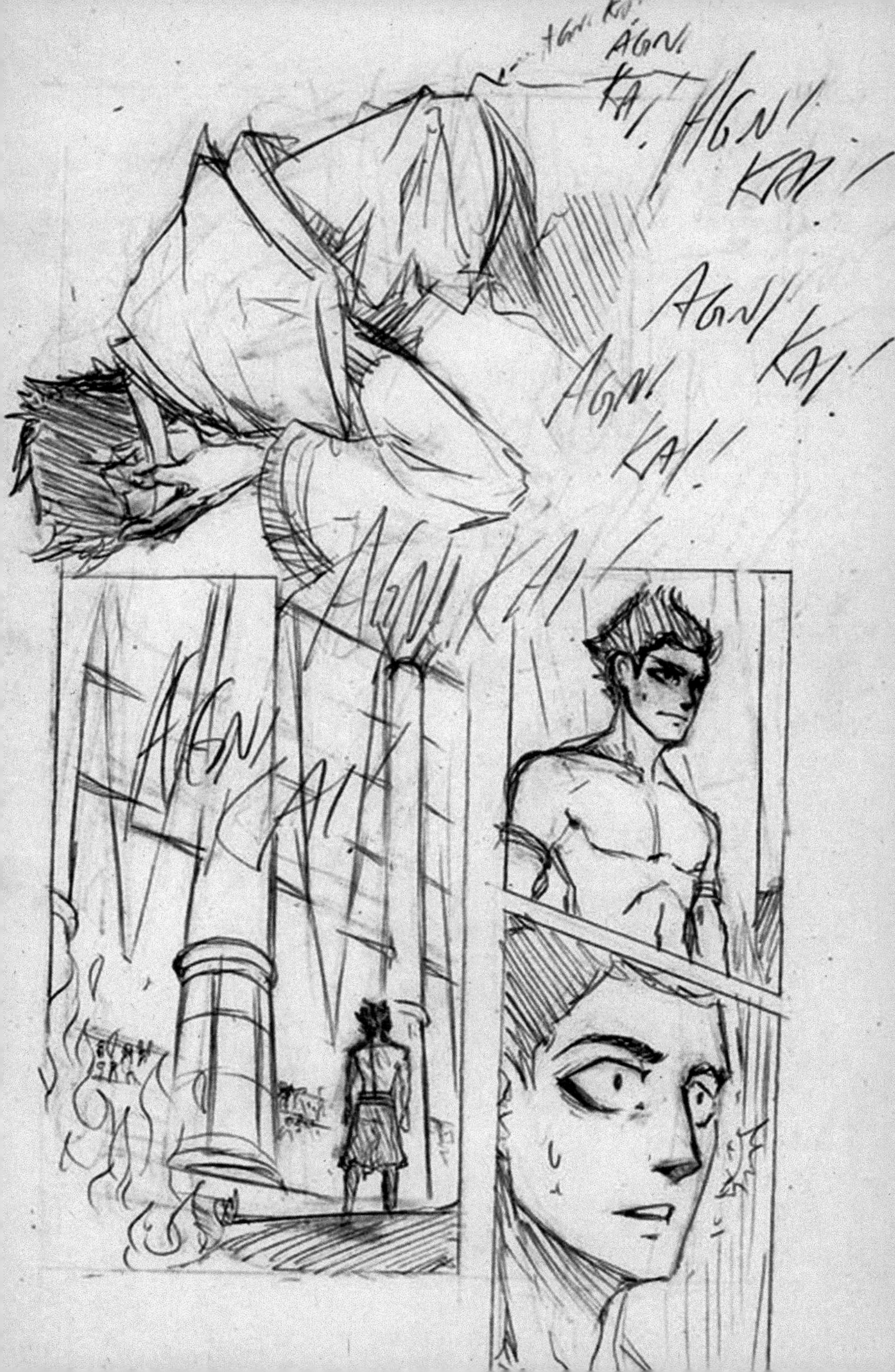
...Agni Kai!
AGNI KAI!
AGNI KAI!
AGNI KAI!
AGNI KAI!
AGNI KAI!
AGNI KAI!

PAGE 7

Panel 1
Fire Lord Ozai steps out of the shadows, naked from the waist up. The contrast between the two of them is startling—Ozai is a grown man, tall and muscled and broad-shouldered. There is no mercy or compassion in his expression. A shocked, wordless murmur rises from the crowd—no one was expecting this.

Crowd (as SFX): GASP

Panel 2
Zuko backs away, frightened and uncertain—this can't possibly be happening. There must be some mistake.

Zuko: Father...?

Panel 3
A tight shot of Zuko's face, the flames of his father's attack reflected in his terrified eyes.

SFX: FOOOOOM!

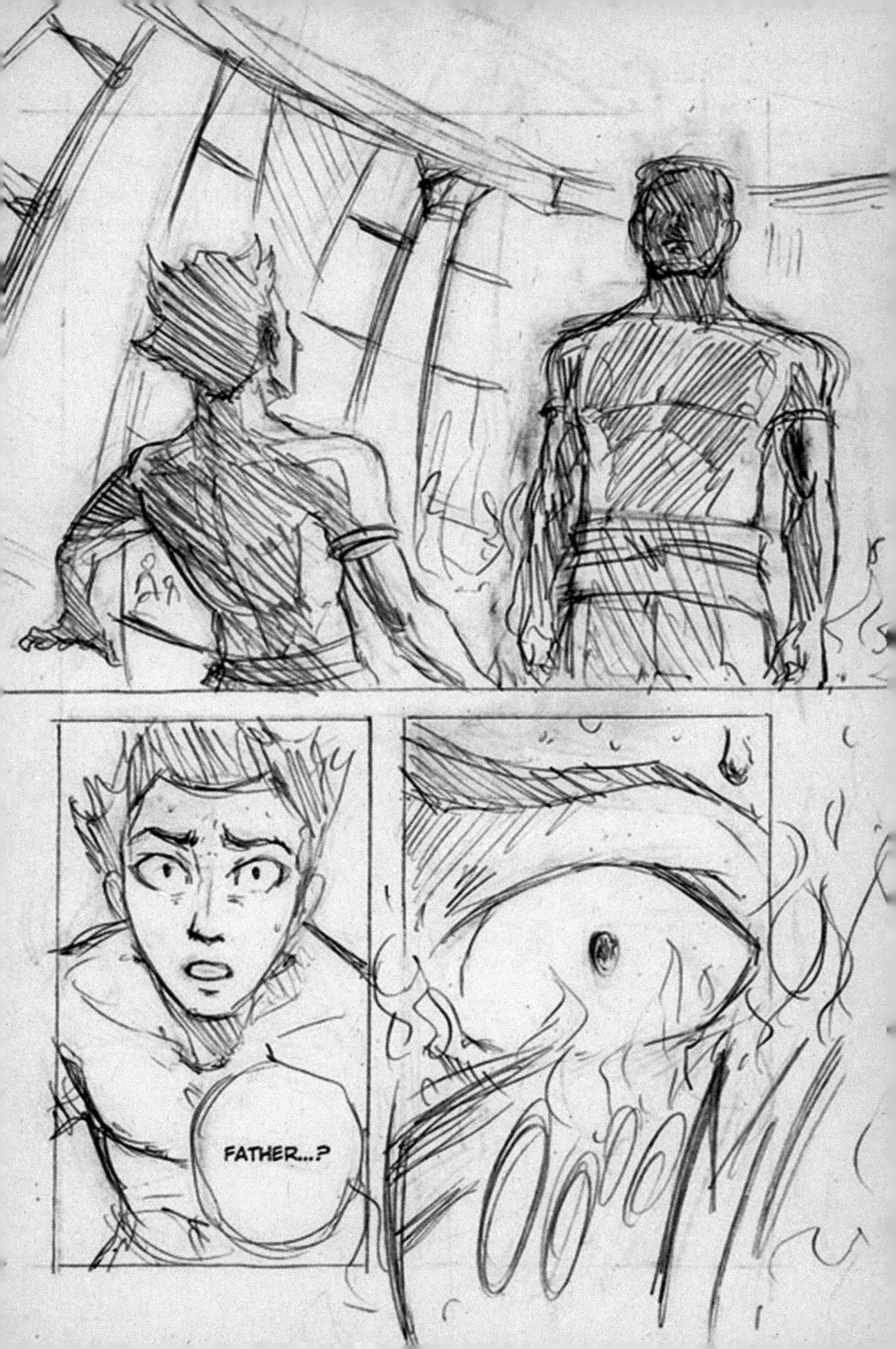
FATHER...?

PAGE 8

Panel 1
The scene returns to Zuko's room. He's no longer sitting with his back to the door—sometime in the last few hours, he slipped the rest of the way down to the floor, curled up into a tight little ball with the undamaged half of his face buried against one arm.

Panel 2
There's a knock at the door. Startled, he pushes himself halfway up.

SFX: KNOCK KNOCK

Panel 3
Zuko scrambles to his feet, trying to make himself look presentable as he does so—his clothes are rumpled and his hair is a mess, made even worse by the bandages. There's a spark of hope in his expression.

Panel 4
He takes a moment to breath deep and calm down.

Panel 5
He opens the door, which we see from the point of view of the hallway. Try as he might, Zuko can't hide how badly he wants this to be good news—an apology, an assurance that this was all an awful misunderstanding. But he only makes it halfway through his greeting.

Zuko: Fath—

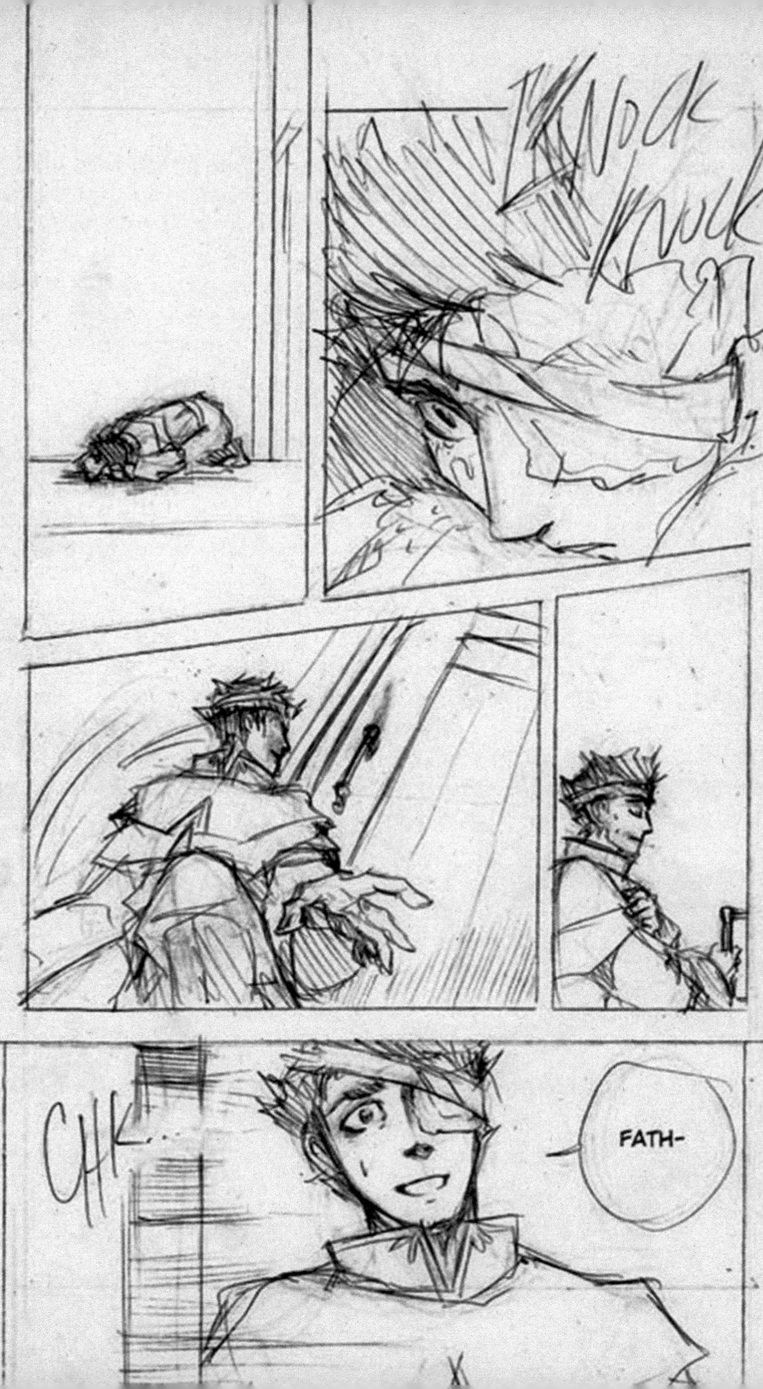
KNOCK
KNOCK!
CHK...
FATH-

PAGE 9

Panel 1
A narrow panel across the top of the page as Zuko's face falls—his visitor is about the last person he wants to see right now.

Panel 2
A reverse shot reveals who's come to see him—a girl in garments similar to his and a small coronet in her hair, her broad smile visible in the shadows. She's still a teenager, but she has the presence and confidence of a woman twice her age.

Azula: Hello, Zuzu.

Panel 3
She breezes past Zuko into the room, as if this evening and her visit are completely unremarkable. Zuko follows her with his eyes, his expression wary.

Zuko: What are you doing here, Azula?

Azula: I thought I'd help my brother pack.

Panel 4
She spots an ornamental knife lying on a table nearby and idly picks it up. It's inscribed and about the size of her hand.

Azula: I wouldn't want you to forget anything important. After all, who knows how long you'll be gone.

Panel 5
Zuko snatches the knife out of her hand, furious both with her and with himself for letting her get to him.

Zuko: I'll be back as soon as I find the Avatar. Then he'll...

PAGE 10

Panel 1
Zuko looks down at the knife in his hand, although we still can't read the inscription. His anger fades as quickly as it flared, eroded by creeping doubt. Beside him, Azula nonchalantly examines her nails.

Zuko: Then Father will welcome me home.

Azula: Well, I suppose the Avatar's only been missing for a hundred years. Maybe you'll track him down in fifty.

Panel 2
Zuko turns his back on her and starts pulling clothes out of a chest, his movements exaggerated by anger. Azula watches him with a feral grin.

Zuko: I'll find him. You'll see.

Azula: Of course you will. I'm sure that when they march you down to the docks, you'll be able to bribe some fisherman into giving you a ride

Panel 3
Close on Zuko as he shoves clothing into a bag. It's clear that Azula's getting to him, however much he tries to ignore her.

Azula: Maybe they'll even give you a job washing down the deck. I've heard that peasants have a soft spot for orphans.

Panel 4
Her words cut deep, and finally Zuko's resistance breaks down. He whirls on her again, furious and ashamed, bending the flame from his bedside lamp toward her in a wild arc.

Zuko: *GET OUT!*

SFX: FOOM!

PAGE 11

Panel 1
Azula smiles at him, triumphant—she got exactly what she came for.

Panel 2
Azula shrugs and turns to leave, waving casually to him over her shoulder.

Azula: The guards will be here to get you in an hour. Better finish packing.

Panel 3
A wide shot of Zuko's dark, empty room. Zuko stands with his arms at his sides, shoulders slumped and head hung low, one hand pressed to his bandaged eye. He looks very young and very scared, the half-packed bag on his bed pathetically small.

PAGE 12

Panel 1

A wide, exterior shot of the palace at sunset. Imperial guards have formed two lines, holding the waiting crowd back from the path to the palace gates. It's a very long walk, and Zuko must make it alone, dressed in simple clothes with his bag over one shoulder. He tries his best to look proud and unconcerned as the crowd watches his progress. No one speaks. It's difficult to believe this is really happening at all.

Panel 2

At the end of the line of guards, the crowd beyond the palace gates moves aside to let Zuko through. No one wants to get too close, as if his dishonor might be contagious. But they stare openly at this "dead man walking"—there's no reason for them not to. He has no power over them anymore.

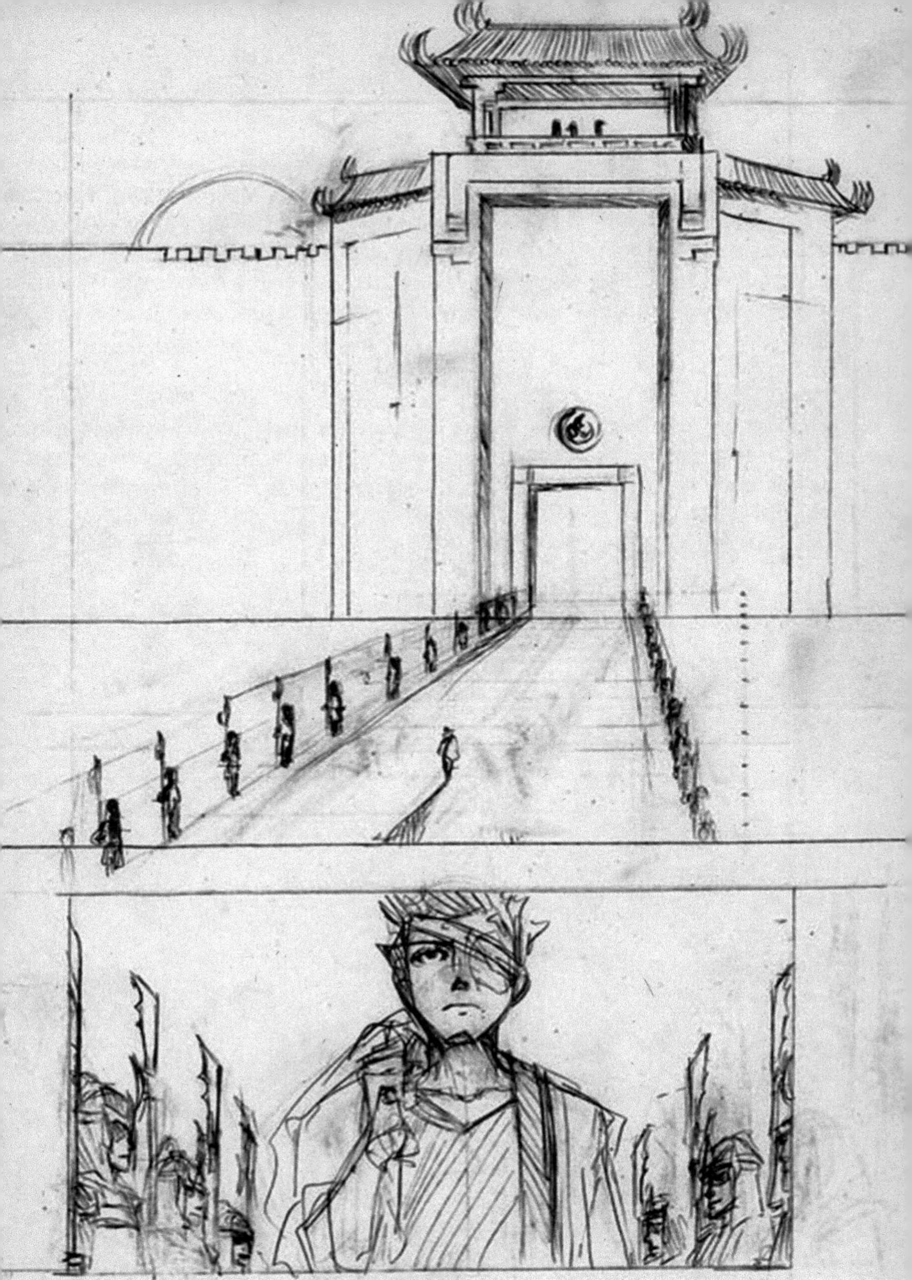

PAGE 13

Panel 1

A wide shot of Azula and Iroh, standing on a high balcony that looks out over the courtyard and the crowd that fills it. Mai and Ty Lee are beside and just behind Azula, Ty Lee wide-eyed and tearful and Mai as stone-faced as she can manage to be, trying to put on the strong front that's expected of her. Zhao watches with relish, but there's an empty spot where Ozai would be—he didn't even bother to watch as Zuko walks slowly out of sight.

Panel 2

Closer in on Iroh and Azula, framed so we can see both of their expressions. Azula seems strangely blank, a small and considering frown on her lips and her arms crossed over her chest. Iroh looks heartbreakingly sad—he would give anything to be able to walk with his nephew. Zuko shouldn't have to face this alone.

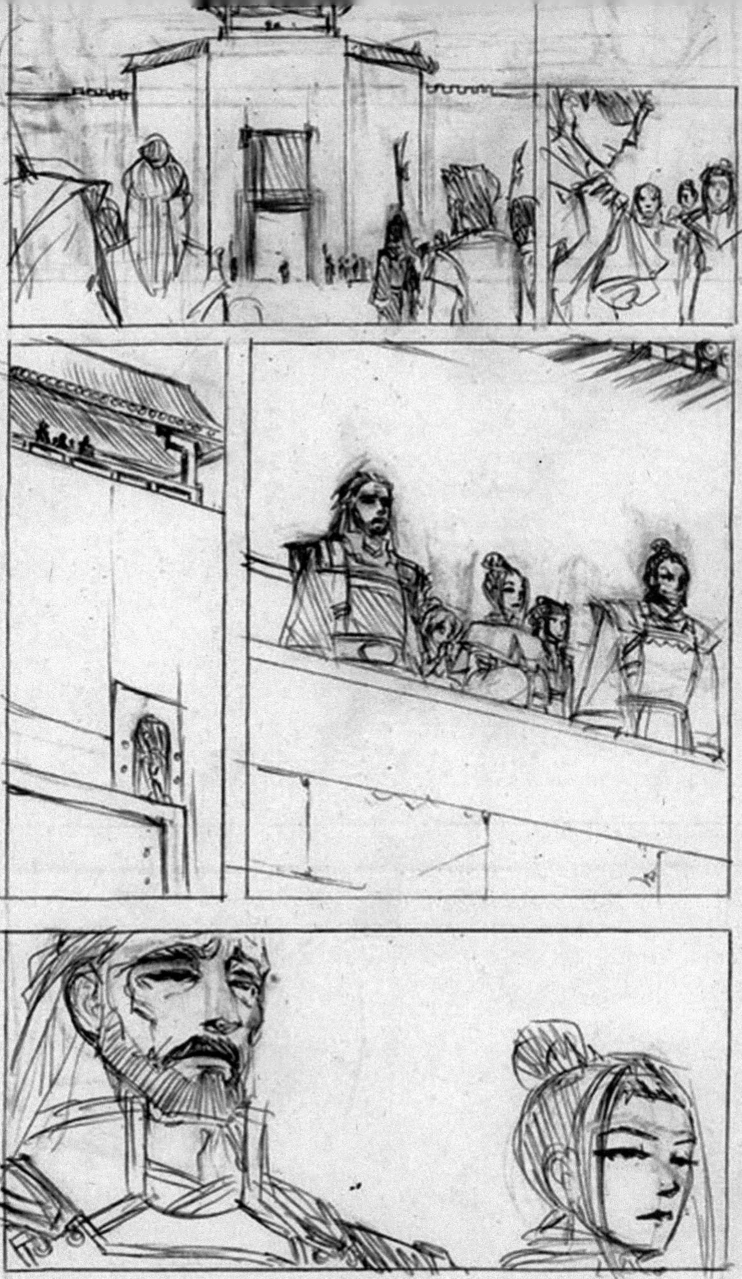

PAGE 14

Panel 1
The flashback continues, although the scene has shifted. It's full dark now, and we're on the docks at the fringe of the Fire Nation capital, outside a seedy-looking bar. Sailors, fishermen, and off-duty soldiers of both genders linger on the pier and outside the lit doorway.

Zuko (off panel): Are none of you brave enough to join my search for the Avatar?

Panel 2
A wide establishing shot of the inside of the bar. Zuko stands defiantly before the gathered patrons. They look like a rough crowd and most are skeptical, but a few seem sympathetic. Zuko's trying very hard to look confident and appropriately royal, but it's clear that he's spent all night talking to people like these, dressed as a commoner with the bag slung across his back. He's visibly exhausted, and blood has seeped through the bandage over his eye. If you were there, you'd find him a chair and tell him to sit down.

Zuko: The Fire Lord himself sent me on this quest. You should be honored to be asked to join me!

Male Soldier: Quest? *Hah.* More like a fool's errand.

Lady Soldier 1: The Avatar's long dead, kid. You'd be better off hiding out in the colonies.

Panel 3
Zuko slams his hand down onto a wooden table, infuriated at the very suggestion.

Zuko: I am honor-bound to bring the Avatar to my father! I ***will not*** turn my back on the task he's given to me!

PAGE 15

Panel 1
An older sailor comes up behind Zuko and rests a large hand on his shoulder. He's grizzled but sympathetic—the kind of guy who probably has children of his own.

Sailor: We aren't heartless, son. We'd help you if we could. But if we sail with a banished prince, we're as good as banished ourselves.

Panel 2
Zuko shrugs the old sailor off—he doesn't want anyone's pity. He tries again, shoulders squared and back straight—he believes he can win these people over with his passion, appeal to their patriotism and their loyalty to the throne. But he's a laughably pathetic sight, and some of his audience has lost patience with him.

Zuko: When I regain my honor, all who helped me will serve in the royal court by my side. Your bravery will be rewarded.

Lady Soldier 2: Nothing brave about lying to yourself. Everyone knows the Avatar's gone. Your own great-grandfather, Sozin, killed him.

Panel 3
Close on Zuko's face, his good eye wide and his brow drawn down in startled fury. The soldier's words are like a punch to the gut.

Lady Soldier 2 (off-panel): Maybe Ozai's just trying to get rid of you.

PAGE 16

Panel 1
Zuko pulls handfuls of flame from a lantern nearby, the movement ungraceful and sloppy in his anger, and the other bar patrons take a hasty step back. This is the first time we've seen Firebending in action, outside of his memories of the Agni Ki, and his display in the following pages is both dramatic and frightening. It's clear that he's only barely in control of what he's doing.

Zuko: *You don't know anything!*

Panel 2
The fire coalesces into daggers above each fist, and Zuko stands as if ready to take on all of them, to force them to see things as he wishes them to be.

Zuko: The Avatar *is* still out there, and I *will* find him. *I'll show all of you how wrong you are!*

Panel 3
The barkeep steps forward and takes hold of Zuko's arm.

Barkeep: All right, kid. I think that's enough recruiting for one night.

PAGE 17

Panel 1
Zuko launches himself at the older man, daggers blazing.

Zuko: Don't **touch** me you **filthy peasant! Don't you know who I am?!**

Panel 2
The man dodges him, and as he spins to face him again Zuko sprays a wave of fire in a wide arc, showering the other patrons with sparks.

Zuko: **I'm the prince of the Fire Nation! Son of Ursa and Ozai and heir to the throne!**

Panel 3
A long, thin panel along the bottom of the page, focusing on the other people in the bar. Many look considerably less sympathetic after his display, although a few still seem to pity him. In the center and closest to us is the grim-faced barkeep, who's had enough of this nonsense.

Barkeep: Yesterday, maybe.

PAGE 18

Panel 1
Cut to a view of the dock outside the bar, where a shaft of light from the doorway cuts across the wooden planks. Zuko is thrown into the frame, the barkeep's shadow looming over him.

Barkeep (caption): Not anymore.

Zuko: Unf!

Panel 2
Zuko pushes himself up halfway from the ground, but the door to the bar has closed and the shaft of light is gone.

Zuko: You can't treat me this way!

Panel 3
Zuko sits up the rest of the way and looks down at his hands, on the edge of tears, his hair hanging over his face and the sodden bandages.

Zuko: I'm the prince...of the Fire Nation...

Panel 4
Zuko looks up. Beyond the dockside rooftops, the swell of a dormant volcano rises up into the sky. The heart of the capital city—and the palace itself—lie inside its crater, and a faint glow rises above the rim and into the night sky.

Panel 5
A close, small panel of Zuko's face as he looks toward home. The people in the bar were right—he's never been away from palace life and his own family. He has no idea what to do.

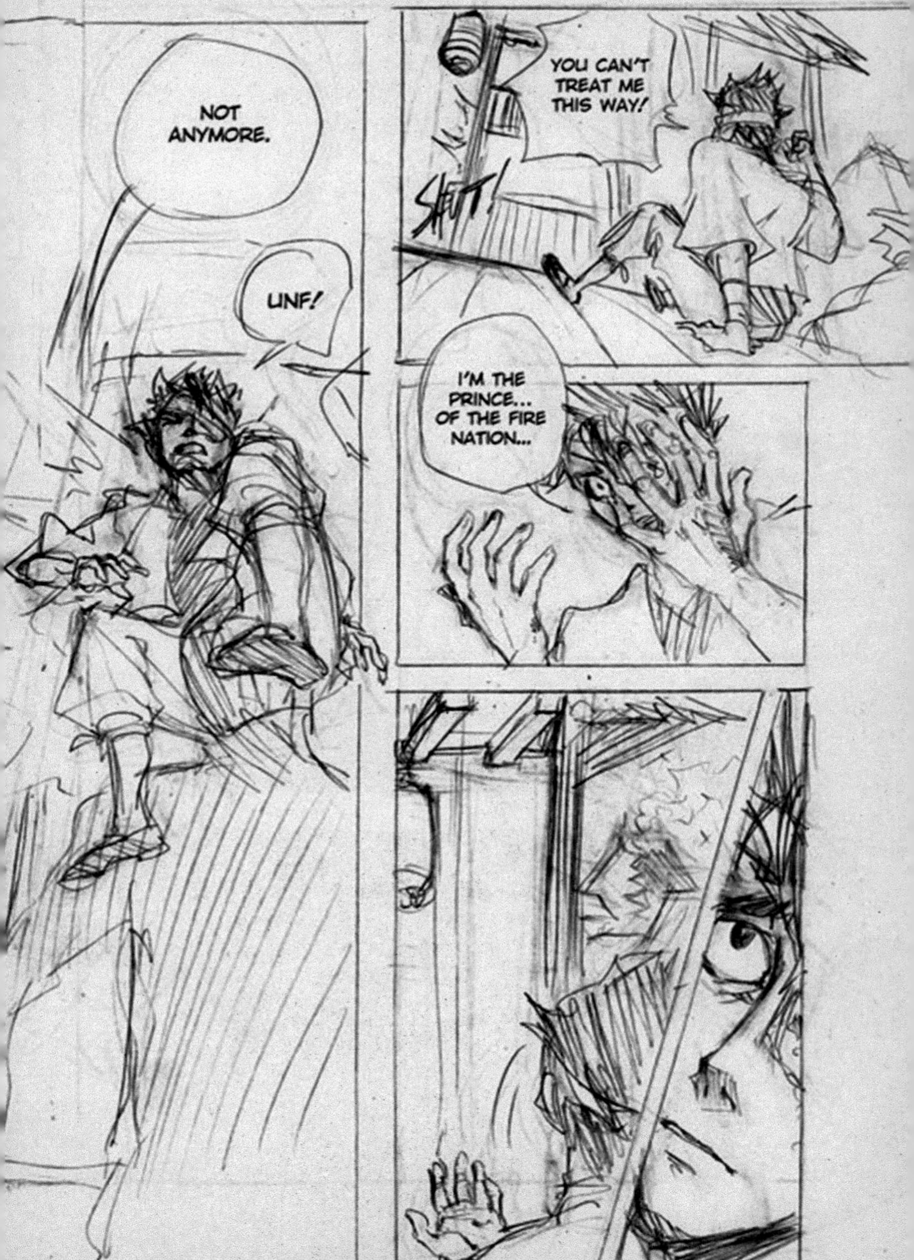
NOT ANYMORE.
UNF!
YOU CAN'T TREAT ME THIS WAY!
I'M THE PRINCE... OF THE FIRE NATION...

PAGE 19

Panel 1

Zuko wanders the docks, aimless and bone tired. As he passes a group of sailors he hunches his shoulders and pulls down the hood of his cloak to cover his bandaged eye.

Caption: I had never been so ashamed.

Panel 2

The first panel melts into this one, implying the passage of time and the daze Zuko is in. Now he's lying in a dark corner of the waterfront, his cloak pulled tight around him.

Caption: And I had never been so alone.

Panel 3

Close on what we can see of Zuko's face, his skin and bandages dirty and his hair a tangled mess. He's begun to dream, and flames creep in on the edges of the frame.

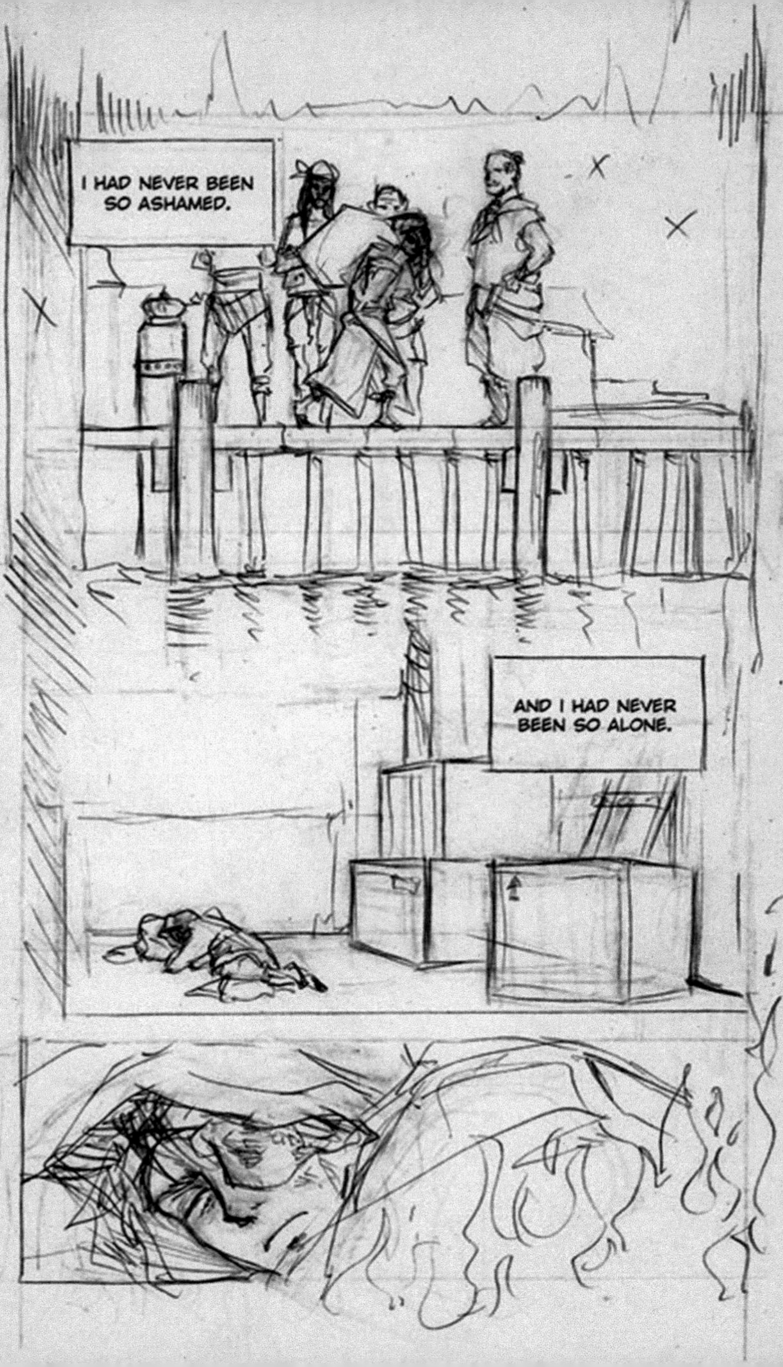
I HAD NEVER BEEN SO ASHAMED.
AND I HAD NEVER BEEN SO ALONE.